Practice Research in the Human Services

POCKET GUIDES TO
SOCIAL WORK RESEARCH METHODS

Series Editor
Tony Tripodi, DSW
Professor Emeritus, Ohio State University

Practice Research in the Human Services
A University-Agency Partnership Model

Michael J. Austin, Mack Professor Emeritus
Founding Director Mack Center
on Nonprofit and Public Sector Human Services School of Social Welfare
University of California, Berkeley
Berkeley, CA
mjaustin@berkeley.edu

and

Sarah Carnochan, Research Director
Bay Area Social Services Consortium
School of Social Welfare
University of California, Berkeley
Berkeley, CA
August 2019

With acknowledgment for the considerable support for this publication from the Bay Area Social Services Consortium, the Zellerbach Family Foundation, and the endowment of the Mack Center on Nonprofit and Public Sector Management in the Human Services at the School of Social Welfare, University of California, Berkeley.

OXFORD
UNIVERSITY PRESS

OXFORD
UNIVERSITY PRESS

Oxford University Press is a department of the University of Oxford. It furthers the University's objective of excellence in research, scholarship, and education by publishing worldwide. Oxford is a registered trade mark of Oxford University Press in the UK and certain other countries.

Published in the United States of America by Oxford University Press
198 Madison Avenue, New York, NY 10016, United States of America.

Library of Congress Cataloging-in-Publication Data
Names: Austin, Michael J., author. | Carnochan, Sarah, author.
Title: Practice research in the human services : a university-agency partnership model / Michael J. Austin, Sarah Carnochan.
Description: New York : Oxford University Press, 2020. |
Series: Pocket guides to social work research methods |
Includes bibliographical references and index.
Identifiers: LCCN 2019053074 (print) | LCCN 2019053075 (ebook) |
ISBN 9780197518335 (paperback) | ISBN 9780197518359 (epub) |
ISBN 9780197518366 (online)
Subjects: LCSH: Human services—Research. | Qualitative research.
Classification: LCC HV40 .A847 2020 (print) | LCC HV40 (ebook) |
DDC 361.0072—dc23
LC record available at https://lccn.loc.gov/2019053074
LC ebook record available at https://lccn.loc.gov/2019053075

1 3 5 7 9 8 6 4 2
Printed by Marquis, Canada

Contents

Preface

The evolution of practice research can be viewed as a 21st-century development. As it is defined and illustrated in this volume, it has been influenced by multiple forces. One of these forces is represented by the wave of interest in evidence-based practice that prioritizes the use of rigorous scientific methods in the form of random controlled trials (RCT) in order to determine service effectiveness. In particular, the central role played by the concept of "fidelity" to the procedures required to guarantee outcomes similar to those demonstrated in multiple RCT studies has generated concerns among researchers and human service practitioners attempting to take into account the diverse needs of service users and the diverse capacities of service providers. These developments have generated renewed interest in qualitative methods and what Flyvbjerg (2001) calls "the science of the concrete," which is defined in the first chapter. We view practice research as a form of evidence-informed practice that involves a wide array of research designs and methods, in contrast to the narrower emphasis on experimental designs that characterizes evidence-based practice.

A second major force at play has been renewed interest in participation, inclusion and the intersectionality of race, gender, sexual orientation, age, and ability, especially when involving service providers and service users in the research enterprise itself. Parallel to the increased attention to the central role of diversity in the delivery and receipt of social services, researchers have become increasingly aware of the importance of a new duality; namely, that the challenges inherent in the delivery of services call for an increase in research-minded practitioners and practice-minded researchers. As Uggerhoj (2014) has noted, the space for practice research can be characterized as highly negotiated when honoring the principle of inclusion means engaging multiple stakeholders in diverse roles (e.g., service users, service providers, researchers, managers, and policymakers).

A third major force relates to research methods. Some might argue that practice research is nothing new given that it relies on using the long-standing social science research tools of interviewing, surveying, observing, conducting focus groups, and reviewing and building upon the existing scientific literature. Although we do not contest this part of the argument, the central role of shared participation in the research enterprise by service users and service providers stands in stark contrast to a more traditional model in which researchers act independently, seeking temporary access to either populations of respondents or secondary data, in the absence of any deeper relationships.

As illustrated in this book, the nature of the negotiated participation of multiple stakeholders in the process of practice research is new with respect to shared involvement in research design, data collection, data interpretation, and research dissemination and utilization. In contrast to the traditional reporting of social science research in peer-reviewed publications, the primary obligation of practice researchers is to share findings with service providers and service users to identify their own applications. The secondary obligation is to contribute to the knowledge development goals associated with defining new, more effective approaches to practice and services, as well as to further the development of interventive theory that complements the extensive development of explanatory theory emerging out of the social sciences.

CONNECTING EVOLVING INTERNATIONAL PRINCIPLES WITH SPECIFIC LOCAL EXPERIENCES

In this book we share our experiences with practice research in ways that researchers, practitioners, service users, and students can find useful and practical. It is important to emphasize that our approach to practice research is just that—our approach. As the field of practice research has developed, it has become clear that local context shapes the forms that practice research takes, and the questions about practice that it sets out to answer. Thus the perspective we bring to practice research may differ from the views of other scholars engaged in this form of research. The research questions, designs, roles and relationships that we have developed are grounded in our local practice research partnership. Our social and institutional context and our interests as researchers shape the specific challenges we encounter, as well as related problem-solving strategies. We believe, however, that it is possible to extrapolate useful lessons from our experience, and this book is intended to communicate those lessons.

By focusing on our practical, tangible experiences that are consistent with the "science of the concrete," we spend time describing small, observable events that illustrate what we mean when we talk about the various processes and activities that constitute our locally negotiated model of practice research Sim et al. (2018); Sim and Lau (2017). We then use these descriptions and stories to construct a comprehensive, detailed picture of the work in which we are engaged. After laying the concrete foundation, we extract from these practice research stories a set of broader principles and guidelines for practice researchers. Although a set of conventions in academic scholarship and writing elevates the abstract and the theoretical, we aim to do the reverse, and focus first on the concrete and practical. We do this in order to share a body of experience that we have found to be immensely rewarding, from an intellectual and professional standpoint, and that we believe will have value for others. We also hope that this book generates discussion in settings that differ from our own, where research funding may be more limited, where theory-informed research plays a more dominant role, and/or where regional and cultural differences preclude our form of practice research.

Finally, we acknowledge the significant support and funding provided by the agency directors and foundation representatives who participate in the Northern California (USA) Bay Area Social Services Consortium of 12 county (local authority) human service agencies, five deans and directors of university social work education programs, and two foundation representatives. If readers of this book are so motivated, we would very much appreciate any and all forms of feedback as we seek to strengthen and refine our approach to practice research.

Michael J. Austin and Sarah Carnochan
School of Social Welfare
University of California, Berkeley
Berkeley, CA

REFERENCES

Flyvbjerg, B. (2001). *Making social science matter: Why social inquiry fails and how it can succeed again.* Cambridge, UK: Cambridge University Press.

Sim, T., Chan, T., Chok, M., Cui, K., Wang, S., Abdullah, F., & Wong, K. (2018). Contextualising the development of practice research in Asia. *China Journal of Social Work, 11*(2), 116–131.

Sim, T. & Lau, V.C.Y (2017). The emergence of social work practice research in the Peoples' Republic of China: A literature review. *Research on Social Work Practice, 27*(1), 8–18.

Uggerhøj, L. (2014). Learning from each other: Collaboration processes in practice research. *Nordic Social Work Research, 4*(sup 1), 44–57.

1

What Is Practice Research and Why Is It Important

INTRODUCTION

The nature of social work practice has been changing in response to the increasingly complex issues facing service users. These issues include finding housing for women on welfare, discovering the unmet needs of the isolated frail elderly, finding safety for children in the midst of domestic violence, and engaging teens caught up in gang violence. At the same time, increased attention has been paid to research methods designed to capture these practice changes and related dynamics. In addition, the increased focus on diversity and inclusion has led researchers to search for ways to amplify the voices of both service providers and service users. Although there is a long history of research *on* social work practice, there has been less emphasis on research *with* practitioners or service users. The emerging principles and practices associated with practice research feature: (1) the inclusion of multiple stakeholders, (2) maximizing and negotiating participation, (3) promoting engagement in all phases of the research process, and (4) adopting new

Practice Research in the Human Services. Michael J. Austin and Sarah Carnochan, Oxford University Press (2020). © Oxford University Press.
DOI: 10.1093/oso/9780197518335.001.0001

identities in the form of research-minded practitioners and practice-minded researchers.

The past two decades have seen growing interest internationally in developing and refining a definition of practice research as carried out within the context of agency-based practice and incorporating the methods of applied research (Fisher, Austin, Julkunen, Sim, Uggerhøj, & Isokuortti, 2016). This evolving form of applied research seeks to understand practice in the context of the relationships between service providers and service users, between service providers and their managers, between agency-based service providers and community advocacy and support groups, and between agency managers and policymakers.

Social work researchers and educators have engaged in an international collaboration to define and refine practice research at a series of international conferences beginning in 2008 (see Note). The latest version of this work-in-progress is described as follows:

> Practice research is a knowledge development process that focuses primarily on the roles of the service provider, service user and the service researcher who all participate in defining the research questions and interpreting the findings. Practice research is often agency-based, service-focused, client-focused, theory-informed, highly interactive (multiple stakeholders), and designed to inform practice, policy, and future research. Practice research plays an important role in a continuing search for ways to improve social services that promote the well-being of service users. It involves collaboration among multiple stakeholders such as service providers, researchers, service users, educators (funders, policymakers, agency directors, etc.) and seeks to take into account the power dynamics between service users and service providers with respect to inclusiveness, transparency, ethical reflexivity, and critical reflection. The goal of practice research is to generate knowledge derived from agency-based practice. The theoretical frameworks and methodological research tools for engaging in practice research often require flexible and collaborative structures and organizational research. In addition, practice research is a negotiated process between practice (providers and users) and research (researchers and educators) within the context of cross-cultural dialogical communications needed to address the gap between research and practice. In essence, for practice and research to be shared, the elements of

co-learning, respect, and curiosity are needed to support an inclusive inquiry and knowledge development process. This process seeks to capture the differences and tensions reflected in fundamentally different perspectives (e.g., service user and provider, service provider and researcher, and researcher and policymaker). In addition, practice research is often funder influenced, outcome focused, and change oriented. (Fisher, Austin, Julkunen, Sim, Uggerhøj, & Isokuortti, 2016)

Although this definition mostly reflects the evolving experiences of practice researchers in the Global North, there is growing interest in the Global South in modifying this definition to account for major differences in community responses to social problems, the organization of services, and the education of future practitioners (Sim, Austin, Abdullah, et al., 2019; Sim & Lau, 2017).

Building upon the emerging definition of practice research, this chapter explores the following questions: (1) How does the evolving definition of practice research inform the discussion in this volume? (2) Is there a platform for conducting practice research that can be adapted in a variety of settings? and (3) How is practice research, rooted primarily in agency-based and community-based social services, related to the concepts of learning organizations and communities of practice? The chapter offers responses to these questions and is designed to inform the rest of the chapters in this volume. In the next section, we explain what we mean by practice research, discussing both its practice and research components.

THE "PRACTICE" COMPONENT OF PRACTICE RESEARCH

A central feature of the delivery of social services is the building of a trusting relationship between those providing services and those using services. Some of the challenges in this relationship relate to confronting the power differential between service users and service providers that complicates their encounters in bureaucratic organizations (Carnochan & Austin, 2015). Other tensions and pressures arise between managers and front-line service providers and are heightened by external demands for performance and accountability (Carnochan, Samples, Myers, & Austin, 2014). The challenges associated with promoting understanding related to the intersectionality of race, gender, sexual orientation, age, and social class, emerge across the multiple relationships that are involved in practice settings and activities (Hancock, 2016).

In a similar way, practice research is based on trusting relationships between those engaged in doing research and those delivering or using services. Therefore, a central feature of practice research is the negotiated relationship among multiple stakeholders needed to carry out research that is directly relevant to the concerns (both concrete and pragmatic) of practice and responsive to the complex challenges involved in everyday service delivery. The multiple stakeholders include service providers, service users, service researchers, service managers, and relevant policymakers and community opinion leaders. The engagement of these stakeholders calls for skillful group facilitation. The negotiated relationships that provide the foundation for practice research are informed by a philosophy of engagement and inclusion. The central aim that guides practice research relates to improving services and questioning current practices. It involves rebalancing power relationships, promoting dialogical communications, and engaging the support of organizational leaders.

A philosophy of engagement and inclusion that is based on the relational nature and organizational context of practice research is an essential element of the foundation for practice research. Practice research is one approach to knowledge development (not "the" approach) and its strength is located in a fundamentally collaborative nature that features well-developed partnerships. It is designed to capture the "art" and "science" of practice by reflecting the central role of curiosity, critical reflection, and critical thinking. The methodological emphasis is on research "with" practice as opposed to the traditional approach of research "on" practice.

The philosophy of engagement often requires a rebalancing of *power relationships* through a process of power sharing based in understanding and respect for the expertise of others. For example, the expertise developed through professional training and experience of service providers differs from the expertise of lived experience demonstrated by service users. Similarly, the expertise of researchers differs from that of both service providers and service users. This rebalancing process often involves elevating the role of service users in the conduct of practice research.

The mechanisms for promoting engagement and power sharing include *dialogical communication* in the form of *open communications without domination* using discussion and democratic dialogue to enhance self-understanding in the practice setting. This form of communication entails the following goals and processes: (1) generate safety and minimize anxiety (for service users, service providers, and researchers); (2) promote open discussion and demonstrate a genuine interest in what each person is saying (following each other's language where words may be ascribed different meanings); (3) generate dialogical communications (creating sufficient time to search for words as well as shared empathy that encourages comments); (4) respond to what the other has said; and (5) speak for one's own sake (wherein each person shares his/her own views and emotions) (Seikkula & Arnkil, 2006, pp. 126–127).

The success of practice research in carrying out a philosophy of inclusion, power-sharing, and open communications relies heavily upon engaging the *organizational support* of service managers. For example, the managerial leadership needed for practice research includes various types of support in the form of released staff time for research, financial support, and demonstrated support for experimentation and innovation for the purpose of improving services and outcomes for service users.

The ultimate goal of practice research is to *improve services* and/or *challenge practice* through research dissemination and utilization. The process of interpreting research findings among stakeholders calls for a candid, safe, and open environment to allow for the emergence of different perceptions and understandings. In addition, the interpretation of research needs to be linked to recommendations for future action. The emphasis on dialogical communications in the beginning of the research process is equally important in the data interpretation process, as well as with community networks beyond those immediately affected by the research.

THE "RESEARCH" COMPONENT OF PRACTICE RESEARCH

Drawing upon many of the elements of applied social science research methods, practice research takes a balanced approach to defining methodological rigor and robustness. It employs both qualitative and quantitative methods of data collection and analysis, dictated by the specific research questions. Some of the key tensions underlying practice research relate to balancing the pursuit of depth and breadth, pursuing rigor within a context of implicit practice wisdom, redefining the roles of knowledge developers for shared learning, and balancing investment in theory-informed research with findings-informed theory development. By working to balance the pursuit of *depth* (e.g., interviews, case records, or field observations) with the pursuit of *breadth* (e.g., surveys, secondary data, controlled trials), the mixed methods utilized in practice research can expand our understanding of specific, local processes and perspectives that are prevalent in the broader community (Creswell, 2015).

From a qualitative data perspective, some of the richest practice data can be found in agency case records where practitioners record/ document detailed aspects of service delivery and the experiences and perspectives of service users. In a similar way, both observational and interview data also can provide for a depth of understanding. Quantitatively oriented practice research typically relies upon large data sets that include surveys, secondary data stored in government and university data archives, and random controlled trials involving experimental research designs.

In contrast to research rigor, the rigor associated with practice leads to another set of tensions. In the context of practice research, rigor can take the form of a challenge to the accepted wisdom found in traditional ways of delivering services. Although more traditional outcome-focused studies may identify challenges related to service effectiveness and impact, challenging the nature of practice methods is one of the key features of practice research. Rigor in practice research can be assessed through the lens of engagement and inclusion as well as the trusting relationships noted in the previous discussion of dialogical communications.

A form of *knowledge development* related to shared learning reveals tensions involved in the roles of the stakeholders engaged in practice research. For example, the focus on shared learning by service providers and service researchers can be seen in the evolution of *research-minded practitioners* and *practice-minded researchers*. In essence, research-minded practitioners are able to demonstrate a curiosity related to exploring new ways of delivering services, a capacity to engage in self-reflective practice in search of ways to improve practice processes, and the ability to engage in critical thinking by clarifying what is being stated, analyze what it might mean, and identify how it might be applied. In contrast, practice-minded researchers reflect a deep curiosity about the evolution and delivery of human services, a capacity to reflect upon how research knowledge and methods can be adapted/applied to complex situations involving multiple stakeholders, and an ability to use their critical thinking skills to identify pathways for practice research findings to inform the development of practice/interventive theory (well beyond the explanatory theories of behavior associated with their research training). Many of these ideas are developed further in Chapter 11.

These role shifts often require considerable time and effort to succeed, especially because most partners in the practice research enterprise have not been exposed to this form of role expansion. This evolution of redefined roles is, however, a critical ingredient in bridging the gap between research and practice. In a similar context, the publishing of practice research findings also needs to include the identification of future areas of practice research emerging from the findings.

And finally, there is little consensus on the role of theory in practice research. Given the inductive and qualitative nature of practice research, to what extent should theory inform the design of practice research and to what extent should practice research findings lead to the expansion of practice or interventive theory? In a similar way, such findings also could lead to explanatory theory that increases our understanding of human behavior and/or the social environment. At least two theoretical perspectives seem directly related to practice research; namely, the *science of the concrete* and *cultural historical activity theory*.

The five elements of the science of the concrete include key concepts related to getting close to reality, focusing on small processes, exploring everyday situations, linking behaviors to the social environment, and engaging multiple stakeholders (Flyvbjerg, 2001). The process of getting close to current realities means designing practice research in a way that involves the perspectives of those persons most closely affected by the focus of the practice research study. For example, the family stabilization study described in Chapter 6 seeks to document the first-hand experiences of service users who are interviewed in coffee shops, their cars, their homes, or the service agency.

Secondly, the emphasis on small phenomena reflects the emergence of major themes derived from what might be viewed as minor activities. The child welfare case record data-mining study noted in Chapter 5 illustrates this approach, examining the daily and hourly activities of agency practitioners that are documented in child welfare case record contact notes.

The third concept embedded in the science of the concrete involves the investigation of practical activities and knowledge located in everyday situations by studying concrete cases and contexts. For example, the detailed descriptions of innovative welfare-to-work services highlighted in Chapter 4 provided a foundation for engaging in cross-case analysis to explore the similarities and differences for future practice implications. The fourth concept within the science of the concrete relates to linking the "agency" of individual behaviors with the structure of the "social environment." The contracting study described in Chapter 7 exemplifies this concept, examining social environment and characteristics of the service organization along with the perspectives and activities of individual contract managers.

The fifth component of the science of the concrete relates to a key element of practice research; namely, engaging in dialogue with a wide range of voices (where no voice claims final authority). The involvement of multiple stakeholders can include exploring the various perspectives of senior managers, service users, service providers, and policymakers. Although all of these elements provide an important context for conducting practice research, they also could guide traditional social science research.

A second promising theoretical development relates to Cultural Historical Activity Theory (CHAT), a practice-based framework for analyzing and informing collective and complex human practices at multiple organizational levels (Engeström, 2000; Foot, 2014). Grounded in place, time, and materiality, CHAT outlines six key concepts: subject, object, tools, rules, community, and division of labor. CHAT helps to identify the systemic contradictions that shape the ways that people work together. It is based upon the following components of human interaction: (1) people act collectively, learn by doing, and communicate in and via their actions; (2) people make, employ, and adapt tools of all kinds to learn and communicate; and (3) the concept of community is central to the process of making and interpreting meaning that contributes to all forms of learning, communicating, and acting (Vygotsky, 1978).

The CHAT model proposes an activity system that is constantly evolving through collective learning actions (often in response to systemic contradictions), and thereby enables the multirelational analyses of the complex practices of professional work over time. Through the use of a CHAT framework, the interactions between service providers and users can be analyzed in terms of the evolving interpersonal/communicative aspects of those relationships within a cultural, political, and historical context. The methods used to implement the CHAT framework include "change laboratories" that identify the need for change, document past and present contradictions, envision a new model of practice, design–test–implement a new model, and codify the experience in order to share new rules of engagement and teach others.

Based upon the use of the science of the concrete and cultural-historical activity theory, it is possible to identify how the findings of practice research can inform theory development, especially interventive theory (e.g., leading to new practice principles for service providers) as well as explanatory theory (e.g., finding new ways to understand the behaviors, interests, and empowerment of service users).

PRACTICE RESEARCH AS LOCALLY NEGOTIATED PARTNERSHIPS

Practice research is grounded in the recognition that we need to identify ways to improve practice in the complex and uncertain situations that characterize human services. In order to identify good practice and challenge troubling practice, it is critical to develop knowledge that emerges directly from the complexity of everyday practice. Practice research in agency settings can serve to test new ideas, try new research approaches, and explore new ways of delivering services. It is relevant to all levels of practice, including micro practice (service provider and service user), mezzo practice (groups of service providers, service users, managers, and community stakeholders), and macro practice (featuring management, community, and policy practice). It is relational by its very nature and is based upon committed and locally based collaborations between researchers/research organizations and practitioner/practice settings in planning, generating, and disseminating research. Practice research represents an inclusive approach to developing professional knowledge, generated through a partnership characterized by equal dialogue between the worlds of practice and research, and involving many different interest groups that may represent different positions, experience, and expertise.

As practice research has evolved, it has become clear that it does not represent a specific research method but rather a meeting point between practice and research that needs to be negotiated every time and every place it is established (Uggerhøj, 2011a, 2011b, 2014). In essence, practitioners are unlikely to become researchers, nor will most researchers become practitioners, but their respective understandings of practice research can certainly expand as they exchange perspectives that are informed by professional practice and academic research standards, as well as a shared desire for rigorous data collection and robust generalizability to other practice settings.

Julkunen (2011) describes four emerging types of practice research (practitioner-oriented, democratic, generative, and method-oriented) that differ with respect to roles, processes, and central aims as follows:

> *The practitioner-oriented model* is located in a service setting where the workload of practitioners is divided between practice and research. The work processes derived from a practitioner's/researcher's own experiences are described and evaluated through analyses of critical incidents, monitoring and interviews and disseminated to other contexts through reflective dialogue with other practitioners including external reference groups representing different types of expertise within the field.

> *The democratic PR model* is a bottom-up research model involving the continuous involvement of practice reference groups, including users, practitioners and leaders. The aim is to change practice locally at the same time as liberating the actors within the research context by empowering them to create their own knowing-in-action in collaboration with other actors.

> *The generative PR model* is a process involving alternative periods of field practice and research related to analysing, conceptualising and

theorising. The aim is to acquire knowledge through action (e.g. the researcher/social worker uses his experience in child protection that informs his regular interaction with the child-protection workers and the way he tests the possible conceptual innovations and develops them further within the research).

The method-oriented model involves the development of new methods in partnership with service users and practitioners where research and practice overlap and proceed simultaneously in pursuit of knowledge for action related to a future practice where both practitioners and service users are considered co-producers of knowledge, often using the methods of action research and ethnographic investigation. (Julkunen, 2011, pp. 66–67)

Although each of these approaches feature the initiative of individual research-minded practitioners, sometimes captured by the role of doctoral students seeking to utilize a practice research model in their dissertation, they differ from the approach featured in this book in several ways. First, the most senior practitioners (often the agency director or deputy directors in consultation with middle-management and line staff) play a significant role in helping to frame the research questions and provide access to the data, such that the priority given to the research topic emanates from the top of the organization. Second, very little, if any, resources are available inside public social service organizations described in this volume to provide line staff with time off to pursue the practitioner-oriented or generative models of practice research. In contrast, the democratic and methods-oriented models come closest to those described in this book.

Increasingly, researchers and practitioners involved in practice research recognize the importance of infrastructure supports for practice research, including organizational structures to support varied forms of learning networks. Within organizations, spaces (physical and intellectual as well as protected time) need to be provided for the exchange of practice research ideas. Most importantly, social capital (e.g., trust, respect, and opportunities to meet regularly) needs to be built to create a platform for practice research, as described in the next section. Over time, it has become increasingly clear that more attention needs to be given to the societal context of practice research given both the diverse political and cultural contexts and the various stages of social work development as a profession throughout the world.

BUILDING A PLATFORM FOR PRACTICE RESEARCH

This section addresses the second question outlined in the chapter introduction: Is there an organizational platform for conducting practice research that can be adapted in a variety of settings? Although platforms for practice research operate inside some large public social service organizations (see Appendix B in Chapter 12 for an example from Finland), this section describes a platform developed by a regional consortium of public social service agencies, schools of social work, and a local philanthropic foundation, that is based at a local university. The platform traces its origins to 1987 in the Northern California region known as the San Francisco Bay Area. At that time, a group of county (government) social service agency directors formed a regional Bay Area Social Service Consortium (BASSC) that included eleven county directors, five university deans or directors of social work education programs, and two foundation representatives (Austin, Martin, Carnochan, Berrick, Goldberg, Kelley, & Weiss, 1999). Thirty years later, the consortium continues to meet five times per year as both a think tank for exploring current and future policy and practice issues as well as a support group for addressing organizational and managerial challenges (Austin, 2017). This regional venue provides a unique opportunity to address the mission of the consortium that includes identifying and investigating research questions, exploring the implications of policy implementation, and specifying emerging topics for educating middle managers.

In order to support an ongoing research budget, the participating counties contribute annual dues on a sliding scale according to the size of the county service population and annual budget. Over time, the consortium has expanded to establish regional groups of managers organized by types of service programs (child welfare, welfare-to-work, and adult and aging services) as well as by senior management roles (human resources, finance, research and policy, public information, regional training advisory board) that meet regularly to exchange information. One university is the focal point for the practice research, but other university faculty inside and outside the region participate as well.

It is important to acknowledge that the research platform used to describe practice research in this volume is unusual in terms of its funding and longevity. However, the types of practice research noted in the succeeding chapters, as well as the lessons learned that are identified in more detail in Chapter 8, should be replicable, in part or in whole, in other agency and/or university settings, provided that the enlightened leadership needed for success is in place.

Exploring the Dynamics of Intermediary Organizations

The unusual structure of this collaborative partnership is worth noting. As an intermediary organization among universities, human service agencies, and foundations, BASSC is ideally suited to help facilitate the transformation of public human services organizations from traditional governmental bureaucracies into learning organizations. Lavis (2006) suggests that intermediary organizations operate "at the interface between researchers (i.e., the producers of research evidence) and users of research evidence . . . to play critically important roles in knowledge translation, in addition to using research evidence to inform their own activities" (p. 37). BASSC influences research and practice by serving several distinct functions, including the following: enhancing research resources, using a network of relationships to promote creativity and innovation, and providing a regional forum to address local, state, and national policy issues. By linking regional resources, county organizations are able to combine their limited financial resources to conduct research that few individual counties could afford to conduct on their own.

From the university perspective, faculty involvement in practice research helps to bring practice issues into the classroom as a way of promoting evidence-informed curricula related to current service delivery issues. For doctoral, master's-level, and postdoctoral students involved in practice research, this exposure involves them in a unique research–policy–practice partnership that significantly complements their fieldwork and coursework experiences. At the same time, practice research offers faculty and students the opportunity to produce publishable research.

The growing interest and investment in evidence-informed practice by the social service professions calls for innovative approaches to bridging the gap between research and practice. The ability of intermediary organizations such as BASSC to operate with research funding helps to promote creativity and innovation as well as educate opinion leaders who can help to support the sustainability of practice research. Intermediary organizations supported by universities represent a promising approach to ensuring the relevance of practice research in relationship to the changing needs of clients and practitioners.

Intermediary organizations have emerged in a variety of fields (e.g., education, workforce development, and social services for children, youth, and families) to support individual and group empowerment in order to connect practice and policy (Wynn, 2000). Intermediary organizations may serve a variety of functions, including: (1) engaging, convening, and supporting partners, such as those needed for practice research, in order to close the gap between research and practice; (2) promoting quality standards and accountability; (3) brokering and leveraging resources; and (4) promoting effective policies (Blank et al., 2003). Intermediary organizations also can function as agents of change by building capacity at individual, relational, and organizational levels needed to improve services as well as practices (Lopez, Kreider, & Coffman, 2005, p. 79).

In addition to the examples of the Cochrane and the Campbell Collaborations, which assess and disseminate research through the development of systematic reviews of health care and social service interventions, respectively (Lavis, Davies, & Gruen, 2006), other models more closely associated with practice research have emerged in the United Kingdom (Research in Practice—RiP) and in Canada (Practice and Research Together—PART) (Graaf, McBeath, Lwin, Holmes, & Austin, 2017).

The Evolution of a Research Platform for Exploratory Practice Research

In the early discussions within the regularly scheduled regional meetings, several county directors became increasingly concerned about the amount of external reporting required by state and federal funding agencies. They noted that they were complying with requests for a wide range of client data while receiving little or no feedback from the funding sources about how those entities were using the data. They also each lacked sufficient internal capacity to analyze and utilize such data. With the goal of framing their own accountability-oriented research questions, four counties were so invested in developing their own practice research capacity that they agreed to jointly fund a new university-based BASSC Research Response Team to be staffed by a doctoral-level researcher and student researchers engaged primarily in qualitative exploratory studies. Box 1.1 provides a brief description of the early studies.

After spending several years completing these exploratory studies, a review was conducted to assess the impact of these efforts (Austin, Dal Santo, Goldberg, & Choice, 2001). The review identified three types of research use by participating agencies as noted in Table 1.1: conceptual, persuasive, and instrumental (Reid & Fortune, 1992). Exploratory studies that reflected conceptual impact were defined as producing insights for future application but not immediately useful in daily practice. Persuasive studies were those that could be used immediately to advocate for change either inside or outside of the organization in the form of influencing future local policy development, statewide legislation, and/or funding needs. And finally, instrumental studies reflected the capacity of the organization to use the findings from the exploratory studies to alter or improve current practices.

These nine initial exploratory studies provided important lessons for future research activities related to positive impacts and areas for improvement. The positive results included the importance of staff participation, especially the involvement of a senior manager in the planning and implementation of research projects, which was instrumental in promoting the dissemination and utilization of the research. In addition, the exploratory studies helped to increase the level of informed decision-making and reduce the level of confusion or lack of information within the agencies as well as the community.

Box 1.1	BASSC Launch of Exploratory Research Projects and Objectives

1. *Homeless Needs Assessment.* Initiated by the county to better understand the service needs of homeless adult individuals and their families to plan for county-wide homeless services.
2. *General Assistance Client Demographics Study.* Initiated by the county to better understand the demographic characteristics and service needs of GA applicants and recipients in order to develop program plans and policies.
3. *Assessing Quality of Care in Kinship and Family Foster Care.* Initiated by the county to examine various dimensions of quality of care in kinship foster care and family foster care in order to develop guidelines for child welfare workers to use when making initial placements for children.
4. *Considerations Relating to the Placement of Children in Gay/Lesbian Foster and Adoptive Homes.* Initiated by the county at the request of Superior Court judges to assess the existing literature relating to gay and lesbian parenting in order to more thoroughly consider issues pertaining to the placement of children in gay and lesbian foster and adoptive homes.
5. *Developing a Public Information and Community Relations Strategy.* Initiated by the county to examine how public relations is currently carried out in the public and private sectors in order to assist the Social Service Department in developing a formal public information function.
6. *Factors Associated with Family Reunification Outcomes: Understanding Reentry to Care for Infants.* Initiated by the county to identify various characteristics (child, family, service, environmental, court, and caseworker) associated with success or failure in family reunification in order to further inform the planning of child welfare services.
7. *Foster Care Recruitment, Retention, and Rate Setting.* Initiated by the county to compare and assess the various approaches used by states to recruit and retain foster parents and to understand how state and county governments determine payment rates for foster parents.
8. *Service Use and Unmet Needs Among Long-Term AFDC Recipients.* Initiated by the county to better understand the service needs of long-term AFDC clients in order to develop programs to help promote their financial self-sufficiency.
9. *A Review of Managed Care as a Tool for Child Welfare Reform.* Initiated by the county to investigate approaches for reforming the delivery, management and financing of child welfare services, by critically assessing current managed care principles and practices.

Table 1.1 Types of Research Utilization (empirical and literature reviews)

Research Projects	Conceptual "Insights for later application"	Persuasive "Used to advocate"	Instrumental "Altered practices"
1. Homeless Needs Assessment	X	X	X
2. General Assistance Client Demographics	X	X	X
3. Gay/Lesbian Foster and Adoptive Homes	X	X	X
4. Developing a Public Information Strategy	X	X	X
5. Assessing Quality of Care in Kinship Foster Care	X		X
6. Family Reunification Outcomes	X	X	
7. Foster Care Rates	X	X	
8. Long-Term AFDC Recipients	X		
9. Managed Care as a Tool for Child Welfare Reform	X		
Total	**9**	**6**	**5**

The areas for improvement emerging from the assessment included the following lessons:

1. Given that there are shared responsibilities across a number of different agency departments or stakeholders that can significantly delay the research process, increased coordination between agency staff and the practice researchers is essential.
2. Successful dissemination of reports requires that researchers invest substantial time and energy in identifying and understanding the interests of internal and external audiences.
3. Successful utilization of research reports requires recognizing that agency managers have different levels of capacity when it comes to using research findings, as well as translating findings into recommendations for policy and program development.
4. PowerPoint presentations, beyond the distribution of the written research reports, were seen by busy staff as the most useful

way to present research results and explore the feasibility of implementing the recommendations.

5. Increased investments in communications are necessary to: (a) clarify the study aims and expectations for the type of information that will be generated, (b) specify types of research and dissemination methods to be used, and (c) identify strategies to address key issues related to cooperation, shared accountability, conflict, and the translation of findings and recommendations into action steps.

One of the most important lessons learned by the university researchers emerged from the complexity of conducting distinct studies in different counties with limited research staff. As a result, it was agreed that the BASSC members would select a topic of common interest that could be explored at the regional level in multiple counties, using a sliding scale of funding where smaller counties contributed less than larger counties. Following this decision, the first two regional studies focused on child welfare services (Carnochan, Taylor, Abramson-Madden, Han, Rashid, Maney, Teuwen, & Austin, 2007; Stone, D'Andrade, & Austin, 2006). In addition to joint topic selection, it was necessary to adjust the time expectations of the participating agencies from the rapid response of 9 to 12 months for a single county department study to the need for 12 to 24 months to complete multi-county studies.

After four years of conducting multi-county studies, new approaches to practice research began to emerge as county directors and senior managers became increasingly interested in evidence-informed practice and wanted to learn more from the existing literature in contrast to supporting single county or multi-county exploratory studies. Learning from the literature became the next arena of inquiry, leading to over 20 structured literature reviews for which the process is described in Chapter 3.

BUILDING LEARNING ORGANIZATIONS AND PROMOTING EVIDENCE-INFORMED PRACTICE

In building this platform for practice research, it became clear that social service organizations would be strengthened by becoming learning organizations that engaged in evidence-informed practice and promoted communities of practice. A learning organization is an organization that is "skilled at creating, acquiring, and transferring knowledge, and at modifying its behavior to reflect new knowledge and insights" (Garvin, 1998; p. 51). A learning organization values continuous quality improvement in both services and organizational processes and is able to define where it wants to go and can systematically identify the steps to get there, using knowledge and the principles and practices of continuous learning. Not only did the BASSC agency directors want to learn more about the breadth and depth of existing knowledge, they wanted to explore ways of building staff capacity to engage in evidence-informed practice. The staff skills associated with the development of a learning organization include Senge's (1990) five concepts: (1) engaging in systems thinking (seeing multiple relationships related to people, ideas, and things); (2) acquiring personal mastery (clarifying what is important); (3) developing mental models (clarifying and adjusting underlying assumptions); (4) promoting a shared vision (agreeing on goals and a course of action); and (5) fostering team learning (thinking insightfully and generating new learning).

Organizational learning is the process of improving actions through better knowledge and understanding (Fiol & Lyles, 1985). The organization's commitment to using the capabilities of all of its members is reflected in policies and procedures that support learning activities, as well as the dissemination of best practices across the organization, so that everyone learns and can make improvements in what they do. (Preskill & Torres, 1999). A learning culture is an environment that promotes and fosters individual, team, and organizational learning through processes that include: (1) information gathering and problem-solving, (2) experimentation, (3) learning from the past, (4) learning from best practices, and (5) transferring knowledge (Garvin, 1998; Austin & Hopkins, 2004).

In addition to connecting practice research with central tenets of a learning organization, it is also important to view the organization as a community; namely, as multiple communities of practice. Communities of practice are groups of people who share a concern or passion for what they do and learn how to do it better as they interact regularly (Wenger, 1998). This learning process is based on shared interests within a context of shared activities and discussions where participants learn together through shared stories, experiences, and tools. The process generates a repertoire of shared resources (sometimes called a shared practice) that may be located inside or outside of an organization. Although the knowledge sharing process is an important dimension of communities of practice, other activities include problem-solving, inventing new approaches, creating new knowledge, and developing a collective voice (Wenger, 2015). Communities of practice have become the foundation for promoting shared learning in the form of learning systems that operate in a single organization, in organizational partnerships, in local communities, and at all levels of government (Wenger, 2015).

The development of practice research reflects an international community of practice composed of practice researchers who update the evolving definition of practice research as noted in the chapter Introduction. In a similar way, the local development of practice research represents a community of practice that can include service providers, researchers, service users, government officials, the community, and those engaged in interdisciplinary research and practice. The evolution of "team science" in the conduct of practice research is an example of a community of research practices where agency and university participants engage one another in both planning and problem-solving. Within social service organizations, the ad hoc teams formed to address major organizational changes emanating from new federal or state legislation provide opportunities for both shared learning as well as shared practices.

CONCLUSION

This first chapter provides a foundation for understanding the principles and challenges of practice research. The challenges facing those engaged in practice research are both multiple and manageable, and include: (1) providing tangible evidence that practice research contributes to service improvement, enhanced practice skills, and social policy development; (2) demonstrating how practice research supports the evolution of learning organizations and the education of future research-minded practitioners; (3) demonstrating how to promote interdisciplinary research, not just between researchers but also between practitioners and service users (linking professional expertise with the service user's expertise of experience); and (4) identifying the connections between the evolving forms of practice research and the new directions underlying survivor research carried out by service users. In essence, the following chapters synthesize the learning derived from over two decades of practice research across multiple fields of practice. Each of these chapters describes the specific topics that we studied and how we carried out the research. Particular attention is given to providing an account of the methodological aspects of practice research in order to illustrate and contextualize approaches to designing, implementing, and disseminating practice research.

Chapter 2 features the learning derived from extensive individual interviews that often resulted in teaching cases or from engaging and observing groups that often resulted in program redesign. Chapter 3 highlights the importance of knowledge development in the form of learning from the research of others and describes the process and products related to our structured literature reviews. Chapter 4 features the learning derived from cross-case analysis applied to organizational cases. This form of practice research opened up opportunities for agency directors to learn more about the experiences of other agencies and to compare those experiences to their own. The cases related to implementing welfare reform in county human service organizations, building knowledge-sharing systems in public sector organizations to promote evidence informed decision-making and practices, and the dynamics associated with sustaining nonprofit human service organizations over time.

Chapters 5 to 7 describe examples of practice research reflecting both qualitative and quantitative research methods in various practice domains. Chapter 5 focuses on two child welfare studies. The first study examined the challenges of promoting interdisciplinary collaboration in juvenile dependency courts where differences in the professional culture and values among social workers and legal professionals play a prominent role. The second project drew upon the richness of client case records, using the methods of qualitative data-mining to explore issues related to child welfare practice and service users. Chapter 6 focuses on the dynamics of welfare-to-work services within the context of subsidized employment programs and services to help families experiencing destabilizing crises. The practice research focus in Chapter 7 addresses aspects of managerial practice, first describing research that explores the complexities faced by organizations when managers seek to use evidence to inform decision-making. Similar issues emerged in a study of human service managers seeking to promote contractual relationships between public and nonprofit organizations.

Based on the examples of practice research provided in the first seven chapters, we developed a set of principles and challenges explained in Chapter 8. The principles relate to all phases that include launching, sustaining, and completing practice research. In contrast, the challenges surface in direct relationship to the complexities of working with representatives of different cultures (e.g., service providers, service users, researchers) and within the context of continuous organizational, community, and policy change.

Many of the broader issues related to the implementation of practice research are featured in the remaining chapters. Chapter 9 describes some of the research methodologies that overlap with those of practice research. Chapter 10 provides additional elaboration of the data-mining methods illustrated in Chapter 5. The final two chapters address the roles played by service providers. In Chapter 11, special attention is given to the evolution of research-minded practitioners along with the organizational supports needed to promote evidence-informed practice. Chapter 12 captures the recognition that an integrated curriculum is needed to help future practitioners integrate the principles of effective practice methods with effective research methods.

FURTHER READING

Evidence of the evolving definition of practice research as an international collaborative work-in-progress:

Epstein, I., Fisher, M., Julkunen, I., Uggerhof, L., Austin, M.J., & Sim, T. (2015). The New York Statement on the Evolving Definition of Practice Research Designed for Continuing Dialogue: A Bulletin from the 3rd International Conference on Practice Research—2014. *Research on Social Work Practice*, 25(6), 711–714.

Salisbury Forum Group (2011). The Salisbury Statement on Practice Research—2008. *Social Work & Society*, 9(1), 4–9.

Second International Conference Scientific Committee (2014). Helsinki Statement on Social Work Practice Research—2012. *Nordic Social Work Research*, 4(1), S7–S13.

Sim, T., Austin, M.J., Abdullah, F., Chan, T.M.S., Chok, M., Ke, C., Epstein, I., Fisther, M., Jourbert, L., Julkunen, I., Ow, R., Uggerhoj, L., Wang, S., Webber, M., Wong, K., & Yliruka, L. (2019). The Hong Kong Statement on Practice Research—2017: Contexts and Challenges of the Far East. *Research on Social Work Practice*, 29(1), 3–9.

REFERENCES

Austin, M.J. (Ed.) (2010). *Evidence for child welfare practice*. London: Routledge.

Austin, M.J. (2017). *BASSC@30*. Mack Center on Nonprofit and Public Sector Management in the Human Services: University of California, Berkeley School of Social Welfare. Downloaded on January 15, 2019. https://mackcenter.berkeley.edu/sites/default/files/bassc30.pdf

Austin, M.J., Dal Santo, T., Goldberg, S., & Choice, P. (2001). Exploratory research in public social service agencies: As assessment of dissemination and utilization. *Journal of Sociology and Social Welfare*, 29(4), 59–81.

Austin, M.J., & Hopkins, K. (Eds.) (2004). *Supervision as collaboration in the human services: Building a learning culture*. Thousand Oaks, CA: Sage Publications.

Austin, M.J., Martin, M. Carnochan, S., Duerr Berrick, J., Goldberg, S., Kelley, J., & Weiss, B. (1999). Building a comprehensive agency–university partnership: The bay area social services consortium. *Journal of Community Practice*, 6(3), 89–106.

Blank, M.J., Brand, B., Deich, S., Kazis, R., Politz, B., & Trippe, S. (2003). *Local intermediary organizations: Connecting the dots for children, youth, and families*. Boston, MA: Jobs for the Future.

Carnochan, S., & Austin, M.J. (2015). Redefining the bureaucratic encounter between service providers and service users: Evidence from the Norwegian HUSK Projects. *Journal of Evidence-based Social Work*, 12(1), 64–79.

Carnochan, S., Samples, M., Myers, M., & Austin, M.J. (2014). Performance measurement challenges in nonprofit human service organizations. *Nonprofit & Voluntary Sector Quarterly*, 43(6), 1014–1032.

Carnochan, S., Taylor, S., Abramson-Madden, A., Han, M., Rashid, S., Maney, J., Teuwen, S., & Austin, M.J. (2007). Child welfare and the courts: An exploratory study of the relationship between two complex systems. *Journal of Public Child Welfare*, 1(1), 117–136.

Creswell, J. (2015). *Educational Research: Planning, Conducting, and Evaluating Quantitative and Qualitative Research.* New York: Pearson.

Engeström, Y. (2000). Activity theory as a framework for analyzing and redesigning work. *Ergonomics, 43*(7), 960–974.

Fiol, C., & Lyles, M. (1985). Organizational learning. *Academy of Management Review, 10*(4), 803–814.

Fisher, M., Austin, M.J., Julkunen, I., Sim, T., Uggerhøj, L., & Isokuortti, N. (2016). Practice Research. In E. Mullen (Ed.), *Oxford bibliographies in social work.* Oxford, UK: Oxford University Press. http://www.oxfordbibliographies.com/view/document/obo-9780195389678/obo-9780195389678-0232.xml

Flyvbjerg, B. (2001). *Making Social Science Matter: Why Social Inquiry Fails and How It Can Succeed Again,* Cambridge, UK: Cambridge University Press.

Foot, K. (2014). Cultural-Historical Activity Theory: Exploring a Theory to Inform Practice and Research. *Journal of Human Behavior in the Social Environment, 24,* 329–347.

Garvin, D. (1998). Building a learning organization. In Harvard Business Review (Ed.), *Knowledge management* (pp. 47–80). Boston, MA: Harvard Business School Press.

Graaf, G., McBeath, B., Lwin, K., Holmes, D., & Austin, M.J. (2017). Supporting evidence-informed practice in human service organizations: An exploratory study of link officers. *Human Service Organizations, 41*(1), 58–75.

Hancock, A. (2016). *Intersectionality: An intellectual history.* New York, NY: Oxford University Press.

Julkunen, I. (2011). Knowledge-production processes in practice research: Outcomes and critical elements. *Social Work and Society, 9*(1), 60–75.

Lavis, J.N. (2006). Research, public policymaking, and knowledge-translation processes: Canadian efforts to build bridges. *The Journal of Continuing Education in the Health Professions, 26,* 37–45.

Lavis, J.N., Davies, H.T., & Gruen, R.L. (2006). Working within and beyond the Cochrane Collaboration to make systematic reviews more useful to healthcare managers and policy makers. *Healthcare Policy, 1*(2), 21–33.

Lopez, M.E., Kreider, H., & Coffman, J. (2005). Intermediary organization as capacity builders in family educational involvement. *Urban Education, 40,* 78–105.

Preskill, H., & Torres, R. (1999). *Evaluative inquiry for learning in organizations.* Thousand Oaks, CA: Sage.

Reid, W., & Fortune, A. (1992). Research utilization in direct social work practice. In A. Grasso & I. Epstein (Eds.), *Research utilization in the social services* (pp. 292–314). New York, NY: Haworth Press.

Seikkula, J., & Arnkil, T. (2006). *Dialogical meetings in social networks.* London: Karnac.

Senge, P. (1990). *The fifth discipline.* New York, NY: Doubleday.

Shafer, M.A. (2006). The role of intermediary organizations and knowledge communities in bridging barriers. Presentation at the 86th AMS Annual Meeting, Atlanta, Georgia.

Sim, T., & Lau, V. (2017). The emergence of social work practice research in the peoples' republic of china: A literature review. *Research on Social Work Practice, 27*(1), 8–18.

Sim, T., Austin, M.J., Abdullah, F., Chan, T.M.S., Chok, M., Ke, Cui, Epstein, I., Fisher, M., Joubert, L., Julkunen, I., Ow, R., Uggerhoj, L., Wang, S., Webber, M., Wong, K., & Yliruka, L. (2019). The Hong Kong Statement on Practice Research: Contexts and Challenges of the Far East. *Research on Social Work Practice, 29*(1), 3–9.

Stone, S., D'Andrade, A., & Austin, M.J. (2006). Educational services for children in foster care: Challenges and opportunities. *Journal of Public Child Welfare, 1*(1), 53–70.

Sweeney, A., Beresford, P., Faulkner, A., Nettle, M., & Rose, D. (2009). *This is survivor research.* Ross-on-Wye, UK: PCCS Books.

Uggerhøj, L. (2011a). What is practice research in social work & definitions, barriers and possibilities. *Social Work & Society, 9*(1), 45–59.

Uggerhøj, L. (2011b). Theorizing practice research in social work. *Social Work and Social Sciences Review, 15*(1), 49–73.

Uggerhøj, L. (2014). Learning from each other—Collaboration processes in practice research. *Nordic Social Work Research, 4*(sup 1), 44–57.

Vygotsky, L. (1978). *Mind and society.* Cambridge, MA: Harvard University Press.

Wenger, E. (1998). *Communities of practice: Learning, meaning, and identity.* Cambridge: Cambridge University Press.

Wenger-Trayner, E., & Wenger-Trayner, B. (2015). *Communities of practice: A brief introduction.* Downloaded October 25, 2018. https://scholar.google.com/scholar?q=Communities+of+Practice:+A+Brief+Introduction,+2015&hl=en&as_sdt=0&as_vis=1&oi=scholart

Wynn, J.R. (2000). *The role of local intermediary organizations in the youth development field.* University of Chicago: Chapin Hall Center for Children.

2

Learning from the Experiences of Practitioners

A long with the significant impact of technology on the nature of practice, the changing needs of service users also have played a role in the transformation of service delivery (Chan & Holosko, 2016; Goldkind & Wolf, 2015; Stevaert & Gould, 2009; Wareing & Hendrick, 2013). In the midst of these two powerful forces, there has been little time for practitioners to step back and reflect on how their work has changed over time. In addition, there are few rewards in the workplace for transforming the reflections on practice into written documents, let alone published reports. A small subset of practitioners utilize professional conferences to present their experiences, usually in the form of service innovations, and rarely in the form of the changing nature of practice. Without the time, incentives, or publication venues, it is not surprising that the current literature rarely includes the individual observations and insights of a practitioner.

In light of these factors, learning from practitioners represents an important element of practice research. The interviewing of busy

Practice Research in the Human Services. Michael J. Austin and Sarah Carnochan, Oxford University Press (2020). © Oxford University Press.
DOI: 10.1093/oso/9780197518335.001.0001

practitioners to capture their organizationally based stories or narratives provides an opportunity for researchers to capture the past, current, and future dynamics of practice (Wells, 2009).

THE CASE STUDY METHODOLOGY FOR CAPTURING THE CHANGING NATURE OF PRACTICE

The development of case studies often includes four distinct phases (see Chapter 11 for more details). These phases include *preparation, data collection, data analysis, and reporting.* According to Yin (2003), **the preparation phase** can include several parts. The first is to orient/train research staff with the appropriate skills using a standardized protocol. The trained researchers should have the capacity and curiosity to ask good questions and interpret answers, to be good listeners, to demonstrate the capacity to be adaptable and flexible, to acquire a firm grasp of the issue being studied, and to be unbiased by preconceived notions. Each researcher needs to know why the study is being done, the evidence being sought, variations that can be anticipated, and what would constitute supportive or contrary evidence. The second part of the preparation phase is to develop the case study protocol. The protocol can include the project overview, interview and field procedures, a brief set of case study questions with probes for each, a plan for selecting the subjects who will inform the case, plans for a pilot interview with an accessible or congenial subject, and a format for reporting the first draft of the case study.

The second component of conducting case studies is **data collection.** Case studies can be built upon an array of potential data sources including documents, archival records, interviews (with key informants and respondents), direct observation, participant observation, and physical artifacts. While direct observation may be the most important form of case-based data to reflect "activity" and "experience" of the case, multiple sources of data represent the ideal (often referred to as triangulation) in order to capture a broad range of historical, attitudinal, and behavioral issues. According to Yin (2003), there are at least four types of triangulation: (1) the convergence of different data sources, (2) data collected by different research staff, (3) consideration of different theoretical perspectives, and (4) use of different research methods to develop the case. One approach to strengthen triangulation is to create a case study database that allows investigators to trace the evolution of data for framing the conclusions. The database could include the case study notes of investigators (organized, categorized, and longitudinal) as well as collected case study documents, tabular materials, and narratives. Finally, Yin (2003) recommends creating a chain of evidence in order to increase reliability. The chain of evidence includes (1) case study questions, (2) case study protocol, (3) sources of evidence, (4) database, and (5) case study report.

Data analysis can be one of the most complicated aspects of conducting a case study when applying one or more analytic techniques. Yin (2003) identifies three analytic techniques; namely, *explanation building*, which seeks to describe and explain the arc of the story underlying the case; *logic modeling*, which is designed to describe a complex chain of events over time where one element leads to another (sometimes used in program evaluation to identify the underlying theory of change); and *cross-case synthesis*, based upon multiple case studies in order to identify major themes or patterns reflecting both commonalities and differences as well as credible assertions supported by the evidence and sometimes supported by the experience or expertise of the cross-case analyst.

The final phase of case study development is the **written report**. Yin (2003) describes three steps for writing a case study; namely, identifying the audience and ways to generate interest and address needs, specifying the report structure (explanation-building, logic model, cross-case), and creating a guide or outline to compose the case study. Yin identifies the following six potential structures for a case study report: (1) the **linear analytic structure** or standard structure for research reports (i.e., problem description, literature review, methods, findings, conclusion; (2) the **comparative structure**, in which cases are discussed from multiple perspectives wherein the facts of the case study are described multiple times within a similar or different conceptual mode; (3) the **chronological structure**, in which the content of the case is organized over time (e.g., early, middle, and late phases) as a form of explanation in search of causality; (4) **theory-building structure**, in which each theme supports a different part of the theoretical argument being made; (5) the **suspense structure** where the linear analytic structure is inverted in order to present the case outcome in the beginning; and (6) the **unsequenced structure**, wherein the evidence-based themes are presented in random order, because the structure of the report is not important. In addition, special consideration needs to be given to the anonymity of cases and participants, as well as to providing an opportunity for contributors to the case description to review the case study draft as a way of participating in the validation process.

LEARNING FROM INDIVIDUAL PRACTITIONERS

Through careful documentation by researchers from outside of the practice setting, it is possible to engage in a form of organizationally focused narrative inquiry or investigative journalism to capture practitioner experiences and lessons learned in their own voices (Wells, 2009). Careful documentation involves a process of amplifying the voices of busy practitioners. It includes conducting multiple ethnographic interviews, editing recorded transcriptions, sharing draft versions with the interview subject, and finalizing the editing process. This highly descriptive form of practice research has the goal of capturing the perspectives of practitioners and often generates ideas about future areas for practice research. For example, case studies of the recurring challenges faced by managers in the public and nonprofit sectors who contract for the delivery of services provided the foundation for a large practice research study described later in Chapter 7. In this section we focus primarily on individual practitioners, primarily those in senior management positions.

The documentation of practice experiences can be used for the development of teaching cases as well as cross-case analysis, and examples of both are provided in this section. The knowledge gained from developing cases can be captured in several domains. The first domain relates to the concept of "practice wisdom" that often is acquired over many years of practice, rarely recorded anywhere, and potentially lost to future generations (except possibly in memoirs, which are quite rare in the human services). A second domain relates to documenting institutional memory where the "tricks of the trade" can be captured (especially those learned over many years of experience related to organizational finance). Included in the area of institutional memory are the multiple organizational changes that occur over time and are not documented and shared with future generations of staff who are likely to "trip over the ghosts of the past" ("we always did it this way") if they are unaware of the changes that preceded their tenure in the organization.

One of the most interesting times to capture the reflections of busy practitioners is when they retire. As they leave their agencies, they are filled with institutional history and memory that rarely gets captured in a form that is useful to other practitioners. The first two examples come from the experiences of agency directors retiring from county public human service organizations. For example, Dick O'Neil retired after 30 years in the same organization, already an unusual phenomenon in an age of multiple career moves (O'Neil, 1995). It is increasingly rare that a social work practitioner spends an entire 30-year career in one agency. When invited as a visiting practice professor to a school of social work to provide lectures, O'Neil was encouraged to reflect on the breadth and depth of his career.

One of the major lessons emerging from his reflections relates to the process of being assigned to a position in a program area where he had no experience or knowledge. As he moved up the career ladder in the agency, he cited this assignment (managing the food stamps program) as a key event in his career, one in which he learned how to take on a challenge (despite an initial reluctance to do so) that led to more opportunities. Once he demonstrated that he could manage the challenge, he was seen as someone capable of handling other challenges en route to his final position as agency director. Many discussion questions related to this teaching case can provide students and practitioners with broader perspectives that reach beyond their current experiences. For example, in an age of rapid career mobility, what are some of the lessons lost from not expanding one's skills over time in one agency? What are some of the adaptive leadership issues connected with taking on an organizational assignment when one does not feel prepared to do so? Questions such as these were used in the pre-service education of future social work managers as well as in the in-service training context of an executive development program for experienced middle-managers.

A second example relates to an agency director who was given the challenge of integrating several county programs into one public human service organization (Borland, 2009). She was pleased with the opportunity to reflect on her experiences after a thirteen year investment but was not sure that others would be interested in her reflections. As with others with her extensive career experience, there is a willingness to share but less of an interest in writing about it, unless someone assumed the practice research responsibility for conducting the interviews, editing the recorded transcriptions, and constructing the first draft of the case for review and comment.

Maureen was known for her innovative approaches to organizational restructuring and service delivery. One of her challenges over the years was finding enough senior and middle managers who could keep up with her pace of change. As an extremely innovative leader, she occasionally generated staff resistance to change. One of her lessons learned related to measuring the frequency and pace of change efforts. Some staff provided pushback with regard to needing more time to implement the latest change project before being asked to begin another one. The questions linked to this teaching case provided students and practitioners with opportunities to reflect on the limits of organizational change and the needs of staff to fully understand and implement new practices. While multiple discussion questions were inserted throughout the teaching case, the following concluding questions provide a few examples: What key principles of organizational change can you draw from this case? And what specific leadership skills do you think would be most important to you as a leader in a human service agency? This teaching case was disseminated as part of a casebook on managing the challenges in human service organizations (Austin, Brody, & Packard, 2009).

The next two examples relate to experiences in nonprofit human service organizations that operate with a different culture than the public agencies. The first example is based on the more than 40-year career of an agency senior manager and is related to experiences in moving up the ladder of increased responsibility while also managing issues of gender and race. As an African-American social work manager, Antoinette Harris (Harris, 2013) found herself engaged in ongoing challenges provided by superiors who found it difficult to understand the complexities of gender and race in the workplace.

The issues of race and gender emerged in the context of university education programs that prepare students for careers in human service organizations that serve increasingly diverse vulnerable populations. Learning from the experiences of senior practitioners provides the opportunity for students from a variety of backgrounds to engage an experienced practitioner on subject matter that can be both sensitive and emotionally intense. The recorded interviews, along with reviewing the edited transcript, provided her with a safe and supportive environment to share her experiences with a white male age-group peer.

In reflecting upon her workplace experiences, Antoinette recounted the continuous need to educate others about discrimination related to both racist and sexist behaviors. This became her second job (unpaid) along with helping staff manage the daily pressures of changing client needs and shifting service priorities. While this teaching case can generate many discussion questions, the greatest learning value can be acquired by those who have never experienced these pressures or have experienced them in a different way. The discussion questions included: (1) What is it like to be true to yourself, your culture, and your value system? (2) How do education, knowledge, and understanding provide a key to integrating gender and race into the workforce without using gender and race as excuses for poor performance? And (3) why is the desire to be the most effective provider/director of services a more important motivator than the lack of gender and race representation within the organization?

The last of these four cases relates to managing organizational change in a very traditional nonprofit family service agency that was continuing to use written case notes placed in case record file folders late in the era of automated, computer-based record keeping. Bob Bennett (2017) was hired away from his successful consulting organization to become the director of an agency that had become both inefficient and very expensive to operate. His reflections captured the process of training staff to engage in new systems of record keeping along with the introduction of documenting and measuring service outcomes. Both changes generated significant staff resistance, which led to a significant proportion of the staff leaving the agency as new, more computer-literate staff were hired to fill the vacancies. This process resembled the old story of "trying to change a flat tire while the car was moving at 60 miles an hour." Maintaining high-quality services while also managing significant staff changes required intensive leadership patience, persistence, and extended time horizons.

The discussion questions associated with this teaching case provide students and practitioners with the challenges associated with managing complex change. Some discussion questions include: Given the creation of a joint management and staff team, what might have been done to anticipate and address the resistance he encountered? What team-building strategies might he have employed? What might be some ways to manage the "clash" between evidence-based practice (EBP) developed and tested in carefully structured environments and the complex demands of providing services in community settings? All of the cases noted above are published in either casebooks or articles that provide students with a wealth of practice experience that often differs from textbook literature, research literature, or exposure to the practice experience of fieldwork instructors. The last section of the chapter explores the process of learning from multiple practitioners.

Learning from Multiple Practitioners

While there are similarities between developing cases based on the experience of one practitioner and cases that involve multiple practitioners (identifying the theme, creating a safe interviewing space for reflection, providing opportunities to review and correct the written version), there are also significant differences, as is illustrated in this section. Learning from multiple practitioners is based on engaging in similar experiences as well as capturing the uniqueness of each participant. As a result, the criteria for including multiple practitioners is directly related to similar or shared experiences, local access, and/or prior relationships (e.g., participants in a local think tank or participants in a local training program), as well as a willingness to reflect upon similar experiences. While the capturing of individual experiences is not necessarily designed to inform the reflections of other practitioners, the goal of the contributions from individuals is for the practice researcher to engage in cross-case analysis to identify themes that emerge from both similar and different experiences.

The first example of learning from multiple practitioners relates to the topic of boundary spanning, which emerged within the context of think tanks for agency directors working in the public sector of local government. Sharing perspectives on various service delivery issues frequently reflected prior work experiences, often related to different sectors; namely, public sector administrators drawing upon their experiences in the nonprofit sector or nonprofit executives drawing upon their public sector experiences. These exchanges became even more enriched by experiences in the for-profit sector.

Little attention has been given to the boundary-spanning capabilities of human service managers seeking to manage the relationship between public and nonprofit sector programs effectively. This exploratory study sought to identify those capabilities by documenting the boundary-crossing career trajectories of senior human service managers and directors in the United States and United Kingdom. The overall purpose of the study was to identify the lessons learned by senior managers as they reflected, in retrospect, on their careers in both sectors. The specific purposes of the study included capturing: (1) the dynamics of people's career trajectories between the sectors; (2) how their personal, role, and integrative perspectives develop across the nonprofit and public sectors; and (3) the means to strengthen the capacity of both sectors. The cross-national perspective was enhanced by a practice researcher who had completed previous research on boundary-spanning in a developing country and had created a conceptual framework for use in analyzing cross-case situations (Lewis, 2008).

Lewis (2008) notes that the types of boundary crossers varied in their adaptive "sense-making" at the individual, organizational, or sector levels, and categorizes their motivations for boundary crossing as *reactive, opportunistic,* or *proactive* strategies. The proactive strategy at the individual level is essentially goal-oriented entrepreneurial behaviors by managers with the goal of either improving their own job satisfaction or increasing their leverage to bring about change. At the organizational level, managers innovate by applying ideas from one sector to another, and at the sector level managers view the boundary crossing as career enhancing. In contrast, the opportunistic strategy comprises less planned activity and more situation-specific behaviors (individual) that respond to unexpected opportunities (organizational) and purposely seek to straddle both sectors (sector). And, finally, the reactive strategy is less a response to the "pull" of opportunity and more of a "push" related to leaving a less than satisfactory situation at all three levels (individual, organizational, and sector). As a distinctive form of "boundary spanning,"' boundary crossing provides an opportunity to see how workplace knowledge is created and shared.

While this exploratory study sought to capture the boundary-crossing changes in the personal and role perspectives of senior human service managers and agency directors, the major findings, based on a cross-case analysis of the major themes, led to three types of boundary crossers: (1) client advocates, (2) organizational change agents, and (3) team leaders.

Client Advocates

The client advocate type of administrator often has a proactive management style that was developed in a nonprofit career and utilized in public sector experiences as demonstrated by a commitment to professional values. The traditional roles played by individuals in the nonprofit sector include serving as an early warning system that can identify problems or service gaps and advocate for correcting them so that government can understand and address them. Their nonprofit sector roles can also inhibit them from engaging in advocacy because of their current funding contracts with the public sector.

Organizational Change Agents

Boundary-crossing administrators with an orientation to organizational change and policy advocacy display an array of skills and abilities necessary to improve organizations and address the needs of their various stakeholders. Their training and experience often motivate them to move from one sector to another in order to use the organizational strengths developed in their former sector to make real changes in their new sector. The challenge of innovating and developing flexibility in policies and practices seems to inspire these boundary crossers. In their efforts to use knowledge, connections, and skills in the new sector that they have entered, they tend to focus more on the organizational issues and less on interpersonal issues. Despite their successes as organizational change agents, these boundary crossers encounter significant political challenges that often lead them to relocate either in a politically congruent public agency or back in the nonprofit sector.

Team Leaders

Boundary crossers who function as team leaders display significant adaptive competencies as illustrated by their self-confidence and role responses to the ever-changing demands of the environment. They can effectively scan and read the environment (inside and outside of organizations) to identify when changes are needed and new skills required. For these individuals, the motivations to cross boundaries were often external to their professional or role identities and included family relocation, recruitment, or an opportunity to closely align their professional and organizational identities.

In summary, the case vignettes of boundary crossers illustrate the important role they can play in bringing the "client voice" from the nonprofit sector to the attention of the public sector. When administrators who reflect a client-advocate, team leader, or organizational change agent orientation cross over from the nonprofit sector to the public sector, they help to sensitize government to its mission of service to the community and its citizens within the context of regulation, politics, and power.

The nonprofit boundary crossers to the public sector also provide firsthand knowledge of the impact of public policies on individuals and groups in the community as they negotiate and implement contracted services. The public sector often does not have the capacity to see firsthand the consequences of its policy decisions. As a result, the public sector can benefit from an infusion of the nonprofit sector's service delivery values of listening, consensus building, cultural competence, and client satisfaction. In contrast, the case studies of individuals with government experience reported that their work revolved around roles and activities such as developing procedures, writing reports, monitoring services, developing policy, requesting proposals, and briefing leaders. The nonprofit-sector boundary crossers help to soften the bureaucratic approach to policies and procedures by interjecting the community's experience and the importance of service values.

In contrast to boundary crossers from the nonprofit sector who can sensitize the public sector, boundary crossers from the public sector often bring with them a big-picture perspective related to policy development and implementation regarding the major social problems facing society (e.g., homelessness and housing, child welfare, domestic violence, prisons, and health care reform). In addition to bringing an understanding of how to interpret public policies and funding practices, those with public-sector experience were able to demonstrate a range of expertise in promoting accountability and measuring outcomes.

Finally, experience in the public sector provides administrators with an understanding of how personal troubles are translated into public policy. In being responsive to the entire community, public sector administrators learn how to deal with multiple stakeholders, including advocacy organizations, business interests, multiple levels of government, and political constituents. In addition, multiple interest groups often lobby public sector administrators, and these sources of information need to be managed.

Practice Implications

Creating a mechanism that would support career transfers between the nonprofit and public sectors could address one or more of the following objectives: (1) strengthen management capabilities to be able to operate effectively in both sectors; (2) assist the transfer and use of new technologies for organizational problem solving within and between the sectors; (3) create an environment for more effective government policy and program development; and (4) provide experience that would strengthen the capacities of both sectors, especially enhanced interorganizational relations.

Learning from Multiple Practitioners Through Participation in a Learning Lab

Another approach to learning from multiple practitioners is illustrated by engaging and observing a group of middle-managers experiencing a leadership training program. The program emerged from the interests of nonprofit human service agency directors interested in providing learning opportunities for their middle-managers. As part of monitoring and evaluating the program, the staff collected periodic feedback from the participants as well as engaged in observations of the group learning experience. Given that agency-based observational data is quite complex (e.g., expensive, time intensive, and multifaceted) to collect within the context of practice research, a partially controlled learning environment provided an ideal locale for infusing observation data with program monitoring data. The observational data were collected by the program trainer along with the program coordinator with numerous opportunities to compare notes and to debrief overall program experiences through a debriefing process that involved a doctoral student. A learning lab provides another setting for engaging in practice research with practitioners away from the intensity of the agency workplace (Austin, Regan, Samples, Schwartz, & Carnochan, 2011; Austin, Regan, Gothard, & Carnochan, 2013).

The transition from direct service to management in human service organizations requires newly promoted managers to engage in a significant role transformation that calls into question their self-concept and identity. Yet, new managers are rarely provided training opportunities that address the formation of a managerial identity. The for-profit and nonprofit literature was used to construct a conceptual model of managerial identity formation. The model was then applied to a case vignette of a managerial leadership development training program developed by a regional network of nonprofit human service agency directors. The goal was to identify implications for managerial training and leadership development in human service organizations.

Based upon a conceptual framework located in the business management literature, the data collected from the learning lab was organized within the existing key concepts developed by Hill (2003). The framework provided a structure to capture the professional and psychological transformations that accompany the transition from direct service to management in human service organizations, where new managers seek to renegotiate their professional role and adjust their own self-perceptions. The framework identifies four stages that characterize the transition: (1) Emerging, (2) Becoming, (3) Acting, and (4) Thriving. Organizations are called to plan and provide for adequate time and a safe space for reflection and learning during these stages (Dubouloy, 2004). An organization's culture and context, including the quality and quantity of training offered, affect the ease with which new managers form a managerial identity. This transformation requires the personal capacity to: (1) cope with increased stress, isolation, and emotion associated with the construction of a managerial identity; (2) engage in honest self-reflection and assessment; (3) recognize personal style; and (4) adjust style/approach in order to meet the demands of the role. In addition, the ability to engage in experiential on-the-job learning is often critical to making a successful transition.

The first stage, *Emerging*, marks the period in which a specialist is identified as a prospective generalist for a role in management. An "emergent manager" is one who is encouraged to: (1) reflect on past experiences and future goals, (2) seek stretch assignments, (3) ask questions and observe activities to get an accurate picture of managerial work, and (4) actively develop professional and support networks (Watson, 2001; Hill, 2003).

The second phase, *Becoming a manager*, often begins at the point of promotion and is marked by negotiating the role and reconstructing elements of identity. The five substantial identity-related shifts that characterize this phase include what Hill (2003) describes as: (1) moving away from technical or clinical mastery and toward generalist competencies, (2) shifting from the role of a specialist or an independent practitioner to that of an interdependent manager, (3) learning to adjust one's locus of responsibility from individual-level task completion to team-level success, (4) shifting from building credibility primarily with clients or customers to learning how to develop credibility with one's staff, and (5) letting go of the need to be personally *liked* and moving toward reliance on being respected in a role, a shift that often is associated with the loss of peer camaraderie and a well-defined reference group (Barnes, 1981; Cohen, 2005).

As new managers gain role clarity and begin *Acting* in a role, they often are confronted with competing demands. New managers continue to construct their managerial identity as they learn to balance the processes of: (1) managing individuals as well as an overall team (Fleming, 2008; Hill, 2004; Hill, 2007); (2) offering support while developing an ability to effectively confront problematic behavior; (3) setting high expectations for performance as well as opportunities for growth and development; (4) acknowledging managerial authority while striving to empower team autonomy (Hill, 2003); (5) relying on personal power while recognizing their new positional power (Hitt, Black, & Porter, 2005); and (6) managing up and down, as well as out (both in the agency and the community) (Austin, 1981, 1988, 2002).

While this model depicts a linear framework, new managers often learn to "become" and "act" as managers simultaneously by thriving in one area and continuing to construct a managerial identity in another. New managers find themselves *Thriving* as they begin to move away from crisis management toward managerial leadership, marked by comfort and competence in planning ahead while effectively managing the present. In order to thrive as leaders in human service organizations new managers are called upon to engage in the following managerial roles: (1) analytic roles that include leveraging resources, managing resources, creating and influencing policy, and evaluating outcomes; (2) leadership roles that include boundary spanning, future planning, aligning process and structure, team building and management, and coalition building; and (3) interactional roles that include facilitating, communicating, advocating, and supervising (Austin & Kruzich, 2004; Menefee & Thompson, 1994). In order to maintain and renew their ability to thrive, managers need to engage in an ongoing process of self-reflection and continuous on-the-job learning (Hill, 2003; Hill, 2004; McCall & Hollenbeck, 2007; McCall & Hollenbeck, 2008; Watson, 2001).

Reflections of an Accidental Manager: The following vignette was developed by a middle manager in a children's residential treatment agency who was struggling with her identity as a manager after many years as a clinician. The story was used in a reporting context where participants shared a key management challenge with the other training program participants. It also was used within the context of research on leadership-identity formation (Regan, 2016).

> I was terrified by each new promotion into administration because I never conceived of myself as a director or even a supervisor because I really loved doing social work in the form of case management and delivering school-based services. So when the agency director and deputy director (my immediate boss) encouraged me to focus on refining my management skills by enrolling in a new leadership development program for middle and senior managers in nonprofit human service agencies, I seized the opportunity for further professional development.
>
> In the program I found myself building upon some advice I had received from the deputy director who supervised my work. My job included a lot of coordination with city department heads of children's programs that include a great deal of politics that made me very nervous because I never wanted to say the wrong thing and thereby jeopardize any of our service contracts. He advised me to remember the "Three S's" related to style, substance and strategy by reflecting on the work of our CEO. She had her own style and sense of authenticity in her interactions with others (e.g., warmly sharing information about her daughter or garden) where the essence of her personality comes out in every interaction. My supervisor described my style and encouraged me to trust it because sharing the essence of who I am can be really powerful in fostering effective communications. The second "S" related to substance requires one to know what they are talking about in order to effectively advocate for human services based on doing one's homework. The third "S" relates to strategy where every time you open

your mouth, the comments shared are strategic. So when the CEO is chatting with me, for instance, about our own kids, you know that her comments are designed to support my professional growth as well as gaining my opinion on some agency issue.

So, the three "S's" have been a really helpful tool for me to use when I was feeling unsure of myself in certain situations. I was also urged to take care of myself as a manager so that I would not absorb or internalize all the stress related to the job. Because social work involves our hearts and souls, as well as our skills, we need to replenish ourselves every day. We need to find something that we love that nourishes us on a daily basis. For me it's walking up hills, like it's my great joy to go into nature and walk up a really big hill and I do it everyday. I walk up a hill and I am puffing and I am thinking about work and problem solving. And then I get to the top and I put my iPod on and I just wander on the hill thinking about everything I want to think about. And it's incredibly nourishing and important for me to do. And that enables me to do the other things like searching for a "high spot" where I can go mentally (i.e., it is not a physical place) and be able to separate myself from the helter-skelter of daily work to find space to think strategically in order not to get lost in the "woods of the work" and ultimately burn out.

These illustrations of learning from a cross-case analysis of career trajectories (using interviews) and from participants in a learning laboratory (using observations and self-report exercises) inform our understanding of practice research from a group or population perspective. In the case of the learning laboratory, the breadth and depth of the observational and self-reflective data contributed to new insights emerging from this form of practice research. For example, the process of becoming a manager involves making the transition from being a specialist (working directly with clients) to becoming a generalist (working primarily with staff) and includes several component parts that all involve some aspect of an identity-formation process. These parts include "emerging" (assessing future potential and fit for becoming a manager), "becoming" (seeking role clarity and constructing a new identity), "acting" (learning to balance competing forces and values), and "thriving" (planning ahead and managing the present). This form of practice research provides further insights for staff members who become supervisors or program managers, especially those who do not have the opportunity for additional training (Austin, Regan, Samples, Schwartz, & Carnochan, 2011; Austin, Regan, Gothard, & Carnochan, 2013; Regan, 2016).

In addition to the value of in-depth case descriptions and cross-case analysis of these descriptions, the cases emerging from practice research also can be used in the teaching process of case-based learning. The preparation of future practitioners is enhanced by learning from experienced practitioners, a process that often is valued by students when guest speakers share their experiences and perspectives in university classrooms. Many of the cases emerging from practice research that are referenced throughout this book have been used in the teaching of practice courses (Austin, Brody, & Packard, 2009; Austin & Packard, 2009; Cossom, 1991).

CONCLUSION

This chapter features an aspect of practice research that seeks to capture the changing nature of practice. While the data collection tools are traditional (interviews, observations, etc.), this form of practice research includes the documentation of practitioner experiences in order to improve our understanding of career trajectories in human service organizations and the challenges of assuming new roles. It includes examples of learning from the experiences of individual practitioners as well as learning from the training-laboratory experiences of groups of practitioners.

This chapter also builds upon the themes in the previous chapter that feature the emerging definition of practice research. It also provides examples of the science of the concrete (gets close to reality, emphasizes little things, features practical activities and knowledge in everyday situations, focuses on both the human behavior of the actors and structural levels found in the social environment, and engages in dialogue with a wide range of voices). The process of learning from the practice experiences and acquired wisdom of individuals serves as a foundation for the next chapter, which features the process of learning from researchers and practitioners as they have reported their findings in the literature. The construction of literature reviews, as either free standing contributions to practice research or as components of a practice research study, is a critical component of all applied research in order to build upon what is already known.

REFERENCES

Austin, M.J (1981). *Supervisory Management for the Human Services.* Englewood Cliffs, NJ: Prentice-Hall.

Austin, M.J. (1988). Managing up: Relationship building between middle management and top management. *Administration in Social Work, 12*(4), 29–46.

Austin, M.J. (2002). Managing out: The community practice dimensions of effective agency management. *Journal of Community Practice, 10*(4), 33–48.

Austin, M.J., Brody, R.P., & Packard, T. (Eds.) (2009). *Managing the challenges in human service organizations: A casebook.* Thousand Oaks, CA: Sage.

Austin, M.J., & Kruzich, J.M. (2004). Assessing recent textbooks and casebooks in human service administration: Implications and future directions, *Administration in Social Work, 28*(1), 115–137.

Austin, M.J., & Packard, T. (2009). Case-based learning: Educating human service managers. *Journal of Teaching in Social Work, 29*(2), 216–236.

Austin, M.J., Regan, K., Gothard, S., & Carnochan, S. (2013). Becoming a manager in a nonprofit human service organization: Making the transition from specialist to generalist. *Administration in Social Work, 37*(4), 372–385.

Austin, M.J., Regan, K., Samples, M., Schwartz, S., & Carnochan, S. (2011). Building managerial and organizational capacity in nonprofit human service organizations through a leadership development program. *Administration in Social Work, 35*(3), 258–281.

Barnes, L.B. (1981). Managing the paradox of organizational trust. *Harvard Business Review, 2,* 107–116.

Bennett, B. (2017). Building an organizational culture to support evidence-informed practice: A teaching case. *Human Service Organizations: Management, Leadership & Governance, 41*(5), 560–566.

Borland, M. (2009). The leadership challenges in transforming a public human services agency. In M.J. Austin, R.P. Brody, & T. Packard (Eds.), *Managing the challenges in human service organizations: A casebook* (pp. 242–269). Thousand Oaks, CA: Sage.

Chan, C., & Holosko, M.J. (2016). A review of information and communication technology enhanced social work interventions. *Research on Social Work Practice, 26*(1), 88–100.

Cohen, S. (2005). Smoothly transition from friend to manager. *Nursing Management, 36*(2), 12–13.

Cossom, J. (1991). Teaching from cases: Education for critical thinking. *Journal of Teaching Social Work, 5*(1), 139–155.

Dubouloy, M. (2004). The transitional space and self-recovery: A psychoanalytical approach to high-potential manager's training. *Human Relations, 57*(4), 467–496.

Fleming, R.S. (2008). Survival Skills for the New Manager. *The Business Renaissance Quarterly: Enhancing the Quality of Life at Work, 3*(2), 127–137.

Goldkind, L., & Wolf, L. (2015). A digital environment approach: Four technologies that will disrupt social work practice. *Social Work, 60*(1), 85–87.

Harris, A. (2013). *Reflections on race and gender throughout the career of a senior human service manager: Teaching case.* Berkeley: Mack Center on Nonprofit and Public Sector Management in the Human Services, School of Social Welfare, University of California, Berkeley.

Hill, L.A. (2003). *Becoming a manager: How new managers master the challenge of leadership (2nd ed.).* Boston, MA: Harvard Business School Publishing Co.

Hill, L.A. (2004). New manager development for the 21st century. *Academy of Management Executive, 18*(3), 121–126.

Hill, L.A. (2007). Becoming the boss. *Harvard Business Review, 85*(1), 48–56.

Hitt, M.A., Black, S., & Porter, L.W. (2005). *Management* (2nd Ed.). Upper Saddle River, NJ: Pearson Prentice Hall.

Lewis, D. (2008). Using life-work histories in social policy research: The case of third sector/public sector boundary crossing. *Journal of Social Policy, 37*(4), 1–20.

McCall, M.W., Jr., & Hollenbeck, G.P. (2007). Getting Leadership Development Right. *Leadership Excellence, 24*(2), 8–9.

McCall, M.W., & Hollenbeck, G.P. (2008). Developing the Expert Leader. *People and Strategy, 31*(1), 20–28.

Miles, M.B., & Huberman, A.M. (1994). *Qualitative Data Analysis: An Expanded Sourcebook.* Thousand Oaks, CA: Sage Publications.

O'Neil, R.R. (1995). From vision to reality and back to vision: Reflections on three decades in public social services administration. In M.J. Austin & S. Weisner (Eds.), *Guiding organizational change: BASSC executive development program.* Berkeley: University of California Extension.

Regan, K. (2016). Leadership identity formation in nonprofit human service organizations. *Human Service Organizations: Management, Leadership & Governance, 40*(5), 435–440.

Stake, R.E. (2010). *Qualitative research: Studying how things work.* New York, NY: Guilford Press.

Steyaert, J., & Gould, N. (2009). Social work and the changing face of the digital divide. *British Journal of Social Work*, *39*(4), 740–753.

Thompson, J.J., & Menefee, D.T. (1994). Rural/urban comparisons of social work management competencies. *Human Services in the Rural Environment*, *17*(3-4), 59–64.

Wareing, T., & Hendrick, H.H. (2013). 5 Trends Driving the Future of Human Services. Downloaded on December 21, 2018. http://www.govtech.com/health/5-Trends-Driving-the-Future-of-Human-Services.html

Watson, T.J. (2001). The emergent manager and processes of management pre-learning. *Management Learning*, *32*(2), 221–235.

Wells, K. (2009). *Narrative inquiry*. New York, NY: Oxford University Press.

Yin, R.K. (2003). *Case study research: Design and methods (3rd ed.)*. Thousand Oaks, CA: Sage.

3

Learning from the Literature

OVERVIEW

Although the review of existing literature is a central feature of any research project (as a way of learning what is already known about a topic), the development of independent, freestanding literature reviews designed to inform practice are less common. Such reviews have been a tradition in the academic literature when literature review articles are commissioned to capture a decade or more of recent research, often for the purpose of documenting recent developments as a foundation for projecting areas for future research.

In our work, freestanding literature reviews within the context of practice research emerged from a call from the practice community. Following the initial experience of conducting local exploratory research projects, agency directors commented on the ever-increasing pile of research reports accumulating in their offices. They wondered whether the practice research agenda could include literature reviews on current topics, which would focus on practice or policy implications, and

Practice Research in the Human Services. Michael J. Austin and Sarah Carnochan, Oxford University Press (2020). © Oxford University Press.
DOI: 10.1093/oso/9780197518335.001.0001

incorporate work published think tanks, research institutes, universities, and the federal government. With regard to those reports piling up in their offices, they worried about the following: (1) Where would they find time to read them? (2) Even if they found the time, would they be able to understand them? (3) Even if they had the time to read and understand them, how would they identify implications for managing their own organizations? and (4) even with the identification of the research implications, how would they find the time to develop implementation strategies?

In light of these challenges, the practice research agenda changed from regional exploratory research projects that addressed one topic relevant to many counties to a predominant focus on the development of structured literature reviews. This shift in focus for an evolving practice research agenda was based on several factors impacting the practitioner community of agency directors. Many of the directors noted that they were being inundated with major national reports produced by the Urban Institute, Mathematica, Manpower Demonstration Research Corporation (MDRC), government reports, and reports emanating from universities and national organizations. These reports piled up in the offices of directors with neither the time nor research expertise needed to assess the relevance of the reports for local consideration. In essence, the directors were reacting to the increasing flood of information and wanted to become more proactive in the choice of topic to be explored and array of research findings located in the literature. As a result, they wanted to "hit the pause button" on the evolving local research agenda to redirect attention to existing literature with its implications for agency practice and policymaking. This shift in focus also represented a growing interest in monitoring the expanding knowledge base (often found in journals that these practitioners did not read or have access to) by tracking research dissemination located in multiple databases (also not easily accessible to the practice community except through their university partners). The major theme of this shift in focus is located in a recurring question from the agency directors; namely, "shouldn't we be making better use of the knowledge already documented while also seeking new knowledge through our regional practice research agenda?"

DEFINING STRUCTURED LITERATURE REVIEWS

This definitional process took place in the midst of international interest in systematic literature reviews associated with the Cochrane Collaborative (UK-based and health oriented) and the Campbell Collaborative (US-based and social and economic change oriented) that were both seeking to account for research studies based on the use of random controlled trials (RCTs).

This approach was labeled the "gold standard" of literature reviews, but it was unrealistic for practice research in the human services, where very few RCTs had been completed (Saini & Schlonsky, 2012). As a result a "silver standard" needed to be developed in the form of a structured literature review that cast a wide net when searching the literature for both qualitative and quantitative studies that appeared in the peer-reviewed journal literature as well as in the "gray" literature that included government, research institute, and agency reports of all types. Although this approach is open to legitimate criticism regarding the uneven quality of such research, the rigor of the structured review process can begin to address this issue.

As noted in Figure 3.1, the structured literature review process includes the following components:

(1) *Identifying topics of interest with practice community*: Topics often emerge within the context of meeting discussions when practitioners share their concerns about a particular issue and then check to see if there is sufficient interest among the majority of members for investing shared research resources (funding) in pursuit of learning more about the topic from the existing literature.

(2) *Shared refinement of focus of literature search with the practice community*: When topics emerge, they are often in the form of global or wide-ranging descriptions. Further discussion with the research partners often yields a more focused definition of the topic and the array of related issues. This refinement process may evolve over several meetings as the minutes of previous meetings provide the continuity of discussion, and the refinement process benefits from the intervening time that allows members to devote more thought to the essence of their concerns.

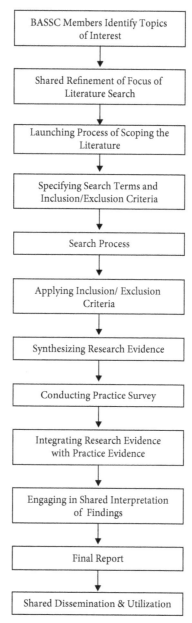

Figure 3.1. Flowchart of a structured literature review process

Anthony, E.K., & Austin, M.J. (2008). The role of an intermediary organization in promoting research in schools of social work: The case of the Bay Area Social Services Consortium. *Social Work Research, 32*(4), 287–293.

(3) *Launching the process of scoping the literature*: This often is enhanced by scanning existing literature-review chapters located in handbooks on specific topics. Scoping the literature often is linked to developing a written research proposal for the practitioners to review and provide final approval for, potentially allowing time for further clarification of the topic and areas of interest.

(4) *Specifying search terms and inclusion/exclusion criteria*: Frequently performed with the help of graduate research assistants, this is an iterative process based on exploring the various terms used in the literature to identify those terms that look most promising in terms of the topic under investigation and the evolution of interests expressed by the practice community. The definition of the exclusion and inclusion criteria for database searching (frequently multiple databases) can include the specification of the rationale for excluding, as well as including, key terms related to the topic.

(5) *Online search process*: The initial search process often generates many more citations from the literature than can be easily managed. As a result, the application of the exclusion and inclusion criteria makes it possible to filter or select the most promising citations (often based only on the title and abstract of an article).

(6) *Applying inclusion/exclusion criteria*: By applying the criteria as rigorously as possible, the search process often yields fewer than one hundred of the most promising citations. Although the focus is frequently on journal articles, the search also includes what often is called the gray literature that encompasses agency and government reports.

(7) *Synthesizing research evidence*: This process involves the application of critical thinking skills when reviewing articles of interest to report on key attributes (topic definition, literature citations worth pursuing, study sample and research methods used, key findings, implications, etc.). Once a set of articles are reviewed with brief descriptions of each, they are clustered by themes that emerge from a critical review in order to synthesize the literature findings into major categories.

(8) *Conducting practice survey* (when feasible): Given the magnitude of the literature review, gathering perceptions of staff is often a luxury and is frequently time consuming. This form of triangulation between the published literature and the current realities of practice can greatly enrich the literature process but is increasingly not feasible, especially as busy staff rarely have time to respond to another survey even if it is brief.

(9) *Integrating research evidence with practice evidence*: When this step in a literature review process is feasible, the integration often relates primarily to the implications section of the literature review.

(10) *Engaging the practice community in a shared interpretation of findings*: In addition to the shared process of defining the study topic, this element related to shared interpretation of the findings might prove to be the most critical element. In practice, the discussion questions frequently relate to the following concerns: Are the themes relevant to current practice? How might the reported data be interpreted differently? What might be the most significant implications of the findings with regard to current practice?

(11) *Compiling final report*: In light of the limited time available for busy practitioners to read reports, the most efficient method of reporting is currently PowerPoint slides along with extensive discussion ("What did we learn? Who should receive this information? What else should be explored?). For those practitioners able to invest more time, a written report also can be shared, given that it is the foundation of the PowerPoint slides. Because of the length of some of the literature review reports, a graphic designer was engaged to lay out the content in the most readable format (e.g., two columns along with improved graphics for the figures) making it more accessible for busy practitioners with limited time to read. While time is needed for practitioners to receive a local version of the report, another form of reporting is publication as a journal article that often benefits from the critical review of an anonymous reviewer.

(12) *Promoting dissemination and utilization*: This is another challenging step in the literature review process. Sharing the

results of the literature review takes time, either in the form
of training others to disseminate the findings or designing
instructional materials for incorporation into agency training
programs. Based upon a request from the practice community,
the researchers who conducted the literature review were
encouraged to create a brief list of recommendations for
organizations to share with their senior management team.
These would serve as a springboard for discussion among
those who often demonstrate greater capacities to react than
time to be creatively proactive with the findings. In essence, a
rationale often emerges during a discussion as to the feasibility
or modification of a recommendation related to implementing
change in the organization.

In some instances, the framing of literature reviews in response
to questions raised by practitioners generated a topic that did not fit
neatly within the boundaries of academic disciplines or fields of study.
Consequently, it was sometimes difficult to specify in advance a comprehensive set of search terms. In these circumstances, it was helpful
to employ additional strategies designed to map the web of scholarship
relevant to a practice-based question. In particular, backward citation
searches drawing on the reference list of a primary article were used to
locate the earlier sources that informed the conceptualization and contribution of the primary article. Similarly, forward citation searching
using Google Scholar assisted in tracing how the understanding of an
issue or topic had evolved through subsequent studies.

The first sets of literature reviews focused on the complex nature
of child welfare practice where practitioners face the daily challenge of
balancing the two service goals of child safety and family preservation.
In the course of multiple discussions, recurring topics emerged (e.g.,
Why are so many children of color entering our service system? What
does research say about the outcomes of referring abusive or neglectful parents to parenting education programs? What does the literature
say about approaching abused or neglected children from a wellness
or strengths perspective?). For example, when the literature on client
assessment instruments was the focus of a literature review, particular attention was given to instrument validity and reliability issues as
well as the search terms used in the process. Our practice partners were

concerned about the current inadequacy of the assessment tools used by their line staff to weigh the very complex decision informed by the evidence for the removal of a child from an abusive or neglectful family for placement in foster care. As for the anticipated outcomes of such literature reviews, the agency directors were hopeful that the process would identify promising practices used in other jurisdictions, evidence that would inform current practices or help to change them, and provide the practice community with information that was generally inaccessible or inadequately assessed. See Attachment A for the array of literature review topics requested by our practice community.

CHILD WELFARE POPULATION ISSUES

The first set of concerns related to various child welfare issues impacting children and parents as well as service outcomes and organizational challenges are noted in Box 3.1. The issues emerged in discussions among the agency directors that were often informed by internal agency discussion among senior managers of child welfare services. The literature reviews were guided by such questions from the practice community as: (1) What are some realistic treatment outcomes for substance abusing parents who abuse or neglect their children? (2) What are the similarities and differences among the instruments used to assess child risk and safety? (3) What are some of the best family assessment tools for promoting family preservation? and (4) given the trauma associated with removing a child from her/his family, what are some of the assessment tools available for assessing child well-being? Although these particular questions focus on the delivery of services, other questions emerged from interests in the outcomes of child welfare services such as measurement issues, parental substance abuse intervention, and parent education programs.

The launching of the structured literature reviews occurred at the same time that there was growing interest in promoting evidence-informed practice. Again, multiple discussions among agency directors included recurring questions about defining the necessary organizational supports needed for staff to engage in evidence-informed practice. The challenges faced by child welfare program managers included the need to address the following questions: (1) What kind

Box 3.1. Evidence for Child Welfare Practice: Building a Foundation for Evidence-informed Practice*

EVIDENCE FOR DIRECT PRACTICE

Assessment in Child Welfare

- Understanding and Addressing Racial/Ethnic Disproportionality in the Front End of the Child Welfare System
- Risk and Safety Assessment in Child Welfare: Instrument Comparisons
- Family Assessment in Child Welfare Services: Instrument Comparisons
- Assessing Child and Youth Well-being: Implications for Child Welfare Practice

Assessing Child Welfare Outcomes

- Understanding and Measuring Child Welfare Outcomes
- Substance Abuse Interventions for Parents Involved in the Child Welfare System: Evidence and Implications
- Assessing Parent Education Programs for Families Involved with Child Welfare Services: Evidence and Implications

EVIDENCE FOR MANAGEMENT PRACTICE

- Evidence-based Practice in the Social Services: Implications for Organizational Change
- Assessing the Evidence on Implementing Evidence-based Practice in Human Service
- Organizations: Preliminary Lessons from the Frontlines
- Dissemination and Utilization of Research for Promoting Evidence-based Practice
- Impact of Organizational Change on Organizational Culture: Implications for Introducing Evidence-based Practice
- Knowledge Management: Implications for Human Service Organizations

*Special Issue, *Journal of Evidence-based Social Work*, 5(1/2), 2008.

of organizational changes need to be considered when promoting evidence-informed practice? (2) What research dissemination and utilization issues need to be addressed related to staff training and education? (3) What changes in the culture of an organization need to be considered when promoting evidence-informed practice? and (4) How is staff knowledge (tacit and explicit) incorporated into evidence-informed practice? All of these questions emerged from ongoing discussions in regularly scheduled meetings of county human service organization directors, often in consultation with their deputy directors in charge of child welfare services.

CHILD WELFARE ORGANIZATIONAL PERFORMANCE ISSUES

In addition to deriving literature review topics from ongoing dialogue with practitioners, there was also interest in learning from the experiences of those engaged in practice research who are located in other countries. One approach included the use of video-conferencing among peers located in the San Francisco Bay Area and a similar group of administrators located in southwest England. This form of exchange greatly enhanced the process of learning from others and led to other forms of learning. For example, considerable efforts were being made by Research in Practice (RiP) in the United Kingdom to assist child welfare staff with their understanding of national government service outcome standards. The RiP publications (Performance Pointers) were developed around a framework that included a description of the national standard, the research underlying the standard, examples of applying the standard, and staff discussion questions designed to increase understanding. When examples of the RiP publications were shared with the local practice community of agency directors, there was considerable interest and support for developing something similar for their child welfare staff members.

Parallel interests in the United States took the form of concerns about the emphasis placed on the use of administrative data to measure service outcomes. In particular, county human service agencies were experiencing difficulties in meeting performance indicators established by the Children and Family Services Review (CFSR) process initiated in 2001, based on federal child welfare performance mandates that were codified in the Social Security Amendments of 1994 and Adoption and Safe Families Act (ASFA) of 1997. Previous evaluation methods focused on the compliance of states with mandated processes, but the CFSRs were intended to tie agency performance to the three broad goals of safety, permanency, and well-being. Based on the emerging interest in replicating the RiP experience in the United States, the county directors decided to select the federal child welfare outcome standards that were causing the most problems with respect to local efforts to meet those standards. In particular, their concerns related to: (1) achieving exits to permanency for children in long-term care, (2) preventing re-entry to foster care, (3) achieving placement stability, (4) achieving timely adoption, (5) achieving timely reunification, and (6) preventing the recurrence of maltreatment.

Following the selection of the federal performance indicators that would be the focus of the literature reviews, we engaged in a series of consultations with a former county human service agency director regarding the framing of the literature reviews aimed at strengthening their relevance for child welfare practitioners. We also consulted a local expert on the federal performance indicators, to explore technical issues related to the measures, as well as the ongoing policy context. Following these discussions, our team of student researchers began to search the literature and develop the reviews.

This series of reviews posed a number of specific challenges. Most notable was the difficulty in dealing with frequently overlapping information in the research literature. Although the federal performance indicators were narrowly defined (focusing on issues such as time to adoption as distinct from time to reunification), many of the relevant studies examined these outcomes simultaneously, leading to the potential for redundancy across the separate reviews. In a similar vein, the student researchers searched for ways to present the research that did not duplicate other sources, such as the California Evidence Based Clearinghouse website. The team also encountered limitations related to locating rigorous evaluative research. These challenges were discussed and addressed in frequent team meetings, where decisions were made about how to draw the boundaries between the reviews, where to place particular studies, and how to develop interpretations and implications that would be relevant and useful to child welfare practitioners in county human service agencies.

Each Performance Pointer included a policy overview, discussion of risk and protective factors, and description of promising practices (see Box 3.2).

Box 3.2. Performance Pointers Outline

- **Policy Overview:**
  - In order to help workers and supervisors better understand the intent behind the measures and standards, the reviews summarized highlights of the policy debate and theoretical rationale relevant to each measure.
  - The intent was to provide context, so that workers could see how their practice is situated within a policy framework.

- **Risk/Protective Factors:**
  - The discussion of risk and protective factors was designed to direct attention to groups of children who are at greater risk.
  - In these sections, the information and findings were presented in language aimed at promoting reflective practice on the part of workers, rather than simply reinforcing existing assumptions or replacing them with new assumptions.

- **Promising Practices:**
  - These sections captured a broad array of practices for workers, supervisors, and agencies to consider.
  - These included practices that an individual worker could implement, as well as practices that require agency-wide implementation, and in some instances, practices that require policy-level reform.
  - The reviews drew upon a broad body of research related to promising practices, consistent with the consortium's emphasis on evidence-informed practice.

As we completed the draft literature reviews and began planning for dissemination, including a presentation to the consortium directors and a pre-test of the materials with county child welfare staff, we met again with our practice partners to refine our dissemination strategies. It was recommended that we engage in discussions with county staff in the form of a collaborative working group designed to gain the perspective and expertise of practitioners, rather than a pilot test of a developed product. This decision also reflected the shared mission of the regional consortium to build participatory knowledge-sharing systems in and across the agencies, and secondarily, emerged as a strategy to ensure that staff groups would engage with the material and avoid the perception that this process was not another externally imposed burden on staff.

It was decided that the agenda for the staff working groups would include: (1) a review of the format and content of the specific literature review, as well as opportunity for feedback on its usefulness; (2) a discussion of the risk factors, as well as the responses/practices in the county that are being used to address these factors; (3) the identification of promising practices occurring within the county related to performance on the measure; and (4) soliciting input on the development of discussion questions to foster discussion and utilization of the Performance Pointers across the region. With the support of five county child welfare directors, local focus groups were created based on a request for a one-time, three-hour, working group session comprised of eight to ten child welfare workers, supervisors, and managers. The request was based on recommendations by their respective agency directors that their staff be consulted, because the topic clearly addressed an area that was particularly relevant for their agency. These agencies shared the search for effective practices and innovative strategies to improve outcomes for children and families, as well as actively gathered the input of practitioners who engage daily in actions that affect the outcomes that were currently being measured. This form of outreach and engagement was seen by the agency directors as essential to ensuring that the performance pointers were useful for them and other agencies.

Over the course of several months, with workers identified by the child welfare directors, we conducted six focus groups related to the following questions: (1) What are the most and least useful aspects of the information presented? (2) What would be the most useful format for presenting this information? (3) What practices are being implemented in your agency to improve performance on this measure? (4) What discussion questions would encourage staff at your agency to think about and make use of this information? and (5) What research questions related to improving performance on this measure do you think are important for researchers to study? The focus groups were well attended (due in part to the lunch and snacks that we offered), and generated rich discussion of the Performance Pointers (see Box 3.3 for a detailed synthesis of the preliminary cross-cutting themes).

In a follow-up meeting with the county directors, we shared a progress report that summarized the input from each of the focus groups and noted preliminary cross-county themes. The groups had identified a series of potential research questions that were categorized

Box 3.3. Preliminary Cross-Cutting Themes Related to Performance
Pointers

1. Tool Format Feedback on the amount of information and how
   presented. Groups generally combined this conversation.
   a. Overall, paper format is not ideal for child welfare stakeholders
   b. Information needs for target audiences
   c. Format of information needs to be broad with option of more
      detailed information
   d. Presentation of information needs to take into account how it
      will be used:
   e. More detailed information for complex situations
   f. Information on best practices needs to be linked to resource
      constraints

2. Tool Content: Promising Practices
   a. Well-being of children and families
   b. Quality of relationships at agency and line-staff levels

3. Building a Research Agenda: What is being done in counties that is
   not measured?

under four broad themes (risk and risk assessment, agency characteristics, service strategies and impacts, and child well-being).
Participants emphasized the importance of access to targeted, locally
relevant, in-depth information, and they proposed multiple strategies
for supporting evidence-informed practice; namely, training agency
staff in the use of technology research and evaluation. Based upon
this report, the directors decided to invite their child welfare directors to their regional meeting in order to reflect on the Pointers and
focus group input and to consider next steps. In the meeting, considerable discussion unfolded about the pressures facing child welfare programs, the importance of developing policies and procedures
to guide practice, the reduction in staff as well as caseloads, and the
need for research to fit into the ongoing needs/interests of child welfare practice.

Some of the challenges cited included: (1) the difficulty of finding research to address the immediate needs of practice; (2) responding to research that generates conflicting results/recommendations;
(3) concern about generating research questions by line staff that may

not conform to the directions being taken by the organization; (4) the need for capturing promising practices emerging within each Bay Area county; (5) the role of unions in the utilization of research to inform practice; (6) the need for immediate online access to information; (7) operating within the constraints of a legalistic, rule-making organizational environment; (8) little staff time to read or engage in discussions of research, whether internal (administrative) or external (research literature); (9) the importance of linking research to the ongoing 3-year cycle of updating System Improvement Plans (SIPs); and (10) the value of capturing promising practices.

Based on the discussion, it was decided that a series of steps would be explored as a way to build upon the work related to child welfare outcomes in order to promote the further development of knowledge sharing systems within and between counties with the goal of expanding evidence-informed practice. Proposed key activities included: (1) creating an online presence for county child welfare (CW) staff to share/access local promising practices throughout the Bay Area using the consortium website; (2) capturing some of the data-mining practices related to administrative data currently in progress; (3) capturing some of the data from periodic case reviews (PQCR and other case review processes) to identify potentials for future qualitative research, along with quantitative research, to inform practice; and (4) participating in regional child welfare meetings and possibly convening child welfare representatives in two groups: small counties and large counties.

The experience with developing the performance pointers led to an increased interest in learning more about how the county agencies mine their own data, in contrast to relying only on external national research findings that tended to focus on quantitative outcome measures and less on qualitative case record data. As a result, a set of four exploratory data-mining case studies in child welfare agencies were developed by our graduate student researchers and featured the following topics: (1) staff supported integrated data mining; (2) multimethod analysis of disproportionality; (3) accreditation-based peer case record review; and (4) administrative and case record analyses. A cross-case analysis of these case studies generated a number of themes that included the importance of strengthening qualitative analyses (see Box 3.4 for summary of cross-case themes).

Box 3.4. Exploratory Data-mining Case Studies: Themes from a Cross-case Analysis

- <u>Responding to Internal and External Demands for Information</u>: Agencies have responded to a diverse set of external and internal pressures and opportunities in developing their data-mining processes as they seek to answer a wide range of service delivery questions through data mining.
- <u>Data Mining as an Evolutionary Process</u>: Important factors contributing to this evolution include: (1) Leadership that values evidence-informed decision-making; (2) Contextual factors, such as external resource availability, negative publicity, and community priorities.
- <u>Importance of Stakeholder Participation</u>: Who participates in data mining, and at what stage, may affect (1) staff engagement and attitudes about evidence-informed practice; (2) quality of data and data analysis; (3) implementation of practice changes based on data-mining findings.
  - *Role of Experts*: Agencies have relied on experts with varied experiences to design, implement, and support their data-mining practices.
  - *Community Involvement*: The nature of community participation in various stages of data-mining processes varies, especially in case review processes.
- <u>Strengthening Qualitative Analyses</u>: Quantitative/administrative data analyses are typically sophisticated and powerful, but methods for qualitative data analyses appear to be less well developed.
- <u>Engaging Staff in Data Informed Practice</u>: Agencies have instituted a number of promising strategies aimed at engaging staff and increasing their willingness and capacity to work with data to inform practice (accessibility, and relevance of data) and these strategies have surfaced the following issues related to changing practice:
  - Balancing accountability with positive rewards.
    - Emphasizes positive rewards.
    - Emphasizes learning.
    - Developing accountability processes.
  - Enlisting supportive data-savvy supervisors.
  - Addressing both systems and individual worker change.
    - Focuses on system level interventions.
    - Focuses on individual worker responses.
  - Identifying ways for data to inform not drive practice.

Based upon this analysis, two options for further research were proposed. One research question explores the relationship between staff involvement in data-mining processes and staff acceptance of evidence-informed practice (Does involvement increase acceptance of evidence-informed practice? What are the factors that lead to different choices about roles/involvement in the data-mining process?). A second research question proposed examining qualitative data mining using the following questions: (1) How should analysis of qualitative case record data be conducted? (2) How is case record data currently analyzed by staff? (3) What are the advantages and disadvantages of using structured data-extraction instruments (e.g., validity and reliability)? (4) How does analysis of qualitative case record data differ from the methods used in applied research studies? and (5) What are effective staff-training strategies on how to analyze qualitative data to answer practice-relevant questions? This second set of research questions is addressed in Chapter 5.

LOW-INCOME FAMILIES AND CHILD POVERTY

In addition to focusing on child welfare, our practice research examples also include the employment and benefits services associated with welfare-to-work programs. As will be noted in the next chapter on learning from the experiences of other organizations, our practitioner community became increasingly interested in learning more about research on low-income families, those not eligible for traditional welfare services. They wanted to think more about how those just above the federal poverty line could be served. Their interests focused on mapping the relationship between poverty and families because the federal welfare reform reflected an emphasis on caseload reduction (moving TANF [Temporary Assistance for Needy Families] participants off of the welfare rolls and into work) rather than addressing poverty reduction or eradication. As a result, the literature review addressed four major areas: (1) the status of low-income families, (2) the status of low-income neighborhoods, (3) promising programs servicing low-income families, and (4) promising practices for meeting the multiple needs of low-income families as illustrated by the executive summary in Attachment B. This literature review was designed to inform the planning for the reauthorization of the federal welfare reform legislation.

CONCLUSION

This chapter began with a discussion of how to structure literature reviews that would cast the widest net for capturing relevant research and agency reports needed to promote learning among agency practitioners. In contrast to the previous chapter on learning from individuals and groups, this chapter features the learning associated with published knowledge in the form of literature reviews. In this chapter, the literature reviews illustrate different aspects of child welfare services; namely, special populations and organizational processes. The second illustration of a literature review relates to populations living just above the poverty line from those receiving welfare benefits.

The last step in the literature review process, related to dissemination and utilization, is proving to be one of the most challenging aspects of practice research; that is, finding ways for the practice community to both understand and make use of the research findings. Most of the methods are either time consuming (e.g., PowerPoint presentations at multiple agency sites) or expensive (e.g., video productions). In addition, the most efficient and cost-effective methods (e.g., webinars, email attachments) require time that is scarce in a busy organizational environment with high service demands and inadequate staff resources. Even the use of graphically designed executive summaries of the practice research study did not address the staff need to read the materials or engage in follow-up staff discussions.

Connections with Previous and Subsequent Chapters

This chapter builds upon the previous chapter by elaborating on the methodology of building upon prior published research. It differs from the previous chapter in the sense that learning from individuals and groups calls for collecting interview data on promising practices in the form of new or unique knowledge development rather than searching databases for existing knowledge.

In contrast to looking back, this chapter provides a foundation for looking forward. In the following chapters (i.e., Chapters 4 through 7), various approaches to collecting data are based upon highly focused reviews of the existing literature in order to identify how a practice research study builds upon existing knowledge.

ATTACHMENT A: EVIDENCE FOR PRACTICE-STRUCTURED LITERATURE REVIEWS (2005–2011)

- Understanding and Addressing Racial/Ethnic Disproportionality in the Front End of the Child Welfare System. Special Issue, *Journal of Evidence-based Social Work,* 5(1/2), 2008.
- Risk and Safety Assessment in Child Welfare: Instrument Comparisons. Special Issue, *Journal of Evidence-based Social Work,* 5(1/2), 2008.
- Understanding and Measuring Child Welfare Outcomes. Special Issue, *Journal of Evidence-based Social Work,* 5(1/2), 2008.
- Substance Abuse Interventions for Parents Involved in the Child Welfare System: Evidence and Implications. Special Issue, *Journal of Evidence-based Social Work,* 5(1/2), 2008.
- Assessing the Outcomes of Parent Education Programs for Child Welfare Populations. Special Issue, *Journal of Evidence-based Social Work,* 5(1/2), 2008.
- Family Assessment in Child Welfare: Instrument Comparisons. Special Issue, *Journal of Evidence-based Social Work,* 5(1/2), 2008.
- Assessing Child and Youth Well-being: Implications for Child Welfare Practice. Special Issue, *Journal of Evidence-based Social Work,* 5(1/2), 2008.
- Impact of Organizational Change on Organizational Culture: The Prospects for Introducing Evidence-based Practice. Special Issue, *Journal of Evidence-based Social Work,* 5(1/2), 2008.
- Implementing Evidence-based Practice: Lessons from the Field. Special Issue, *Journal of Evidence-based Social Work,* 5(1/2), 2008.

- Knowledge Management: Implications for Human Service Organizations. Special Issue, *Journal of Evidence-based Social Work, 5*(1/2), 2008.
- Strategies for Engaging Adults in Welfare-to-Work Programs. *Families in Society, 90*(4), 2009.
- Assessing Elder Mistreatment: Instrument Development and Implications for Adult Protective Services. *Journal of Gerontological Social Work, 52*(8), 2009.
- TANF Child-only Cases: Identifying the Characteristics and Needs of Children Living in Low-income Families. *Journal of Children and Poverty, 14*(1), 2008.
- Re-entering Foster Care: Trends, Evidence, and Implications. *Children and Youth Services Review, 31*(4), 2009.
- Early Detection of Drug and Alcohol Abuse in Pregnant Mothers: Implications for Child Welfare Practice. *Children and Youth Services Review, 32*, 2010.
- Coming Back Home: The Reintegration of Formerly Incarcerated Youth with Service Implications. *Children and Youth Services Review, 32*(10), 2010.
- Reducing Child Poverty by Promoting Child Well-being: Identifying Best Practices in a Time of Great Need. *Children and Youth Services Review, 33*, 2011.

Selected examples of literature reviews are accessible as noted here:

(1) Assessing Child and Youth Well-being Implications for Child Welfare Practice. https://mackcenter.berkeley.edu/publications/assessing-child-and-youth-well-being
(2) Assessing Elder Mistreatment: Instrument Development and Implications for Adult Protective Services. https://mackcenter.berkeley.edu/publications/assessing-elder-mistreatment-instrument-development-and-implications-adult-protective
(3) Coming Back Home: The Reintegration of Formerly Incarcerated Youth with Service Implications. https://mackcenter.berkeley.edu/publications/coming-back-home-reintegration-formerly-incarcerated-youth-service-implications
(4) Reducing Child Poverty by Promoting Child Well-being: Identifying Best Practices in a Time of Great Need.

      https://mackcenter.berkeley.edu/publications/reducing-child-
      poverty-promoting-child-well-being-identifying-best-practices-
      time-great
(5) Preventing Re-Entry to Foster Care. https://mackcenter.
      berkeley.edu/publications/preventing-re-entry-foster-care
(6) Understanding and Addressing Racial/Ethnic
      Disproportionality in the Front End of the Child Welfare
      System. https://mackcenter.berkeley.edu/publications/
      understanding-and-addressing-racialethnic-disproportionality-
      front-end-child-welfare
(7) Strategies for Engaging Adults in Welfare-to-Work
      Activities. https://mackcenter.berkeley.edu/publications/
      strategies-engaging-adults-welfare-work-activities

ATTACHMENT B

Executive Summary: Serving Low-income Families in Poverty Neighborhoods Using Promising Programs and Practices (Hastings, Taylor, & Austin, 2006)

I. The status of low-income families in a post-welfare reform era
The major research on low-income families includes the following:

- One-third of all workers in the United States earn below-poverty wages and of these workers, one-third are persistent low-wage earners who are responsible for the bulk of their family's income (Carnevale & Rose, 2001).
- The primary earner in a low-income family works full-time, year round, and the average income of a single-parent working family is barely above $15,600 (Acs et al., 2001).
- African American and female-headed households earn considerably less than White and male-headed households (Carnevale & Rose, 2001; Johnston, 2002).
- In California, the high cost of living increases the financial hardships of low-income families; more than 16% of households in California spend over 50% of their income on rent alone (Johnston, 2002).

Based on a review of the literature on the status of low-income families, four key themes emerge:

(1) *Low-income families experience severe hardships whether they rely on cash assistance, work, or a combination of both.*
   - Research suggests that over 72% of low-income families earning twice the poverty line (or up to $37,320 using 2003 data for a family of four) experience a serious hardship (affordable housing and lack of childcare) within a12-month period (Boushey et al., 2001).
   - Earnings from government assistance and low-wage labor are inadequate for providing even a minimal standard of living to low-income families; therefore, many families must choose between health care and food, or between other necessary expenditures (America's Second Harvest, 2002).

(2) *Low-income families are resilient and resourceful.*
   - Many low-income families exhibit strengths equal to higher income families (Orthner et al., 2003) and demonstrate a remarkable capacity to employ flexible and creative coping strategies (Edin & Lein, 1997; Zedlewski et al., 2003).
   - Low-income families are able to make use of extensive social networks such that more than 75% report receiving cash assistance from a friend or family member (Edin & Lein, 1997). Low-income families also rely on side work and help from private charities when necessary.

(3) *Low-income families face significant barriers to using public and private services and to increasing earnings from work.*
   - Many low-income families who would otherwise be eligible for government cash or in-kind assistance either do not know they are eligible, or find that the application process is an obstacle to receiving assistance (Zedlewski et al., 2003).
   - For families that do receive government assistance, there are disincentives to increasing their earnings because as earnings increase, other government assistance is reduced (Shipler, 2004).

(4) *The quality of life for families of color and immigrant status is continuously affected by discriminatory practices in the employment and service sectors.*

- Low-income families of color and immigrant families still face the burden of poor educational systems, random crime, gangs, high unemployment, ongoing issues with the police, job and wage discrimination, discrimination within TANF programs, and constant fear of remaining in poverty for generations (Gooden, 2000; Harknett, 2001; Gilens, 1999; Handler & Hasenfeld, 1997; Quadragno, 1994).

II. The status of low-income neighborhoods in a post-welfare reform era

The major research on low-income neighborhoods includes the following:

- Between 1970 and 1990, concentrated neighborhood poverty (defined as those census tracts where more than 40% of the residents are living in poverty), increased, especially among the urban African American population and among poor, female-headed families with children (Wilson, 1996).
- Emerging immigrant communities, especially those from Mexico, the Caribbean, Central America, and Southeast Asia also tend to experience high rates of poverty (CIS, 1999).
- Geographically speaking, of the 34.6 million people in poverty in 2002, 27 million lived in metropolitan areas (78%): 13.8 million in inner cities (40%) and 13.3 million in the suburbs (38%). Among those living outside metropolitan areas, 7.5 million (22%) people were in poverty in 2002 (Jargowsky, 2003).

A review of the literature on the status of low-income neighborhoods reveals four key themes:

(1) *Macroeconomic trends have contributed to the creation of segregated, high-poverty neighborhoods.*
   - A major force shaping low-income neighborhoods has been the transformation of the urban economy, which for the past 50 years and most rapidly, in the past two decades, has become more decentralized, global, and heavily reliant on finance, services, and technology rather than on its once

larger and more powerful manufacturing base (Abramson, Tobin, & VanderGoot, 1995; Massey & Eggers, 1993).

- These macroeconomic changes have fueled the concentration of poverty and joblessness in central cities where low-income minorities tend to be disproportionately located (Coulton, Chow, Wang, & Su, 1996).

(2) *Low-income neighborhoods tend to be characterized by a variety of social problems.*

- The term "neighborhood effects" is used to describe the simultaneous presence of neighborhood socioeconomic disadvantage with other social problems, including high rates of unemployment, crime, adolescent delinquency, teenage childbearing, social and physical disorder, single-parent households, child maltreatment, high levels of mobility, poor child and adult health and mental health, and poor developmental outcomes for children and adolescents (Coulton, Korbin, Su, & Chow, 1995; Policy Link, 2002; Roosa et al., 2003; Sampson, 2001; Sampson, Morenoff, & Gannon-Rowley, 2002).

(3) *There are several possible mechanisms through which the social environments of low-income neighborhoods impact residents.*

- The environmental conditions of low-income neighborhoods may impact residents in several ways: (1) the level or density of social ties between neighbors, the frequency of social interaction among neighbors, and patterns of neighboring; (2) the mutual trust and shared willingness to intervene for the public good; (3) the quality, quantity, and diversity of institutions in the community that address the needs of residents; and (4) the land-use patterns and the distribution of daily routine activities that affect well-being (Sampson & Morenoff, 2002).

(4) *Neighborhood indicators for Bay Area neighborhoods can help inform social service practice and delivery.*

- In 2003, some 72 Bay Area neighborhoods experienced concentrated poverty; the majority of these neighborhoods are clustered around the cities of Richmond, San Jose, Oakland, and San Francisco. These cities are located in the counties of Contra Costa (20 neighborhoods), Santa Clara

(16 neighborhoods), Alameda (11 neighborhoods), and San Francisco (9 neighborhoods) and account for 77% of the concentrated-poverty neighborhoods in the Bay Area. Additional data reveal variations in the social, health, and economic status of these neighborhoods.

- Neighborhood-specific assessment techniques can assist program planners in designing the most appropriate interventions. By developing a set of indicators in the domains of well-being for which significant neighborhood effects have been demonstrated, local institutions may be able to better locate services and target strategies for neighborhood intervention.

III. Promising programs for low-income families living in poverty neighborhoods

A review of the literature on promising programs reveals three key themes:

(1) *Earnings and asset development programs are used to increase the economic self-sufficiency of low-income families.*
   - Programs to increase the earnings and assets of low-income families include employment programs, such as place-based strategies that target employment services to an entire neighborhood, linking low-income parents to "good jobs," and the use of work incentives and supports; as well as asset development programs, including promoting banking and savings accounts, promoting low-income car and home ownership, and linking families to the Earned Income Tax Credit (EITC).
(2) *Family-strengthening programs are used to improve health and educational outcomes, as well as to link families to needed support and benefit services.*
   - Programs that strengthen families include the promotion of healthy child and family development through home visitation programs, parenting education programs, and programs implemented through California's First Five. They also include early childhood educational programs to increase school readiness, as well as strategies to facilitate

the receipt of support services, such as outreach efforts and strategies to streamline eligibility procedures.

(3) *Neighborhood-strengthening programs are used to improve community development and collaboration among service providers, as well as promote resident involvement in neighborhood affairs.*

- Programs that strengthen neighborhoods include community development corporations (defined as neighborhood-based nonprofit business ventures) that most often focus on improving housing options in low-income neighborhoods (Blanc, Goldwasser, & Brown, 2003).
- Comprehensive community initiatives are long-term strategies to increase collaboration, planning, and coordination of funding among community-based organizations in low-income communities (Blanc et al., 2003)
- Community organizing strategies are used to increase resident involvement in community planning, decision-making, and advocacy in order to bring resources into a neighborhood.

IV. Promising practices for low-income families living in poverty neighborhoods

A review of promising practices for meeting the multiple needs of low-income families living in poverty neighborhoods reveals four main themes:

(1) *The challenges facing low-income families living in poverty neighborhoods are multifaceted.*

- The parent who needs living-wage work is often the same parent who needs services to promote healthy child development and resides in a neighborhood that needs more resident involvement, community collaboration, and economic development.
- Promising practices to address the multiple and complex challenges facing poor families and poor neighborhoods are increasingly using a more holistic approach that brings together various levels of intervention.

(2) *Integrated family and neighborhood strengthening practices represent innovative strategies to address the multifaceted issues facing low-income families living in high-poverty neighborhoods.*
   - The Annie E. Casey Foundation's Making Connections (MC) Initiative and the Harlem Children's Zone (HCZ) are two programs that currently implement the following integrated approaches:
     - Earnings and asset development,
     - family strengthening,
     - neighborhood strengthening, and
     - an emphasis on collaboration, capacity building and producing tangible results.

(3) *The organizational structure, challenges, and successes of the MC and HCZ provide insight into the nature of integrated family and neighborhood approaches.*
   - The organizational structure of MC sites tends to be characterized by a loose and flexible structure, and many sites are hosted by local organizations with an emphasis on collaborative committees with strong resident participation.
   - Challenges facing integrated approaches are related to keeping residents engaged in the process, forming and maintaining collaborations with partners, dealing with certain characteristics of the community, and handling the expectations of the funding sources.
   - Overall, the major success reported by staff included the development of resident leaders to direct the course of programs.

(4) *A framework for the design of an integrated family and neighborhood program includes the following features:*
   - *Internal processes* include reformulating service models, organizational strategies, and a responsive organizational structure.
   - *Neighborhood processes* include targeting the neighborhood and the scope of service, and assessing neighborhood characteristics.
   - *External processes* include structured and strategic partnerships, community buy-in, community leadership development, and tracking outputs and outcomes.

This framework can assist social service agencies in moving their services toward a more integrated family and neighborhood approach for all low-income families, not just welfare-to-work participants. All references cited in this Executive Summary of a literature review are available in:

Austin, M.J. (2006). Low-income families [Special issue]. *Health and Social Policy, 21*(1), 33–117.

REFERENCES

Abramson, A., Tobin, M., & VanderGoot, M. (1995). The changing geography of metropolitan opportunity: The segregation of the poor in U.S. metropolitan areas, 1970 to 1990. *Housing Policy Debate, 6*(1), 45–72.

Acs, G., Ross Phillips, K., & McKenzie, D. (2001). Playing by the rules, but losing the game: Americans in low-Income working families. In M. Miller (Ed.), *Low-Wage Workers in the New Economy* (pp. 21–44). Washington D.C.: The Urban Institute Press.

America's Second Harvest. (2003). *State Fact Sheets (California)*. Retrieved June 29, 2004, from http://www.secondharvest.org/site_content.asp?s=69

Anthony, E.K., & Austin, M.J. (2008). The role of an intermediary organization in promoting research in schools of social work: The case of the Bay Area Social Services Consortium. *Social Work Research, 32*(4), 287–293.

Anthony, E.K., King, B., & Austin, M.J. (2011). Reducing child poverty by promoting child well-being: Identifying best practices in a time of great need. *Children and Youth Services Review, 33*(10), 1999–2009.

Austin, M.J. (2006). Low-income families [Special issue]. *Health and Social Policy, 21*(1), 33–117.

Austin, M.J. (Ed.). (2008). Evidence for child welfare practice [Special issue]. *Journal of Evidence-based Social Work, 5*(1/2), 1–389.

Austin, M.J., & Carnochan, S. (2013). Performance measurement in the child welfare system: Policy and performance pointers [Special issue]. *Journal of Evidence-based Social Work, 10*(3), 147–264.

Blanc, S., Goldwasser, M., & Brown, J. (2003). From the ground up: The Logan Square Neighborhood Association's approach to building community capacity. Paper presented on COMM-ORG: The Online Conference on Community Organizing and Development. Retrieved July 1, 2004 from: http://comm-org.utoledo.edu/papers.htm.

Boushey, H., Brocht, C., Gundersen, B., & Bernstein, J. (2001). *Hardships in America: The real story of working families*. Washington, D.C.: Economic Policy Institute.

Carnochan, S., Lee, C., Lawson, J., & Austin, M.J. (2013a). Achieving exits to permanency for children in long term care: Performance pointers. *Journal of Evidence-based Social Work, 10*(3), 220–234.

Carnochan, S., Lee, C., Lawson, J., & Austin, M.J. (2013b). Achieving timely reunification: Performance pointers. *Journal of Evidence-based Social Work, 10*(3), 179–195.

Carnochan, S., Moore, M., & Austin, M.J. (2013). Achieving timely adoption [Special issue]. *Journal of Evidence-based Social Work, 10*(3), 210–219.

Carnochan, S., Moore, M., Lawson, J., & Austin, M.J. (2013). Achieving placement stability: Performance pointers. *Journal of Evidence-based Social Work, 10*(3), 235–253.

Carnochan, S., Rizik-Baer, D., Lawson, J., & Austin, M.J. (2013a). Preventing the recurrence of maltreatment: Performance pointers [Special issue]. *Journal of Evidence-based Social Work, 10*(3), 168–178.

Carnochan, S., Rizik-Baer, D., Lawson, J., & Austin, M.J. (2013b). Preventing re-entry to foster care: Performance pointers [Special issue]. *Journal of Evidence-based Social Work, 10*(3), 196–209.

Carnevale, A., & Rose, S. (2001). Low earners: Who are they? Do they have a way out? In M. Miller (Ed.), *Low-Wage Workers in the New Economy* (pp. 45–66). Washington D.C.: The Urban Institute Press.

Carnochan, S., Samples, M., Lawson, J., & Austin, M.J. (2013). The context of child welfare performance measures [Special issue]. *Journal of Evidence-based Social Work, 10*(3), 147–160.

Chow, J.C, Johnson, M., & Austin, M.J. (2006). The status of low-income neighborhoods in the post-welfare reform environment: Mapping the relationship between poverty and place [Special issue]. *Health and Social Policy, 21*(1), 1–32.

Coulton, C., Chow, J., Wang, E., & Su, M. (1996). Geographic concentration of affluence and poverty in 100 metropolitan areas, 1990. *Urban Affairs Review, 32*(2), 186–216.

Coulton, C., Korbin, J., Su, M., & Chow, J. (1995). Community level factors and child maltreatment rates. *Child Development, 66*, 1262–1276.

Edin, K., & Lein, L. (1997). *Making ends meet: How single mothers survive welfare and low-wage work*. New York: Russell Sage.

Gilens, M. (1999). *Why Americans hate welfare*. Chicago: University of Chicago Press.

Gooden, S.T. (2000). Examining employment outcomes of White and Black welfare recipients. *Journal of Poverty, 4*(3), 21–41.

Handler, J.F., & Hasenfeld, Y. (1997). *We the poor people: Work, poverty, and welfare*. New Haven, Conn.: Yale University Press.

Harknett, K. (2001). Working and leaving welfare: Does race or ethnicity matter? *Social Service Review, 75*, 359–386.

Hastings, J., Taylor, S., & Austin, M.J. (2006). The status of low-income families in the post-welfare reform environment: Mapping the relationships between poverty and family [Special issue]. *Health and Social Policy, 21*(1), 33–63.

Jargowsky, P.A. (2003). Stunning progress, hidden problems: The dramatic decline of concentrated poverty in the 1990s. In A. Berube, B. Katz, & R.E. Lang (Eds), *Redefining urban and suburban America: Evidence from census 2000, volume two* (pp. 327–369). Washington, DC: Brookings Institution Press.

Johnson, C. (2002). *Census 2000 highlights.* San Francisco, CA: San Francisco Department of Public Health.

Lemon, K., & Austin, M.J. (2006). Promising programs to serve low-income families in poverty neighborhoods [Special issue]. *Health and Social Policy, 21*(1), 65–94.

Lemon, K., Leer, E., & Austin, M.J. (2006). Promising practices for meeting the multiple needs of low-income families in poverty neighborhoods [Special issue]. *Health and Social Policy, 21*(1), 95–117.

Massey, D., & Eggers, M. (1993). The spatial concentration of affluence and poverty during the 1970s. *Urban Affairs Quarterly, 29*(2), 299–315.

Orthner, D., Jones-Sanpei, H., & Williamson, S. (2003). Family strengths and income in households with children. *Journal of Family Social Work, 7*(2), 5–23.

Policy Link. (2002). *Reducing Health Disparities Through a Focus on Communities.* Oakland, CA: Policy Link.

Quadagno, J.S. (1994). *The color of welfare : how racism undermined the war on poverty.* New York: Oxford University Press.

Roosa, M.W., Jones, S., Tein, J.-Y., & Cree, W. (2003). Prevention science and neighborhood influences on low-income children's development: Theoretical and methodological issues. *American Journal of Community Psychology, 31*(1-2), 55–72.

Saini, M., & Schlonsky, A. (2012). *Systematic synthesis of qualitative research.* New York, NY: Oxford University Press.

Samples, M., Carnochan, S., & Austin, M.J. (2013). Using performance measures to manage child welfare outcomes: Local strategies and decision-making. *Journal of Evidence-based Social Work, 10*(3), 254–264.

Sampson, R.J. (2001). How do communities undergird or undermine human development? Relevant contexts and social mechanisms. In A. Booth, & Crouter, A. C. (Eds.), *Does It Take a Village? Community Effects on Children, Adolescents, and Families* (pp. 3–30). Mahwah, NJ: Lawrence Erlbaum Associates, Inc., Publishers.

Sampson, R.J., Morenoff, J.D., & Gannon-Rowley, T. (2002). Assessing "neighborhood effects": Social processes and new directions in research. *Annual Review of Sociology, 28*, 443–478.

Shipler, D. (2004). *The working poor: Invisible in America*. New York: Alfred K. Knopf.

Zedlewski, S., Nelson, S., Edin, K., Koball, H., Pomper, K., & Roberts, T. (2003). *Families coping without earnings or government cash assistance* (No. 64). Washington, D.C.: The Urban Institute.

4

Learning from the Experiences of Other Organizations through Cross-case Analysis

OVERVIEW

One of the ways of becoming a learning organization is to look for opportunities to learn from other organizations. This chapter is devoted to three examples of practice research that feature cross-case comparisons in order to identify practice implications. By learning from the experiences of others, senior managers were able to identify innovations and perspectives that could be applied to their own organizations. Except through random and informal conversations among practitioners, there is rarely an opportunity to gather the practice details, documented by research partners, that are relevant to one's own organization.

The first example of practice research involves the implementation of national legislation related to welfare reform at the local county

Practice Research in the Human Services. Michael J. Austin and Sarah Carnochan, Oxford University Press (2020). © Oxford University Press.
DOI: 10.1093/oso/9780197518335.001.0001

level. Captured in the form of case studies of innovative practice, this form of *qualitative* practice research provided a significant complement to the nationally collected *quantitative* data on the nature of caseload reduction.

The second example features the efforts of county human service agencies to promote knowledge sharing as a way of supporting evidence-informed practice. The cross-case analysis is built upon a set of 'works-in-progress" that feature the ongoing nature of organizational learning and change.

The third example represents a shift from public to nonprofit human service organizations with a focus on organizational histories as the database for understanding organizational sustainability. The practice research dimensions of this cross-case analysis provided practitioners with insights about other agencies in the community as well as the potential for building upon innovative practices.

The chapter concludes with implications for the use of practice research to promote interorganizational learning as well as findings that can be used to improve internal organizational operations. Before describing the three examples related to learning from other organizations, the practice research methods are identified.

METHODS FOR CASE STUDY DEVELOPMENT

The purpose of a case study is to analyze in detail an individual, a situation, or a single phenomenon in order to identify new understandings and/or lessons learned for both practitioners and researchers (Dufour & Fortin, 1992). According to Yin (1992), a case study represents an empirical investigation of a contemporary phenomenon within its real-life context using multiple sources of evidence (agency documents, staff perceptions, and client perceptions). Karbo and Beasley (1999) would characterize the cases in our studies as descriptively *holistic* (not guided by hypothesis testing) in that the programs and practices, as well as organizational histories, are fully described and as *interpretive* when designed to systematically examine patterns within and across cases in order to trace change over time and offer cross-case interpretation of the findings.

In this chapter each case study is based on information obtained from interviews with local social service agency staff and consumers as well as written documents (along with a brief literature review) relevant to each program or practice. The data collected for these case studies used such general questions and follow-up probes as: (1) How did the program or organization get started? (2) What have been some of the implementation difficulties or barriers? And (3) what were some of the program or organizational successes as well as the lessons learned?

The development of a case study in the human services is essentially a storytelling process; namely, what is the history of the story? Who was involved in the early days or at the outset of the program or initiative? What evidence exists to help tell the story? How is the story viewed by those looking back and engaged retrospectively? These are some of the questions used by investigative reporters. They collect information from various sources in order to identify the major "threads" or "themes" buried in multiple forms of evidence. Storytelling also involves a form of triangulation as the author seeks to confirm various findings or conflicting narratives by using several different sources, as in people and/or documents. Investigative journalists also rely on their editors to review drafts of their work to see or not the logic of the story is clear, the themes or threads are supported well, and the conclusions are based on the evidence collected.

The data in these case studies were collected by graduate research assistants under the editorial assistance of a university faculty member. The students were oriented to the data-collection process by making reference to the methods of investigative journalism. In addition, they were given the background rationale for developing the case along with the relevant contacts needed to enter the organization at the level of the agency director.

When one particular researcher was focusing on the history of a human service organization, she was told by the agency director that she could find all relevant records in boxes located in the attic of the agency's building, much like searching through boxes of family albums. For example, each student researcher was encouraged to locate the archive of meeting minutes that recorded the deliberations of the board of directors in each nonprofit organization as well as to consult with those in charge of finance in order to locate the size of the annual budget. These budget figures were plotted on a chart to reflect the various changes from one year to the next over the life of the organization. In many situations, this process of locating old documents was challenging, especially in organizations that were not oriented to careful record keeping. In a similar manner, when it came to locating people with long associations with the agency, student researchers were encouraged to locate former board members *and* staff members who had retired, as well as the member of the current staff with the greatest longevity with the agency. All of these sources could play an important role in uncovering the history of the organization.

The students selected for the conduct of organizational research were primarily interested in careers that involved managing human services. They were also interested in acquiring more research experience as part of the Social Work Masters (MSW) program. Upon graduation, many of these students commented on the research experience as one of the highlights of their graduate school experience. The case study research provided the students with an in-depth view of a human service organization along with many learning experiences associated with the detective work needed to gain access to people and documents. They were able to demonstrate the key ingredients of becoming a research-minded practitioner with regard to the importance of an insatiable curiosity, critical self-reflection about their own understanding of the details, and the opportunity to refine their critical thinking skills needed to write the case study under supervision.

The nature of the supervision included various forms of problem-solving related to the organizational barriers encountered in the pursuit of people and information. In addition, multiple drafts of the case studies were reviewed by the faculty supervisor in order to provide feedback with regard to missing information, statements needing additional evidentiary support, and the flow and clarity of the narrative that sought to capture the unique aspect of the story. From the initial recruitment interview designed to assess the fit between the interests of students and the challenges associated with each case to the exit interview at the end of the process, the goal was to develop a substantial case study (30 to 60 pages) as well as a meaningful learning experience.

Because the ideas for the case studies came from discussions with agency administrators, the drafts were shared with them as part of the data interpretation process. The most talented graduate student researcher was selected to assist the faculty member with the cross-case analysis. This process included an independent review of each case in order to locate major themes. The lists of themes created by the student researcher and faculty member were then compared to arrive at a consensus in order to begin drafting the cross-case analysis.

After sharing and editing several drafts, the completed version became the basis of a presentation to the agency administrators. Ideas from this discussion were incorporated into the final version of the cross-case analysis. With the collected histories of pioneering nonprofit organizations, the researchers were encouraged by the agency administrators to use the cross-case analysis as the basis for locating current literature on organizational assessment tools that were available online (Austin, 2013). In a similar way, the recurring interest in the budgets and the funding of nonprofits, based in part on mapping the budget history of each organization, led to two new fields of inquiry. The first involved performance management related to documenting and assessing service outcomes, and the second led to an exploration of the nature of government contractual relations with local county human service organizations, known as the funder–fundee project and described in Chapter 7.

The cross-case analysis of organizational development and change provided another opportunity to reflect on the evolving methods of practice research. The methods included the following components or sequence:

(1) Facilitating the dialogue and negotiation process involving the university researcher with the practice community of agency administrators by convening several meetings each year (five for the public sector administrators and three for the nonprofit sector administrators under the auspices of a dues-paying collaborative or consortia)

(2) Using the minutes of meetings over time to frame the scope of research projects as well as identify relevant staff liaisons to facilitate access to agency data

(3) Sharing the scope of work with the practice community in order to gather multiple perceptions, expectations, goals, and outcomes

(4) Identifying and recruiting student researchers and project consultants, where needed

(5) Consulting with the practice community as the research project evolves in order to address unexpected barriers as well as recalibrate the scope of work, especially with agency staff liaisons

(6) Sharing preliminary findings in order to begin the process of data interpretation and analysis

(7) Sharing highlights of the final research report in order to launch a discussion of recommendations for future action as well as potential staff training opportunities

(8) Converting final report into a publishable article (or a series of cases into a Special Issue of a journal)

(9) Engaging in a debriefing process (after-action review) regarding future research directions that build upon the recently completed study

(10) Stepping back from the entire research process with both the practice community and the research staff to identify lessons learned (e.g., moving from multiple solo county research projects to single topic multiple-county projects) and possibilities of further synthesis (e.g., capstone paper featuring elements of multiple reports/articles).

IMPLEMENTING WELFARE REFORM: CROSS-CASE ANALYSIS #1

Overview

The 1996 federal welfare-to-work program (Temporary Assistance to Needy Families, or TANF) contains a variety of policy measures designed to reduce dependency and promote self-sufficiency. Within these policy constraints and opportunities, social service agencies and their community partners were transforming themselves as they made the change from eligibility determination to employability enhancement. The shared goal was to build a more comprehensive social service system that enabled low-income individuals and families to become self-sufficient.

The passage of TANF legislation required social service organizations to engage in a substantial reassessment of their mission and organizational structure. The major outcomes of this assessment included the findings that: (1) cultural change was a critical component of implementing a family self-sufficiency service model; (2) the demands of delivering new services required substantial organizational restructuring; (3) interagency partnerships with a wide range of partners, including other county departments, community-based organizations, and for-profit businesses were needed; (4) integrated services and interdisciplinary teams should receive increased attention; and (5) the demands of welfare reform increased the importance of data-based planning and evaluation.

Methodology

The purpose of a case study is to analyze in detail an individual, a situation, or a single phenomenon in order to identify new understandings and/or lessons learned (Dufour & Fortin, 1992; Firestone & Harriott, 1984). According to Yin (1992), a case study represents an empirical investigation of a contemporary phenomenon within its real-life context using multiple sources of evidence (agency documents, staff perceptions, and client perceptions).

According to Karbo and Beasley (1999) the cases in this study can be characterized as both descriptively *holistic* (not guided by hypothesis testing) in that the innovative programs and practices are fully described with "lessons learned" and as *interpretive* case studies designed to systematically examine patterns within and across cases in order to trace change over time and offer an interpretation of the findings.

Each case study is based on information obtained from interviews with local social service agency staff and consumers as well as written documents (along with a brief literature review) relevant to each program or practice. Data were collected by social work graduate students using such questions and follow-up probes as: (1) How did the program get started? (2) What have been some of the difficulties or barriers to implementing the program? And (3) How would you describe the program's success as well as lessons learned from implementing the program?

As noted in Box 4.1, the cases are clustered into three areas. The first set features new approaches to service delivery that help low-income individuals find employment and become self-sufficient. The second group includes neighborhood and community-wide partnerships that help to provide low-income individuals with affordable housing, education, and job training, as well as a variety of social, health, and behavioral health services. The third cluster involves organizational changes inside social service agencies brought about by implementing welfare reforms.

Box 4.1. Changing Welfare Services: Case Studies of Local Welfare Reform Programs*

An Overview of Welfare Reform Implementation and Practice

- Implementing Welfare Reform and Guiding Organizational Change
- Overview of Innovative Programs and Practices

Redefining Service Delivery

Removing Barriers to Workforce Participation

- Connections Shuttle: Transportation for CalWORKs Participants
- The Guaranteed Ride Home Program: Transportation Services for Welfare-to-Work Participants
- Training Exempt Providers to Deliver High-Quality Child Care Programs
- Integrating Mental Health and Substance Abuse Services into a County Welfare-to-Work Program

Self-Sufficiency Support Services

- Combining Business with Rehabilitation in a Public Work Center for Disabled and Low-Income Participants
- The Family Loan Program As a Public Private Partnership
- The Adopt-A-Family Program: Building Networks of Support
- Utilizing Hotline Services to Sustain Employment
- Hiring TANF Participants to Work in a County Human Services Agency
- Promoting Self-Sufficiency through Individual Development Accounts (IDAs)

Enhancing Community Partnerships

Neighborhood Partnerships

- Fostering Neighborhood Involvement in Workforce Development: The Alameda County Neighborhood Jobs Pilot Initiative
- Neighborhood Self-Sufficiency Centers

Community-wide Partnerships

- A Community Partnership Approach to Serving the Homeless
- Wraparound Services for Homeless TANF Families Recovering from Substance Abuse

- Building a Coalition of Nonprofit Agencies to Collaborate with a County Health and Human Services Agency
- Collaborative Partnerships Between a Human Services Agency and Local Community Colleges

Promoting Agency Restructuring

- Introducing Organizational Development (OD) Practices into a County Human Service Agency
- Preparing Human Service Workers to Implement Welfare Reform: Establishing the Family Development Credential in a Human Services Agency
- Merging a Workforce Investment Board and a Department of Social Services into a County Department of Employment and Human Services
- Blending Multiple Funding Streams into County Welfare-to-Work Programs
- Crossover Services between Child Welfare and Welfare-to-Work Programs
- Managing Out: The Community Practice Dimensions of Effective Agency Management

*Austin, M.J. (Ed.) (2004). *Changing welfare services: Case studies of local welfare reform programs*. Binghamton, NY: Haworth Press.

Creating and maintaining collaborative partnerships is also a major challenge, as coalition building takes time and is often difficult due to diverse political perspectives and personalities. Furthermore, when relying on several different agencies for service delivery, it is often difficult to maintain consistency across the agencies in terms of the services that consumers receive, staff responsibilities, and organizational objectives. Finally, sustaining a collaborative vision is challenging when program implementation is often found to be more difficult than program design, especially when there is a loss of momentum following the institutionalization of the innovation.

Lastly, several challenges relate to organizational restructuring. First, when new policies and procedures have not been fully implemented or staff positions have been changed, there can be considerable confusion. Second, maintaining highly qualified staff members is difficult for most human service agencies, in the midst of increased staff turnover where new employees need to be trained. Third, it has been difficult to structure multifunctional service delivery teams to deliver a wide range of employment and human services within the guidelines of welfare-to-work policy and, more generally, difficult to address the needs of local residents within categorical funding constraints.

Practice Lessons Learned from the Findings

The implications of this cross-case example of practice research includes the following set of lessons learned:

- Extra staff support and transitional time are needed to assist individuals making the transition from welfare to work,
- Teams of staff members are needed to promote effective change, which includes anticipating and proactively addressing personnel issues as well as scheduling a substantial number of staff meetings to clarify changing roles in an evolving system,
- With respect to developing partnerships, all potential stakeholders (especially local government officials whose support is needed for implementing new practices) need to be included in program planning meetings and team-building opportunities,
- The building of a practice-research community often calls for: (1) minimizing bureaucratic procedures and costs in order to facilitate consumer access to services, (2) a comprehensive assessment of community needs, (3) availability of unrestricted funding for pilot projects and services, and (4) enhanced media relations to increase public awareness of new services as well asculturally and linguistically appropriate outreach efforts.

BUILDING KNOWLEDGE-SHARING SYSTEMS: CROSS-CASE ANALYSIS #2

Overview

One of the major organizational lessons learned from implementing a comprehensive national welfare reform program was the need for bureaucratic organizations to become more adaptive learning organizations. Human service organizations began to realize that in order to promote evidence-informed practices, they needed to build knowledge-sharing systems within their organizations. This section illustrates the process of sharing innovative approaches to building such systems through the use of cross-case analysis designed to capture works-in-progress that are noted in Box 4.2 (Lee & Austin, 2012).

As standards for accountability and service outcomes are increasingly common in public human services, the question of how to effectively incorporate the management of administrative data and relevant research into daily practice becomes increasingly useful to practitioners. One of the biggest challenges is to identify ways of systematically incorporating such information in the midst of work overload and limited resources. This cross-case analysis is based on the following practice research questions: (1) What does it look like? (2) What barriers exist in public human service organizations related to collecting, analyzing, and utilizing administrative data? And (3) How is new evidence systematically integrated into the daily provision of services?

METHODOLOGY

Given that effective knowledge-sharing processes and mechanisms in human service organizations are not yet well understood, the cross-case analysis method was especially useful for this study of building knowledge-sharing systems in public human service organizations (PHSO). Case study research is particularly useful in acquiring a better understanding of a phenomenon as it occurs in its natural context, or providing insight into a theory in need of further substantiation (Hancock & Algozzine, 2006; Stake, 1995; Yin, 2003).

Each of the 12 case examples included in this illustration was the result of content review of agency documents, supplemented with face-to-face interviews conducted by three social work graduate research assistants. Interviews were conducted with senior social service staff from 10 Bay Area county human service organizations during May to September 2008, resulting in the 12 case studies.

Box 4.2. Building Knowledge-sharing Systems to Support Evidence-informed Practice: Case Studies of "Works-in-Progress" in Public Sector Human Service Organizations*

Data-Mining in Children and Family Services: The Contra Costa County Experience

Building a Culture of Learning through Organizational Development: The Experiences of the Marin County Health and Human Services Department

Linking an Agency Strategic Review to Increase Knowledge Management: San Francisco County Human Service Agency

Linking Departmental Priorities to Knowledge Management: The Experiences of Santa Cruz County's Human Services Department

Using Evidence-based Accreditation Standards to Promote Continuous Quality Improvement: The Experiences of the San Mateo County Human Services Agency

Transforming Data into Action: The Sonoma County Human Services Department

Knowledge Capture and the Retirement of the Director of Finance: Succession Planning in the San Mateo County Human Services Agency

A Senior Manager with a Knowledge Management Portfolio: The Santa Clara County Experience

Quality Management as Knowledge Sharing: Experiences of the Napa County Health & Human Services Agency

Learning from Staff to Share Knowledge and Inform Decision-making: The Contra Costa County Experience

The Use of Key Indicators as a Foundation for Knowledge Management: The Experiences of Monterey County's Social and Employment Services Department

Using Agency-wide Dashboards for Data Monitoring and Data Mining: The Solano County Health & Social Services Department

Building Organizational Supports for Research-minded Practitioners

*Lee, C., & Austin, M.J. (2012). Building organizational supports for knowledge sharing in county social service agencies: Cross-Case analysis of works-in-progress. Special Issue, *Journal of Evidence-based Social Work*, 9(1/2), 3–18.

Practice Lessons Learned from the Findings

In addition to strengthening their capacities as learning organizations, each of the 12 case examples illustrated the various ways that knowledge sharing can emerge in a public human service agency. Though the sharing and transferring of information is the most obvious motivation for developing a knowledge-sharing system, the idea of "knowledge sharing" requires further conceptualization. Emerging from the cross-case analysis were three themes that represented organizational level outcomes that can help to define an organization's larger knowledge-sharing structure; namely, transparency, self-assessment, and knowledge dissemination and utilization.

The first outcome, *transparency*, may be located within and outside of the agency in the form of horizontal transparency among similar level personnel (e.g., line worker to line worker), vertical transparency between personnel of different agency levels (e.g., line worker and manager), or transparency with members in the larger public community. Transparency also can provide greater clarity about existing agency data and thereby reduce/eliminate staff confusion and other barriers to integrating evidence into practice.

The second outcome is related to *self-assessment* and reflects an organization's efforts to assess the current status of services and operations in order to learn and improve organizational performance. The third outcome relates to knowledge or evidence *dissemination* and *utilization*.

The results from this cross-case analysis of the 12 "works in progress" revealed that public human service organizations were pursuing unique and innovative ways to effectively and efficiently incorporate evidence into everyday practice and service provision. Agencies also were committed to and focused on developing their work environments into learning organizations, even amidst high-stress conditions. In addition, the case examples demonstrated how knowledge-sharing systems could be incorporated into daily practice in the form of increased transparency inside and outside the agency, learning from agency self-assessment, and increasing the dissemination and utilization of data and evidence.

ORGANIZATIONAL GROWTH AND RESILIENCE AMONG PIONEERING NONPROFIT HUMAN SERVICE ORGANIZATIONS: CROSS-CASE ANALYSIS #3

Overview

Knowledge of organizational history is important for recognizing patterns in effective management and understanding how human service organizations respond to internal and external challenges. A cross-case

analysis of 12 histories of pioneering nonprofit human service organizations contributes an important *longitudinal* perspective on organizational history, complementing the case studies that dominate the
existing research on nonprofit organizations (Kimberlin et al., 2011;
Austin, 2013). Based on analysis of the 12 organizational histories, a
conceptual model was developed that captured the key factors of leadership, internal operations, and external relations that emerged from
the cases and influenced the organizational growth and resilience that
enabled these nonprofit organizations to survive and thrive over time.

An organization's history can be difficult to untangle. Organizational
history or "memory" is stored within an organization in various locations, ranging from the memories of individual employees, to the rules
and norms of the organizational culture, to the hierarchical structures
of staffing and programs, to the physical layout of workplaces, to the
patterns apparent in ongoing operations and processes by which change
is implemented. In addition, external documents and individuals retain
certain aspects of an organization's history. By presenting a longitudinal
view of organizational history over multiple decades, this analysis identified patterns and themes that emerge as nonprofit organizations grow
and change over time.

Methodology

To explore the issue of nonprofit organizational history from a holistic and longitudinal perspective, a series of organizational histories of
human service nonprofit organizations were compiled. The organizations were selected on the basis of several criteria: a human services
mission, location in the San Francisco Bay Area, a minimum 20-year
existence, diversity of clients served, size of budget (from under $1 mil-
lion to over $20 million), and a willingness to participate by facili-
tating data collection. Each organization signed a Memorandum of
Understanding that granted permission for the public sharing of the
completed and agency-approved organizational history. The researchers worked closely with an agency contact person to locate important
historical documents (e.g., board meeting minutes, newsletters, agency
memos) and identify individuals to be interviewed (such as past and
current board members, past and current employees, and executive

directors). Agency contacts also facilitated agency review and approval of the completed histories.

Data collection for each organizational history was relatively unstructured, following a traditional qualitative case study research design (Firestone & Herriott, 1984). The research team of students and faculty conducted interviews and analyzed organizational records to gain an understanding of the life of the organization over time. Based on access to a wide selection of historical materials (e.g., agency publications, media coverage, and documents that had previously detailed the history of the organization), in-person and telephone interviews were conducted with key individuals from the organizations' present and past. An informal interview guide was constructed based upon review of agency documents and discussions with key informants. Most histories were compiled using a combination of document analysis and informational interviews. In addition, financial data were collected to create an historical budget trend line for the organization.

The process of researching and writing each organizational history took approximately three to nine months. Once the narrative history descriptions were completed and reviewed by the research team, copies were sent to the executive directors of the respective agencies for review and comment. Each agency then received a copy of the final organizational history.

The next step in the research process was the cross-case analysis of the 12 organizational histories. The major challenge in a multi-case analysis is balancing the need to identify cross-cutting themes and generalize findings across multiple cases without sacrificing attention to the uniqueness of individual cases. For example, over time, each organization changed in structure, leadership, programs, and other characteristics, often radically, adding a layer of differences within each case in addition to the differences between cases.

Each case, noted in Box 4.3, was examined for key themes that reflected concepts derived both deductively from a review of the literature related to organizational change over time, and inductively, from themes that emerged from a thorough review of each history. The analysis proceeded through a combination of strategies that included identifying themes that cut across cases and examining the ways that themes played out in individual cases.

Box 4.3. Organizational Histories of Pioneering Nonprofit Human Service
Organizations*

Growth and Resilience of Pioneering Nonprofit Human Service
Organizations: A Cross-Case Analysis of Organizational Histories
Exemplars of Sustained Leadership
Bananas at 35: A Pioneering Child Care Referral and Family Support
Organization (1973–2007).
The Unity Council at 40: A Pioneering Community Development and
Service Organization (1967–2007).
Girls Incorporated of Alameda County at 50: A Voice for Girls
(1958–2008).
Coleman Advocates for Children and Families: A Pioneering Child
Advocacy Organization (1974–2008)
Exemplars of Reinventing Internal Operations
Larkin Street Youth Services: Helping Kids Get Off the Street for Good
(1982–2007).
Asian Community Mental Health Services at 35: A Pioneering Multi-
ethnic Service Organization (1973–2008).
CompassPoint Nonprofit Services: Strengthening the Capacities of
Nonprofits (1971–2008).
Black Adoption Placement and Research Center at 25: Placing African
American Children in Permanent Homes (1983–2008).
Exemplars of Substantial External Relations
Shelter Network: Serving Homeless Families and Individuals
(1987–2007)
Jewish Family and Children's Services: A Pioneering Human Service
Organization (1850–2008).
On Lok: A Pioneering Long-term Care Organization for the Elderly
(1973–2008).
The Bayview Hunters Point Foundation for Community
Improvement: A Pioneering Multi-ethnic Human Service
Organization (1971–2008).

*Austin, M.J. (Ed.) (2013). *Organizational histories of nonprofit human service organizations.*
London, UK: Routledge.

Practice Findings

Through a review of the literature and an analysis of the collected organizational histories, key themes were identified in order to develop a
conceptual model of factors that contribute to the capacities of these
nonprofits to thrive and survive over time. The emerging key themes

were *organizational growth* and *organizational resilience*. Organizational growth was characterized as a period of expanding services, clients, or capacity. Organizational resilience was displayed during periods of time when an organization was responding to and recovering from a crisis or challenge.

In contrast to the proactive nature of growth, time periods characterized by resilience entail reactivity, as an organization is forced to respond to a usually unanticipated event or circumstance. Resilience represents an organization's ability to survive such challenges. A variety of organizational factors contributes to an organization's capacity for growth and resilience over time; namely, leadership factors, internal operations factors, and external relations factors.

Leadership factors are often central to facilitating growth and resilience. One of the elements is effective individual leadership, which comprises both leadership by staff and leadership by the *board of directors*. The other element is the leadership style of entrepreneurship, especially the components of flexibility and calculated risk-taking.

Internal operations factors are also important for enabling successful organizational growth and resilience. Internal evaluation comprises actions designed to assess the adequacy and effectiveness of organizational structures and activities, and includes evaluation of program effectiveness, administrative capacity, and responsiveness to constituent needs. One important internal factor is investment in infrastructure, including both the establishment of organizational *systems* and the deliberate development of redundancy in resources, leadership, and operations so that a loss in any organizational area does not threaten the organization's overall functioning.

Finally, *external relations factors* are vital to long-term organizational growth and resilience. External engagement generates community stakeholders to support an organization. This concept includes both community outreach (e.g., through the media or volunteer opportunities), as well as policy engagement (e.g., active response to or efforts to influence public policies that affect the organization). Another important external factor is diversified support, including a variety of financial resources as well as political and community support from a broad range of groups and individuals.

Each of these factors related to leadership, internal operations, and external relations contributes to an organization's ability to seize opportunities for growth and exhibit resilience in the face of challenge. Some successful organizations demonstrate strengths in all of these areas, while others show strengths in only some of them. Furthermore, over the history of an individual organization, the vitality and importance of individual factors emerges and recedes, with a period characterized by strong staff leadership, for example, followed by a period characterized by weaker leadership but strong external engagement. Thus all factors need not be present simultaneously and continuously for an organization to survive and thrive. Each factor, however, contributes to growth and resilience, and some or all may be necessary at any given time in an organization's lifespan to enable the organization to continue to succeed over the long-term. An organization seeking long-term, sustainable success, therefore, needs to attend to and invest in each of the three areas of organizational functioning.

Practice Lessons Learned from the Findings

During periods of organizational growth, each of the factors related to leadership, internal operations, and external relations can play an important role in promoting an organization's success in expanding programs, services, or capacities. The same three factors are important during periods requiring resilience, when organizations struggle to deal with crises or unexpected challenges.

While the previous examples illustrate how different organizational factors influenced growth and resilience at particular moments in the histories of nonprofit organizations, it is important to consider how these factors interrelate over time within a single organization. Throughout its lifespan, an organization can alternate between periods of growth and periods of crisis that require resilience. As an organization shifts between a focus on growth and a focus on resilience, and back, different organizational factors emerge and recede in strength and significance to enable the organization to seize opportunities for growth and to survive when resilience is required.

By focusing on longitudinal data that encompass 20 to more than 150 years of organizational history, the mapping of the organizational histories of pioneering nonprofit human service organizations helps to fill an important gap in the research on nonprofits, complementing the cross-sectional and time-limited case studies that dominate the existing research. Furthermore, the cross-case analysis of 12 different organizational histories provides a broader view of patterns in growth and resilience over time than is possible through a single case study. This analysis of organizational histories provides evidence for the lifecycle models of nonprofit growth. Moreover, the data support a conceptual model of factors related to leadership, internal operations, and external relations that are important for nonprofit organizations to survive and thrive through alternating periods of growth and resilience over time.

Practice Research Lessons Learned from Organizational Cross-case Analysis

- Articulating the limitations of generalizability

No matter how many cases are explored within a set of diverse human service organizations, there will always be limitations regarding the application or relevance of findings to another set of organizations that vary in size, history, location, policy mandates, mission, and funding. Such a limitation also can be viewed, however, as a strength, given the depth of the practice research findings and the prospect of testing the major emerging themes with a much larger population using survey or secondary administrative data.

- Triangulate case-based data from multiple sources to monitor the bias of the case reporters

Practice research that relies upon interviews and organizational documents calls for continuous monitoring of respondent and document bias, often reflected in self-serving written and verbal statements. The process of triangulation provides one approach to cross-checking data that have been captured in different forms. Knowing that the view of senior management often will differ from that of individuals at the line level of service delivery, those engaged in practice research need to pay attention to the importance of multiple sources—just as a skilled investigative journalist seeks confirmation of a fact or perception from multiple sources.

- Capturing case materials as soon as the subject matter of the case has been completed or experienced

This lesson is difficult to apply, especially when seeking to capture historical facts. The importance of this lesson, however, is critical to practice research in practice situations that are so hectic and fast-moving that practitioners may have difficulty recounting something that occurred six months ago. As a result, collecting data as close to the situation under investigation as possible can clearly increase the richness of the findings.

- Describing the context of a case study is a critical component of practice research

Describing the historical factors that influenced the implementation of a public policy is essential for creating an understanding of the findings reflected by the experiences of practitioners seeking to implement the policy. Similarly, cross-case analysis of efforts to improve organizational performance requires an understanding of the evolution of the issues that called for change. Even more challenging is capturing the multiple dimensions of the local context when seeking to capture the elements of organizational sustainability. It might be argued that "context is everything" when engaging in practice research.

- Accessing the tools of other disciplines

When practice research involves capturing the history of an organization in order to identify key aspects of sustainability, the tools used by historians (historiography) can enhance the case development process. Similarly, the tools of investigative journalism also can be useful in regards to fact checking, networking with key informants, and making ongoing efforts to promote triangulation among multiple sources.

CONNECTIONS WITH PREVIOUS AND SUBSEQUENT CHAPTERS

This chapter on organizational cross-case analysis builds upon the previous chapters in several ways. For example, as noted in Chapter 3, when constructing the cross-case analyses of organizations, it is important to contextualize the analysis with a review of the relevant literature that informs the case studies. Although the focus of attention is on the organization in this chapter, similar methods of interviewing are used when accessing the experiences of practitioners, as noted in Chapter 2.

In addition to building upon previous chapters, the discussion in this chapter on implementing welfare reform provides another context for the practice research related to staff and clients discussed in Chapter 6, where we address the issues of subsidized employment and family stabilization. In a similar way, the cross-case analysis of building knowledge-sharing systems relates to the organizational study of evidence-informed practice described in Chapter 7. And finally, the cross-case analysis of nonprofit organizational sustainability informs the relational contracting study in Chapter 7, which features the connections between public and nonprofit sector human service organizations.

The issues identified in this chapter receive additional attention in Part II, where other practice research methods are described, including the organizational challenges associated with case record data mining. Similar organizational challenges are featured in the chapters on defining and supporting research-minded practitioners in a human service organization along with the educational processes that can used to address these challenges. One of the biggest organizational challenges related to practice research involves the dissemination and utilization of research findings (Austin, Dal Santo, Goldberg, Choice, 2001; Graaf, McBeath, Lwin, Holmes, & Austin, 2017). In essence, how were the findings shared with staff? How well were they understood? What impact did they have on modifying practice? And how were services to clients improved as a result of practice research? All these questions relate to the impact of practice research, and there is renewed interest in the human services when it comes to addressing impact (Kania & Kramer, 2011).

REFERENCES

Austin, M.J. (Ed.) (2004). *Changing welfare services: Case studies of local welfare reform programs.* Binghamton, NY: Haworth Press.

Austin, M.J. (Ed.) (2013). *Organizational histories of nonprofit human service organizations.* London, UK: Routledge.

Austin, M.J., Dal Santo, T., Goldberg, S., & Choice, P. (2001). Exploratory research in public social service agencies: As assessment of dissemination and utilization. *Journal of Sociology and Social Welfare, 29*(4), 59–81.

Dufour, S., & Fortin, D. (1992). Annotated bibliography of case study method. *Current Sociology, 40*(1), 166–181.

Firestone, W., & Herriott, R. (1984). Multi-site qualitative policy research: Some design and implementation issues. In D. Fetterman (Ed.), Ethnography in educational evaluation (pp.63–88). Beverly Hills, CA: Sage Publications.

Graaf, G., McBeath, B., Lwin, K., Holmes, D., & Austin, M.J. (2017). Supporting evidence-informed practice in human service organizations: An exploratory study of link officers *Human Service Organizations, 41*(1), 58–75.

Hancock, D.R., & Algozzine, B. (2006). *Doing case study research: A practical guide for beginning researchers.* New York, NY: Teachers College Press.

Kania, J., & Kramer, M. (2011). Collective impact. *Stanford Social Innovation Review, 9*(1), 36–41.

Kimberlin, S., Schwartz, S., & Austin, M.J. (2011). Growth and resilience of pioneering nonprofit human service organizations: A cross-case analysis of organizational histories. *Journal of Evidence-based Social Work, 8*(1/2), 4–28.

Lee, C., & Austin, M.J. (2012). Building organizational supports for knowledge sharing in county social service agencies: Case studies of works-in-progress. *Journal of Evidence-based Social Work, 9*(1/2), 3–18.

Stake, R.E. (1995). *The art of case study research.* Thousand Oaks, CA: Sage Publications.

Yin, R.K. (2003). *Case study research.* Thousand Oaks, CA: Sage Publications.

5

Learning from the Staff and Clients of Child Welfare Services

Following the early years of the research program, in which we carried out single-county studies, addressing research questions that an individual agency wanted to pursue, the consortium decided to expand the scope of the research to involve multiple counties in regional studies of the same topic. This decision was based on factors related to the efficient use of resources, as well as the aim of increasing the rigor of the research. Regional studies enabled us to consolidate and streamline the costs and time associated with framing study questions, developing the study design and instrumentation, and managing the process of obtaining approval from the University Institutional Review Board (IRB). Implementing studies in multiple counties enhanced the rigor of the studies by increasing sample size, increasing the variation related to county context, and increasing the diversity of agency and client population characteristics.

The high proportion of our studies focused on child welfare is attributable to a number of factors. This is a complex field of practice, in which

Practice Research in the Human Services. Michael J. Austin and Sarah Carnochan, Oxford University Press (2020). © Oxford University Press.
DOI: 10.1093/oso/9780197518335.001.0001

clients are mandated participants, services are evaluated by federal and state performance measurement systems, and a professionalized workforce experiences high levels of job stress and low retention rates. As a result, there are both high levels of demand for research evidence, and a relatively high level of resources to support that research as compared with employment and self-sufficiency or adult and aging services.

EARLY EXPERIENCES WITH REGIONAL RESEARCH: CHILD WELFARE AND THE COURTS

One of our first regional child welfare studies focused on the interprofessional relationships among judicial, legal, and social work professionals in the juvenile dependency system. The Adoption and SAFE Families Act, enacted in 1997, emphasized the role of the court in achieving the mandated goals of ensuring that children were safe, reunified with their parents as soon as possible, and supported with respect to their healthcare, educational, and other needs (Carnochan, Molinar, Brown, Botzler, Gunderson, Henry, & Austin, 2019). The courts were required to oversee local judicial processes and funding was allocated to each state for the training of judges, lawyers, and social workers. As a consequence, the level of legal practice and judicial expertise in the juvenile dependency system was elevated nationwide, and court hearings shifted from a relatively informal setting to a more traditional courtroom model. In California, the child welfare system is administered at the county level, where the courts play an important oversight role at the individual case level (Carnochan, Molinar, Brown, Botzler, Gunderson, Henry, & Austin, 2018). As a result, professional interactions and communications in the context of court hearings and outside of the courtroom took on heightened importance. Agency child welfare (CW) directors found that they and their staff members were experiencing increasing challenges in their relationships with judges and attorneys, and asked us to initiate a study to examine these challenges.

Framing the Study Question

In order to frame the study aims and specific research questions, we attended the monthly regional meeting of the CW directors to discuss their concerns and what they hoped to learn from the study. At the outset of the discussion, they articulated the questions they sought to address: "Why are lawyers and judges so hostile and rude to us?" and "What can we do to change this dynamic?" Over the course of this meeting with the CW directors, we worked with them to reframe the study questions and consider design options for an exploratory study. The first question they posed was restated as follows: "What are the perspectives of social work and legal professionals in the juvenile dependency system regarding factors that contribute to tensions among professionals." This reframing served multiple purposes. First, the restatement transformed the focus from a negative to a neutral framing of the issue. By doing this, we sought to facilitate buy-in from legal professionals. The reframing also expanded the question in order to guide a broader investigation that would include the contextual factors that shape the interprofessional dynamics operating within the juvenile dependency system. The reframed questions also focused on identifying promising strategies to strengthen and improve interprofessional relationships.

In this case, practice research sought to understand interprofessional practice within a system of care that involves professionals from multiple professions, with divergent values, professional cultures, and intervention frameworks. It was helpful that the university researcher was both an attorney and a social worker and could approach the research question with a grounding in these divergent worldviews. In addition to these practice-based influences that informed the aims of the study, we conducted a review of professional and academic literature that identified a number of potential contributing factors, including organizational culture, professional status, resource availability, role definition, and job stress.

Data Collection Decisions

Once the study questions were finalized, we worked with the CW directors to determine data collection strategies. Given the emphasis in social work values and practice on the importance of collaboration, we decided to conduct focus groups with child welfare workers in each of the study counties. In designing the focus group protocol, we consulted with the CW directors, in order to make sure that the topics and questions were addressing the central issues of interest, as well as reflecting the existing literature.

In making the decision to conduct individual interviews with judges and attorneys, we expected that they would be more likely to participate in interviews than in focus groups based upon concerns related to attorney-client privilege and confidentiality. Logistical considerations also played a role, given that in contrast to child welfare staff, legal professionals do not typically work full-time in a single child dependency office; schedules and work locations, therefore, may vary from day to day, complicating efforts to schedule a focus group. In smaller counties, there may be only one or two children's attorneys, parents' attorneys, or county counselors, making a focus group impractical. Lastly, we were told by a prominent judge that lawyers who represent clients in dependency proceedings do not always specialize in child dependency law. By interviewing purposely selected legal professionals, we were able to ensure that only those possessing substantial dependency law experience were included in the study.

To design the interview guides, we consulted further with an experienced and well-respected juvenile court judge in one of the participating counties, to ensure that the content and wording of the questions were appropriate and would elicit candid perspectives on the issues being investigated. The primary questions asked of each group included the following:

- How would you define your own professional goals and values, and those of the other professionals engaged in juvenile dependency work?
- How would you define your role and the roles of the other professionals engaged in juvenile dependency work?
- How would you describe the character of your relationships with other professionals?
- Are there features of the juvenile dependency system or court process or characteristics of clients that affect professional relationships?

We wanted to gather service-user perspectives in addition to those of practitioners, and made the decision to conduct focus groups with former foster youth and foster caregivers. Although children and foster caregivers are not necessarily in a position to observe all of the interactions among child welfare workers, attorneys, and judges, they do witness these interactions in court as well as in conferences surrounding judicial dependency proceedings. To ensure that information shared by the focus group participants would be received and interpreted appropriately, these focus groups were led by a doctoral student with substantial child welfare practice experience.

Ultimately, we conducted 10 focus groups with 98 social workers, 50 interviews with judges, attorneys, and court appointed special advocate (CASA) volunteers, and two focus groups, one each with children and caregivers. We also conducted a series of key informant interviews with social work, legal, and judicial professionals involved in model court programs in other jurisdictions around the country in order to explore promising initiatives and best practices as a way to supplement the recommendations from the data provided by the regional study participants.

Study Findings

The key findings that emerged from the interviews and focus groups related to structural factors operating in the juvenile dependency system, as well as operational and individual level factors. The structural factors included professional culture, collaborative and adversarial processes, power and status, and resources. Operational and individual factors included communication, competence, consistency, and interpersonal relations. The analysis went on to trace the linkages between these structural and individual level factors and their impacts on interprofessional relationships (see Figure 5.1). Finally, we reported on the following recommendations offered by study participants with respect to strengthening professional relationships:

- Leadership: Promote communication and culture of respect
- Training: Implement joint training opportunities to improve collaboration and increase competence
- Staffing: Improve hiring practices and professional support to increase commitment and consistency
- Resources: Plan more efficient use of space and scheduling to reduce frustration and provide time for collaboration

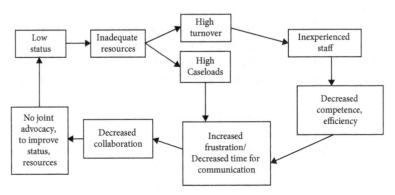

Figure 5.1. Interrelated factors affecting professional relationships.

Disseminating Research Results

The initial dissemination of the study findings was carried out at separate regional meetings with the CW directors and directors of our partner agencies. We sent out the draft summary of findings and recommendations to the groups in advance, noting in the cover email our plan to convert this brief summary into a journal article to promote wider dissemination that would reach a broader audience. We posed several questions to each group to initiate the meeting discussions and to focus their attention. Most importantly, we sought their input on the summary of the recommendations that were offered by participants in the study. The recommendations were organized according to the study participants (e.g., social worker, attorney, judge, client) making the recommendation in response to a request from the CW directors. More broadly, we wanted to know whether there were any findings that did not make sense to them or that were inappropriate for a public audience beyond the consortium agencies. Although the report included a literature review and methods section, we clarified that these would not be a focus of the discussion. The outcome of these discussions enabled us to elaborate on the relationship between the study findings that highlighted factors that contribute to interprofessional tensions and the recommendations offered by study participants for improving relationships (see Figure 5.2).

In addition to sharing findings at regional meetings, two journal articles reporting study findings were published, based on the

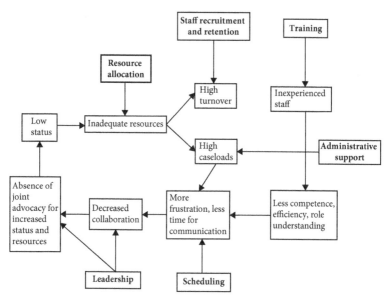

Figure 5.2. Linking results to recommendations.

qualitative component of the study described above, as well as a related quantitative component that involved case record review (Carnochan, Taylor, Abramson-Madden, Han, Rashid, Maney, Teuwen, & Austin, 2007; Han, Carnochan, & Austin, 2007).

CHILD WELFARE DATA MINING

Origins of the Project: Child Welfare Staff Response to Structured Literature Reviews

As described in Chapter 3, following several years of empirical regional studies, the BASSC agency directors asked us to develop a series of structured literature reviews. One set focused on the federal child welfare performance indicators that they believed would be useful tools to inform practice in their child welfare divisions. These literature reviews described a specific federal performance measure, and summarized the research related to the standard, including risk and protective factors as well as relevant promising and evidence-informed practices. In contrast to the expectations of the agency directors, we heard a very different perspective from child welfare managers, supervisors, and line staff when we conducted a series of five focus groups in six of our partner child welfare agencies to discuss the reviews. Feedback from these focus groups raised a number of issues related to the content and potential uses of the reviews, especially the format and extended length that resembled a research paper rather than a tool for practitioners. In addition, participants explained that the reviews: (1) provided insufficient detail to support actual implementation of specific interventions, and (2) summarized studies that were not directly relevant to local county environments, practice settings, and/or client populations. The potential for use was seen as very limited, although some noted that the information could be useful for grant writing or early induction training for child welfare workers.

This focus group experience served as a reminder that the interests of agency administrators do not always correspond to those of their middle-management or line staff, making it important to explore in advance the priorities of the primary target audience. It was important for our practice research partnership that we respond to the differing views held by practitioners at different levels of the agency with respect to the value of structured literature reviews on the national service outcome standards. The subsequent discussions that we held with the agency and CW directors identified an interest on the part of the CW directors in examining the potential for research using their own internal data. This discussion led to the development of a set of case studies exploring existing data mining practices in four agencies. In a cross-case analysis, we identified qualitative data mining as a promising topic for future research, ultimately leading to a project that would develop qualitative data mining methods that can be used to analyze narrative case record data to investigate questions about child welfare practice.

Piloting the Child Welfare Qualitative Data Mining (CWQDM) Project

Following the identification of the shared interest among child welfare directors in strengthening their capacity to engage in qualitative data mining, we developed a pilot project with one of our partner agencies to address the following aims: (1) assess the utility of child welfare case record data for research purposes; (2) develop qualitative data mining methods that could be used to map and analyze the narrative data contained in child welfare case records; and (3) examine the specific issue of case plan alignment, and the extent to which case plan requirements and services related to the initial risks and harms presented in a case. We developed a "memo of understanding" with the pilot agency that laid out our respective roles as partners (see Box 5.1).

Box 5.1. Pilot Agency Memo of Understanding

BASSC research team will carry out the following:

1. BASSC will develop the initial study design but will solicit and incorporate feedback from HSA regarding the design. This includes feedback on sampling, code development, and interpretation of findings.
2. BASSC will staff a research team, including a project manager who will act as liaison for the project and graduate-level research assistants.
3. BASSC will submit a protocol to the university Institutional Review Board and ensure that the study abides by the terms of research ethics upheld by this board. This includes ensuring that all research assistants have been trained in research ethics and ensuring data security requirements are met.
4. BASSC will submit preliminary findings, reports, and presentations to HSA for review and approval prior to dissemination.
5. BASSC will provide agency-relevant reports and presentations as desired by HSA.

HSA staff will carry out the following:

1. HSA will participate in the development of the study design in collaboration with BASSC. This will include one to two meetings to discuss study design.
2. HSA will provide technical assistance with respect to selecting an appropriate sample and querying data, providing the necessary training for and access to CWS/CMS records, and providing access to computer facilities to access these records.
3. HSA will provide a letter of support to the university Institutional Review Board substantiating support for the project.
4. HSA will participate in the interpretation and development of study findings. This includes reviewing and providing feedback on study findings (estimated one to two meetings).

The partner agency had a well-developed research and evaluation team in their child welfare division, which was one of the reasons that we had reached out to them for the pilot project. We worked with two agency-based child welfare analysts as our study liaisons, who assisted throughout the project with data access, determining the sampling criteria, validating the coding scheme, interpreting themes identified in the coded data, and disseminating results at a national practice research conference.

Data Collection and Analysis

A significant component of the pilot involved the design of the proto-col and methods to be used for data extraction and qualitative analysis (Henry, Carnochan, & Austin, 2014), made possible by the agency's electronic case record data system and our access to a web-based qualitative analytic software. In the past, case record review projects required that our team work on site at the agency to review stacks of case files provided by agency staff. Records would sometimes be inaccessible, archived elsewhere in a storage facility, or locked in a social worker's personal file cabinet. Manual coding of the documents could take months, with limited opportunities for follow-up review in situations where there were questions about a case or specific coding decisions. In contrast, the agency's electronic data system and our web-based analytical software allowed our team to log onto the agency's data system over several weeks, quickly locate the cases in the sample, and upload documents (sometimes as many as 60 to 80 per case) containing case data directly to the data storage system of the qualitative data analysis platform.

Gaining this access to the qualitative, narrative data contained in case records (e.g., investigative report, contact notes, case plans, and court reports) allowed us to employ qualitative analytical methods in new ways for case record review. Each case was summarized in a 10 to 15-page overview that described the family configuration, present-ing risks and harms, and the progress of the case through the system, along with the critical reflections of the Master's in Social Work (MSW) student research assistant reviewing the case. In addition, we developed a codebook that integrated the concepts and issues framed by the child welfare literature with categories of characteristics and events that we observed in the case records. Applying these codes to excerpts of the nar-rative data at the level of case documents enabled us to map the contents of the case records, and identify key patterns across the cases. As we developed the codebook and carried out the first round of coding, we communicated with our agency liaisons regularly to confirm our interpretation of the data with respect to the aspects of practice described in the case records. We also elicited their perspective on important practice dynamics and processes that the coding should capture.

Working with successive teams of MSW research assistants, we coded and summarized over 1,500 documents across a total of 105 cases, with each case requiring 15 to 20 hours to complete. It took over two years to complete the analysis for this pilot phase of the project, due to a number of factors. First, we were designing the qualitative data mining methods as we worked, requiring an ongoing iterative process of coding and codebook revisions. The student staffing model also contributed to the long timeline. We hired teams of five to seven MSW students for 75% time summer research positions, with only one student continuing in a paid position at 25% time during the academic year, meaning total staff time was limited. Most importantly, the volume of the data was immense, with hundreds of pages of documentation for each case. Without our long-standing research partnership with the pilot agency, it is unlikely that the project would have been sustainable.

Throughout the pilot, we engaged in regular meetings with our study liaisons, and shared emerging findings with them and the agency's CW director. In the early stages of the pilot, we learned an important lesson when we shared results from our initial review of a small sample of case records in the pilot county with the CW directors at a regional meeting that included the pilot county director. The initial review was designed to determine the viability of the records as a data source for research. Following this initial assessment, we presented what were positive findings about case record quality and content. We did not obtain prior approval from the pilot county, based on an incorrect assumption that sharing positive findings in this setting would not be problematic. This decision, however, generated substantial tension in our relationship with the pilot county CW director. When we discovered the issue in a subsequent meeting with the CW director, we acknowledged the error and apologized. This enabled us to continue the project with the pilot county as we further developed the qualitative data mining methods, including mapping of case record content to inform future research directions that would be supported by the data. The experience demonstrated the importance of ensuring that practitioners play a central role with respect to all dissemination decisions.

This phase of the project generated several MSW student research papers. In response to the agency's research question related to case plan alignment, one of the students examined whether case plans addressed presenting problems, finding that: (1) 80% of case plans included service objectives that completely addressed presenting problems overall; (2) 46.2% of case plans included service objectives that addressed all and only presenting problems; (3) 33.8% included service objectives that addressed all presenting problems as well as additional objectives that did not address a presenting problem; (4) 20% of case plans outlined service objectives that did not address all of the presenting problems; and (5) 13.8% did not address all presenting problems, yet included additional objectives that did not address a presenting problem (Storey, 2014).

We also pursued an analysis that captured forms of skillful practice documented in the case records (Carnochan, Weissinger, Henry, Liner-Jigamian, & Austin, 2018). We chose to focus this analysis on the case records for 39 youth in the sample, owing to the complex practice challenges posed by this age group. We found that child welfare workers were implementing many of the practices that are promoted by child welfare practice frameworks. We identified categories of skillful practice that included: (1) effective communication on the part of social workers, (2) support for client self-determination, and (3) active intervention strategies (Carnochan et al., 2018). We disseminated the qualitative data mining (QDM) methodology more broadly via conference presentations and a journal article (Henry, Carnochan, & Austin, 2014).

Expanding the Data-mining Project to More Counties

Following the initial pilot stage of the project, we embarked on a second phase aimed at using our QDM methods to investigate substantive issues in child welfare practice in other partner agencies. The process of identifying the topics and the participating agencies involved multiple steps and communication strategies with agency directors and their child welfare directors. First, we developed a spreadsheet listing possible future research topics that were identified in our analysis and in subsequent discussions with the child welfare director at the pilot agency. This list was shared with the BASSC directors, and topics were added and subtracted from the list based on their input. The revised list was then disseminated to the child welfare directors. We scheduled in-person meetings with seven or eight interested child welfare directors at their offices. We then identified a subset of topics in which two or more agencies expressed interest, and sent a second round of emails to the interested directors identifying common research interests and proposing two common topics: Parental Substance Abuse and Child Mental Health. Each topic was selected by two agencies for a qualitative data mining study; however, we later learned from one of the smallest counties that the County Counsel would not approve sharing sensitive, non-deidentified case record data with our research team. By investing time in these multilevel communications, and facilitating cross-county shared decision-making, we were able to secure the commitment of agency staff to support the design of the sampling strategy and the onsite data extraction process.

DEFINING SAMPLES AND EXTRACTING CASE RECORD DATA

Similar to the case with the data-mining pilot study, we worked with study liaisons in each participating agency to define the sample, coordinate extraction of the case records, and analyze and interpret the data. In both projects, we made the decision to extract data for a much smaller sample than we had in the pilot project, that is, between 20 and 30 cases instead of over 100. Based on our experience with the pilot, 105 cases were far too many to analyze within a reasonable time frame, and 20 to 30 cases provided sufficient depth and complexity to generate meaningful substantive findings.

In contrast to the pilot experience, working with agency liaisons to define the study sample related to parental substance abuse proved to be challenging when it came to accessing the agency's quantitative administrative data to identify client-level variables of interest. We needed to identify parents impacted by substance use; however, there is no diagnostic or assessment field in CWS/CMS (California Child Welfare Services/Case Management System) database that specifically indicates parental substance use disorder. To work around this limitation, we developed an alternative strategy. CWS/CMS contains drop-down menus for selecting case plan elements, and substance use services is one of the items on the menu. We pulled from this data field cases involving parental substance use. The sample that was generated revealed some of the limitations of administrative data more generally. Busy practitioners who have experience with the high prevalence of substance use among child welfare-involved families, and are making decisions in the early stages of a case based upon incomplete information, may select substance use services as a default option for parental case plans. As a result, a small percentage of cases in the original sample did not involve parental substance use, necessitating further refinement of the sample as we moved into the analysis process.

Fortunately, in the small county where we examined the integration of child mental health and child welfare services, we were able to work closely with our study liaison to implement a purposive sampling approach that reflected the agency's local context and implementation of California's child mental health policy reforms. It was interesting to note that there was some degree of variation in case record documentation across the three counties, particularly with respect to the agency where we examined child mental health integration. Despite the common electronic administrative data system (CWS/CMS) that is used in all California counties, we observed some differences in county approaches to the content of court reports and contact notes, some of which we learned from our study liaison reflected the influence of the local judge on documentation requirements associated with court proceedings.

ANALYZING THE DATA AND DISSEMINATING STUDY FINDINGS

The case record data for the two projects were analyzed using the same methods that we developed in the pilot study, including the creation of individual case summaries, as well as detailed coding based upon a coding scheme informed by the relevant research literature, as well as by input from our practice research partners.

Reporting our findings from the child mental health integration study to our agency partner represented a relatively robust and engaged exchange that unfolded in several steps. We provided the child welfare director and agency liaison with a preliminary report that summarized emerging findings in the following domains: (1) child characteristics, including mental and behavioral health needs; (2) family characteristics; (3) multisystem collaboration; (4) child outcomes; (5) promising practices; (6) practice challenges; and (7) emerging implications for practice. The child welfare director brought in the Child Mental Health (CMH) Director to discuss the report of preliminary findings. Although much of the report was quite positive, the results did indicate delays of four to six months from the initial referral to commencement of services. The observed delays were a central focus of the discussion, which was quite collaborative in nature, based on the close working relationship between the CMH and CW directors. The discussion highlighted possible reasons for the delays, and identified priority topics for the next phase of the analysis, including comparing experiences between immigrant and non-immigrant families, and between in-county and out-of-county cases, as well as how coordination or communication issues between caregiver and child welfare workers affect youth.

We submitted a final report that incorporated these topics, and a second meeting took place to discuss the final report, as well as possible directions for future analysis and research, including our interest in developing an article focused specifically on child trauma, which had emerged as we examined immigration experiences among children in the sample. A program officer from the family foundation that is a member of BASSC attended this meeting as well, because one aim of the meeting was to explore a CW–CMH service integration focused project at the regional level. There was consensus at the meeting that we would present a synthesis of the findings from the pilot, the CMH study and the Parental Substance Abuse study at an upcoming meeting of the child welfare directors' regional group in order to explore interest in a study in multiple counties that would examine experiences with integration of CMH and CW services.

Several months later, we were able to share with the regional group the synthesized findings from the three studies and suggest possible next steps for expanding the project, but the discussion headed in a different direction, as the group noted the length of time involved in case-record data mining. Instead, members of the group turned to focus on supervision in child welfare, which they viewed as playing a critical role in skillful practice and implementation of evidence-based practices. Their response represents a clear example of the difference in perspectives related to practice and research time frames.

Our efforts to engage the county agencies in disseminating the results of the parental substance use study were less successful. The departures of the CW directors in each agency (retirement and transition to director in another agency) made it difficult to gain the attention of the study agencies when preliminary and final results were being shared. We provided an aggregate preliminary report, followed by county-specific final reports to the two agencies. The discussion among the CW directors highlighted the length of time from identifying study aims to presenting study findings.

Each project generated more focused articles and conference presentations, in addition to the comprehensive preliminary and final reports that we provided to the participating county agencies. Building on the study examining child mental health service integration, we pursued more focused analyses of children's experiences of immigration and their experiences of trauma, and the agency's responses to child trauma. Findings from the immigration analysis presented at a national social work research conference provided an example of the kind of case summary that this form of qualitative data mining can generate, tracing the trajectory of a single case over time that is representative of other case trajectories in the data set (Figure 5.3).

The trauma-focused analysis examining 16 cases in the sample was presented in early form at the International Practice Research conference in Hong Kong, and subsequently published in the *Journal of Public Child Welfare* (Taylor, Battis, Carnochan, Henry, Balk, & Austin, 2018). We found that the youth exhibited multiple signs and symptoms of complex trauma which are identified in the literature on childhood trauma, in the domains of attachment, biology, affect regulation, behavioral control, dissociation, cognition and self-concept.

Focusing on the responses of child welfare workers to trauma among children, we found that child welfare workers were applying elements of trauma-informed practice in their work with children and families. Key activities included: maximizing the child's sense of safety; assisting children in reducing overwhelming emotions; addressing the impact of trauma and subsequent changes in the child's behavior, development, and relationships; coordinating services with other agencies; utilizing comprehensive assessment of the child's trauma experiences and their impact on development and behavior to guide services; supporting and promoting positive and

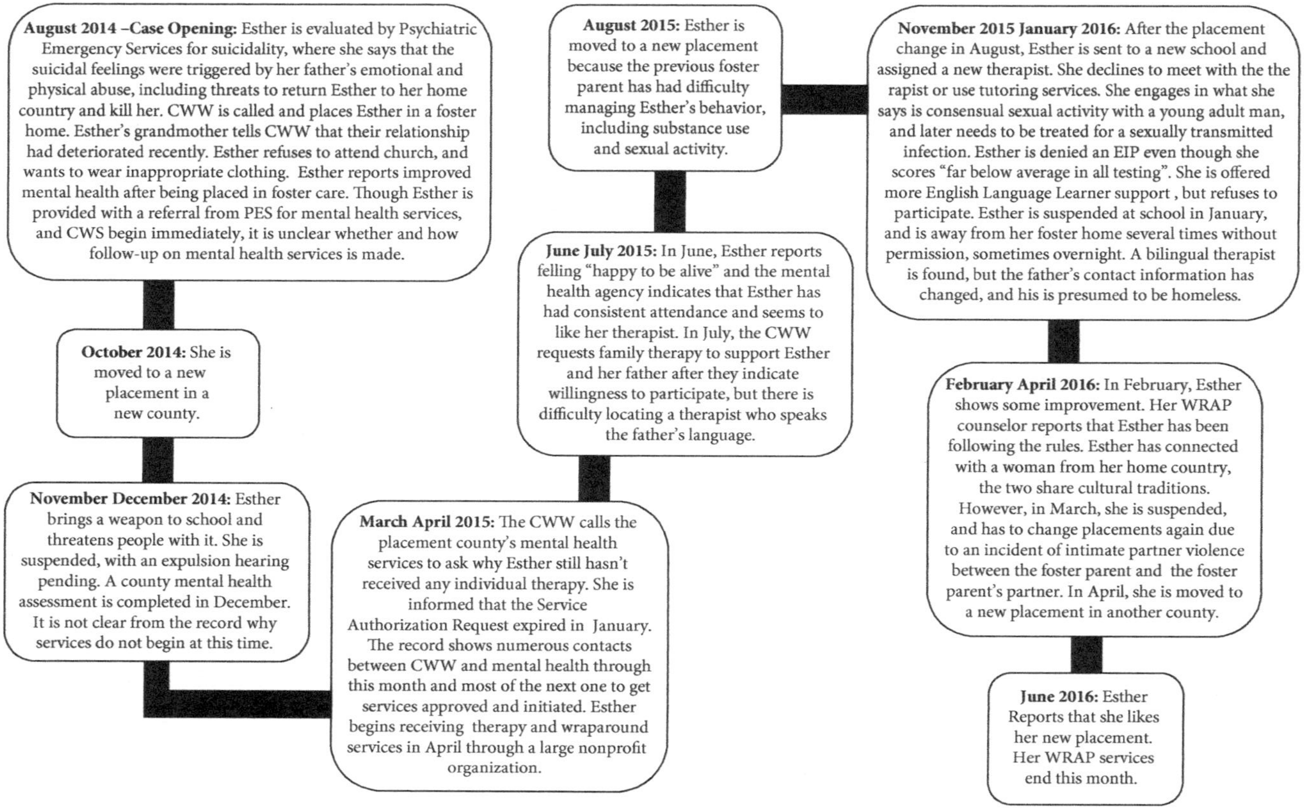

August 2014 – Case Opening: Esther is evaluated by Psychiatric Emergency Services for suicidality, where she says that the suicidal feelings were triggered by her father's threats to return Esther to her home country and kill her. CWW is called and places Esther in a foster home. Esther's grandmother tells CWW that their relationship had deteriorated recently. Esther refuses to attend church, and wants to wear inappropriate clothing. Esther reports improved mental health after being placed in foster care. Though Esther is provided with a referral from PES for mental health services, and CWS begin immediately, it is unclear whether and how follow-up on mental health services is made.

October 2014: She is moved to a new placement in a new county.

November December 2014: Esther brings a weapon to school and threatens people with it. She is suspended, with an expulsion hearing pending. A county mental health assessment is completed in December. It is not clear from the record why services do not begin at this time.

March April 2015: The CWW calls the placement county's mental health services to ask why Esther still hasn't received any individual therapy. She is informed that the Service Authorization Request expired in January. The record shows numerous contacts between CWW and mental health through this month and most of the next one to get services approved and initiated. Esther begins receiving therapy and wraparound services in April through a large nonprofit organization.

August 2015: Esther is moved to a new placement because the previous foster parent has had difficulty managing Esther's behavior, including substance use and sexual activity.

June July 2015: In June, Esther reports felling "happy to be alive" and the mental health agency indicates that Esther has had consistent attendance and seems to like her therapist. In July, the CWW requests family therapy to support Esther and her father after they indicate willingness to participate, but there is difficulty locating a therapist who speaks the father's language.

November 2015 January 2016: After the placement change in August, Esther is sent to a new school and assigned a new therapist. She declines to meet with the the rapist or use tutoring services. She engages in what she says was consensual sexual activity with a young adult man, and later needs to be treated for a sexually transmitted infection. Esther is denied an EIP even though she scores "far below average in all testing". She is offered more English Language Learner support, but refuses to participate. Esther is suspended at school in January, and is away from her foster home several times without permission, sometimes overnight. A bilingual therapist is found, but the father's contact information has changed, and his is presumed to be homeless.

February April 2016: In February, Esther shows some improvement. Her WRAP counselor reports that Esther has been following the rules. Esther has connected with a woman from her home country, the two share cultural traditions. However, in March, she is suspended, and has to change placements again due to an incident of intimate partner violence between the foster parent and the foster parent's partner. In April, she is moved to a new placement in another county.

June 2016: Esther Reports that she likes her new placement. Her WRAP services end this month.

Figure 5.3. Child welfare and immigration—case trajectory.

stable relationships in the life of the child; and providing support and guidance to the child's family and caregivers.

The parental substance use project focused further analysis on exploring the ways in which child welfare workers refer to child mal-treatment statutes, risk assessment tools, and practice guidelines as they frame evidence and make the case to the court that parental substance use is harmful or poses a substantial risk of harm to children. The analysis revealed that workers cited multiple sources and types of evidence to argue that parents had failed to protect their children from harm or risk of harm and/or had failed to provide for their children's basic needs due to substance use. The analysis further suggested that state policy and local practice guidelines influenced the structure of court reports and the arguments that social workers made for state intervention (Henry, Liner-Jigamian, Carnochan, Taylor, & Austin, 2018).

The most recent product generated by the data-mining project is a casebook for use in social work practice courses, child welfare seminars, and agency-based training programs. Drawing from the individual case summaries created from the case record data, the casebook offers 20 cases designed to provide students with real-life examples that demonstrate the complexity and challenges involved in daily child welfare practice (Carnochan, Molinar, Brown, Botzler, Gunderson, Henry, & Austin, 2019).

CONCLUSION

Practice Research Lessons

Based upon our experiences with these practice research studies in child welfare, several lessons can be identified. At the initiation of any study, it is important to develop the study aims and research questions jointly with practice partners. This process may necessitate multiple rounds of communications, both electronic and face to face, to ensure that the study is focused on the high priority issues. In some instances, practice partners may articulate concerns, such as perceived harsh treatment by legal and judicial professionals that require translation into answerable research questions.

Attention also should be given to the different perspectives that may be held by researchers and practitioners with respect to what constitutes timely reporting of study findings. For practitioners in child welfare agencies, policy reforms, program initiatives, and evolving community concerns create an environment in which priorities can change rapidly, resulting in pressure for study results to be reported in three to six months. Even in the second phase of the qualitative data mining project, where parental substance abuse data were extracted in midsummer, and the preliminary reports were shared in December, it proved challenging to engage the staff in a timely manner. In contrast, for researchers, the value placed on attention to theoretical frameworks, responding to identified gaps in the literature, and ensuring methodological rigor led to much longer study time frames. Researchers also may be conditioned by the traditionally slow academic process when engaged in journal manuscript submission from peer review, revise and resubmission, to final publication.

Practitioner and researcher perspectives on what constitutes sensitive information also may differ. Although researchers may consider "positive" findings to be noncontroversial, they can create complications for child welfare agencies that may be in the midst of negotiations with unions and/or responding to community advocates regarding standards for service provision. What constitutes relevant or useful information also reflects some variation across practice and research worlds. Agencies often want a broad and comprehensive accounting of the study results that are most relevant to current practice challenges, while academic journals typically seek more narrowly focused analyses that address novel issues not yet examined by scholars.

Connecting to Other Chapters

The child welfare studies described in this chapter are also related to the literature reviews on substantive child welfare topics noted in Chapter 3; namely, the literature reviews related to child welfare population issues and child welfare organizational performance issues. In addition, Chapter 10 provides a more comprehensive description of the methodology developed in our qualitative data mining studies.

REFERENCES

Carnochan, S., Molinar, L., Brown, J., Botzler, L., Gunderson, K., Henry, C., & Austin, M.J. (2019). *Public child welfare: A casebook for learning and teaching.* San Diego, CA: Cognella.

Carnochan, S., Taylor, S., Abramson-Madden, A., Han, M., Rashid, S., Maney, J., Teuwen, S., & Austin, M.J. (2007). Child welfare and the courts: An exploratory study of the relationship between two complex systems. *Journal of Public Child Welfare, 1*(1), 117–136.

Carnochan, S., Weissinger, E., Henry, C., Liner-Jigamian, N., & Austin, M.J. (2019). Using qualitative data-mining to identify skillful practice in child welfare case records. *Journal of Public Child Welfare, 13*(4), 419–440.

Han, M., Carnochan, S. & Austin, M.J. (2007). Factors contributing to perceived difficulty in child welfare and court inter-professional collaboration: An exploratory study of case records. *Journal of Public Child Welfare, 1*(3), 115–131.

Henry, C., Carnochan, S., & Austin, M.J. (2014). Using qualitative data-mining for practice research in child welfare. *Child Welfare, 93*(6), 7–26.

Henry, C., Liner-Jigamian, N., Carnochan, S., Taylor, S., & Austin, M.J. (2018). Parental substance use: How child welfare workers make the case for court intervention. *Children and Youth Services Review, 93,* 69–78.

Storey, J. (2014). *Do case plans address presenting problems in family reunification child welfare cases?* Student paper, School of Social Welfare, UC Berkeley.

Taylor, S., Battis, C., Carnochan, S., Henry, C., Balk, M., & Austin, M.J. (2018). Exploring trauma-informed practice in public child welfare through qualitative data-mining of case records. *Journal of Public Child Welfare,* 1–20.

6

Learning from Staff and Clients of Public Assistance Programs

In our work with the employment and self-sufficiency (E&SS) divisions of our county social service agency partners that oversee CalWORKs welfare services and benefits, we have focused on program participants and stakeholders, as well as the experiences of agency managers and staff (Stanczyk, Carnochan, Hengeveld-Bidmon, & Austin, 2018; Austin, Chow, Johnson, DeMarco, & Ketch, 2008). One major project investigated the perspectives of employers participating in county administered subsidized employment programs (Carnochan, Taylor, Pascual, & Austin, 2014; Taylor, Carnochan, Pascual, & Austin, 2016). Our county practice research partners continue to identify areas for further research, including most recently the Family Stabilization program providing intensive, whole-family focused services to participants in CalWORKs (California's TANF

Practice Research in the Human Services. Michael J. Austin and Sarah Carnochan, Oxford University Press (2020). © Oxford University Press.
DOI: 10.1093/oso/9780197518335.001.0001

program) who are experiencing destabilizing crises (Stanczyk, Carnochan, Hengeveld-Bidmon, & Austin, 2018).[1]

THE PERSPECTIVES OF EMPLOYERS IN SUBSIDIZED EMPLOYMENT PROGRAMS

In response to the Great Recession that began in 2007, county agencies were authorized and funded to develop subsidized employment programs under the American Recovery and Reinvestment Act–TANF Emergency Funding Act (ARRA-TEF), enacted by President Obama and Congress in 2009 as a strategy to address high unemployment and business distress. In 2010, we carried out a study to examine the experiences and perspectives of employers who participated in these programs by providing subsidized employment positions to CalWORKs clients and individuals with incomes up to 200% of the federal poverty threshold.

Gaining Consensus

During the early months of the Great Recession, we engaged in a series of discussions with the agency directors seeking to define a study that would capture their experiences in responding to the recession. The issues included managing budget cuts, expanding services to address increased community need, developing strategies to do more with less, and sustaining morale among staff who faced increased workloads and loss of colleagues to layoffs. In order to identify a research topic that would not duplicate the current efforts of a number of regional,

---

[1] The Temporary Assistance for Needy Families (TANF) program is a federal program that provides cash assistance as well as employment services and other supports for low-income families with children. Created through the 1996 welfare reform legislation (The Personal Responsibility and Work Opportunity Reconciliation Act), TANF ended the entitlement to aid, imposed work requirements and time limits on benefits, and transferred policy and administrative decision-making from the federal government to the states. California's TANF program—California Work Opportunity and Responsibility to Kids (CalWORKs)—is administered locally by county human service agencies. CalWORKs has historically been more generous and less punitive than most other state TANF programs.

statewide, and national organizations, one of the agency directors proposed an alternative study of county subsidized employment (SE) programs that might identify successful strategies to address the economic and employment consequences of the recession and budget crisis.

As a first step, the research team developed a comprehensive structured literature review on SE programs, which we presented to the directors in the fall of 2010. Despite the uncertainty related to whether Congress would reauthorize the funding, the decision was made to proceed with a study based on regional program experiences. The following month, reauthorization did indeed fail, but member agencies were determined to continue their programs, possibly with additional state CalWORKs funding. With the encouragement of the agency directors, the county employment and self-sufficiency (E&SS) division directors were invited to a meeting in early 2011 to share their experiences with SE services. As a result of this meeting, it was agreed that other agency staff members should be involved in order to identify the specific aims and methods for a regional SE study.

Framing Study Aims

The discussions among the E&SS directors related to identifying effective strategies to engage employers in continued SE programs, as well as tracking longer term participant outcomes to determine program effectiveness. Building upon these topics, the BASSC directors considered an array of more specific issues that might be investigated, including the following: (1) the roles/skills of staff in addressing long-term outcomes, (2) different county economic contexts as they impacted the SE programs, (3) differences in program design and structure across counties that might contribute to variation in program outcomes, and (4) the role of workforce investment boards in SE programs. Regarding the aim of examining employer engagement strategies, the directors highlighted their interest in understanding: (1) employer perceptions of county human service agencies, including whether the agency is a trustworthy source of employee referrals, and (2) the role that case management or other agency-based supports played in employer decisions to participate in SE programs. This extended series of separate and joint discussions carried over approximately 18 months at the director and division-head levels resulted in approval to proceed with a study.

In framing the study aims, the final decision was to focus on employers, based upon several considerations. First, the federal act authorizing the use of TANF funds to operate SE programs was implemented with little to no guidance for agencies with respect to how the funds could be spent, and how programs could be structured. In response, some of the agencies had seized the opportunity to rapidly set up programs to begin placing individuals as quickly as possible. As a result, many of the programs were perceived as works in progress, and the agency directors as well as the E&SS directors were interested in the perspectives of employers on program operations to inform ongoing reforms. Second, they believed that university-based researchers would be in a better position than their own research and evaluation staff to obtain more candid responses from employers. The agencies were interested in the outcomes for employers participating in SE programs, their experiences with employees (e.g., Does the employee perform effectively? Does the employee "fit" in the organization?), and whether employers hire (or intend to hire) the employee permanently. There was also interest in understanding: (1) the reasons why employers decide to utilize the program, (2) whether the application and placement processes were easy to understand, efficient, and effective (e.g., placing employees with appropriate skills in positions within a certain time frame); and (3) the nature of the challenges or barriers faced in relation to applying to or participating in the program.

The initial interests of the directors included evaluating participant employment and earnings outcomes, but the county automated client data systems would not allow us to track the postprogram participation outcomes of the participants and accessing statewide employment and wage data was not feasible. As a result, we agreed with our practice research partners that the study would focus only on understanding employer perceptions of the programs.

Identifying Participating Agencies

In the SE study, three agencies initially elected to participate; after one agency dropped out, two additional agencies joined, and we moved forward with four agencies. This experience illustrates one of the benefits of working with a regional consortium of agencies; namely, the variation and flexibility that the platform provides with respect to identifying participating agencies. For any specific project, each agency makes the decision on whether and how to participate. These decisions are made based upon the degree of relevance or urgency represented by the study topic, along with consideration of agency resources that will be required to support the study, particularly with respect to sampling, participant recruitment, and data collection. As a result, some agencies might be actively involved in discussions related to defining research questions, but they might not participate in the data collection process. Others may begin with the intention of full participation, but later determine that circumstances have changed, and they can no longer devote the necessary staff time.

Methods and Implementation

As with a number of our studies, we engaged a colleague on the social work faculty at a neighboring university to help with the implementation of the project, along with graduate research assistants (MSW students) who carried out the data collection and provided support for the data analysis. A range of data sources were accessed for the study, including: (1) agency materials providing program descriptions, (2) agency administrative data to generate the sample of employers, (3) a brief online employer survey that collected descriptive information about the employer and asked about interest in doing an interview, and (4) semistructured phone interviews with employers that explored program experiences. Random samples of employers in the community were drawn from employer lists provided by the participating agencies; employers who declined to participate were replaced through additional random sampling. The E&SS directors were provided with drafts of the employer materials, including the interview guide and the invitation to participate, and their comments related to content and language were incorporated into the final versions.

The interviews of the employers were the primary component of the study, and interview questions addressed the following topics:

- Description of the employer's company
- Description of the employer's involvement with the SE program

- Positive aspects of the experience
- Negative aspects of the experience
- Incentives that would lead the employer to continue with the program
- Description of one or two successful employees
- Description of relationship with county staff/job developer
- Recommendations for changing or improving the program
- Satisfaction rating: Scale of 1–5

Dissemination to Our Partners

We kept our practice research partners, including the agency directors, updated throughout the duration of the project. The preliminary report that we developed following completion of the interviews noted emerging themes related to motivation to participate, interactions with county staff, the hiring process, employee characteristic, job characteristics employee-employer fit, and overall positive and negative experiences.

After the analysis was completed, we distributed a draft report of final results to the E&SS directors. We then met with them in order to elicit their help with interpreting the findings, commenting on some of our preliminary interpretations, and helping us identify practice and policy implications. The draft report briefly summarized selected findings of interest relating to: (1) satisfaction with the program, (2) subsidy design, (3) hiring/screening processes, (4) employer motivation, and (5) employee skills. In our view, these findings were of particular interest because they seemed to have strong implications for policy and program design. The E&SS directors were invited to highlight findings of particular interest, identify sensitive findings not appropriate for cross-county sharing, and/ or suggest implications for their programs. Their comments, along with those provided electronically by individuals who were not able to attend in person, were integrated into the final report. In the final full report, we provided a brief summary of the initial literature review, followed by a summary of the findings (Table 6.1), and program and policy implications informed by our communications with the E&SS directors.

Table 6.1. Final Report Themes

Program	Overall rating; Preferred subsidy duration; Preferred subsidy amount; Program features
Employers	Decisions to participate; Risk assessment and management; Benefits to the employer; Previous and future subsidized employment participation
Employees	Employee challenges; Employee skills; Employee training
Jobs	Responsibility level; Need for workers who can multitask
Employer–Employee Match	Skill, interest and workplace "fit"; Interplay between employee traits, personal commitment on the part of the employers, and appropriate expectations
Employer Suggestions	Employer services and supports; Employee services and supports; Program features

Disseminating to the Field

After completing the reporting to the consortium members, research staff turned to developing articles for journals that focused on two of the central topics from the final report. The first article examined the role of soft skills in relationships between employers and subsidized employees, in which employers emphasized the importance of motivation, self-presentation, and interpersonal skills (Carnochan, Taylor, Pascual, & Austin, 2014). The article identified the following four processes that can facilitate successful workplace relationships: (1) identifying the particular soft skills required based on workplace and job characteristics; (2) clarifying soft skill expectations with SE employees initially and throughout the placement experience; (3) establishing employer–employee communication processes related to job performance and competing family demands; and (4) working with employers to identify and address negative assumptions in order to promote stronger workplace relationships.

The second article synthesized findings related to employer perspectives on the program design and their interactions with county staff, identifying key themes related to program marketing, program structure, economic climate, and improving the program (Taylor, Carnochan, Pascual, & Austin, 2016). Study participants reported that they were motivated to participate by altruism as well as the financial incentive offered by the subsidy and had generally positive experiences while engaging with the program.

CLIENT PERSPECTIVES ON FAMILY STABILIZATION PROGRAMS

The subsidized employment policy and related county programs were designed to address the challenges experienced by adult participants related to finding and retaining work. A more recent example of our research involving the CalWORKs program sought to understand the implementation as well as participant and worker perspectives on services designed to address barriers to program participation and employment. Established by state Assembly Bill 74 (AB 74) on January 1, 2014, the CalWORKs Family Stabilization (FS) Program was a new component of the CalWORKs program intended to provide intensive case management and services to clients to ensure a basic level of stability within a family—either before or during their participation in welfare-to-work activities. The goal of the FS program was to increase client success in light of California's newly established flexible welfare-to-work policy, which had required CalWORKs participants to find employment within 24 months, by providing more intensive case management and assigning clients to additional activities or services needed to achieve self-sufficiency. CalWORKs recipients were eligible to participate in FS if the county human service agency determined that the family was experiencing a specific situation or crisis that was destabilizing the family and would interfere with the ability of adult clients to participate in welfare-to-work activities and services.

Each county was responsible for implementing the requirements set forth in the authorizing legislation and associated All-County-Letter (ACL) issued by the California Department of Social Services (CDSS). The legislation provided illustrations of the kinds of crises that would make a client eligible to participate (e.g., homelessness, domestic violence, behavioral health needs), but allowed counties to develop their own eligibility criteria. Similarly, although the state offered examples of the additional services that counties could provide under FS (e.g., treatment for family members, if the situation interfered with client's ability to participate in E&SS activities, emergency shelter, day treatment, substance abuse counseling), counties were given considerable latitude to determine the array of services provided to FS clients.

PHASE 1: IMPLEMENTATION OF THE FAMILY STABILIZATION PROGRAM

In an effort to understand how to best provide services to CalWORKs families as outlined in the ACL, county agency directors expressed an interest (a year after the start-up of the state initiative) in exploring several issues. These included: (1) the array of implementation approaches used throughout the Bay Area, (2) potential training needed for CalWORKs staff providing FS services, (3) approaches to meet these training needs, and (4) research from the field regarding best and/or promising practices in the area of family stabilization. The research project was staffed by a retired county staff development director with extensive regional experience who would help us to capture information about the following specific aims: (1) local interpretation of ACL mandates and related service delivery structures, (2) nature of services and employees assigned to deliver them, (3) training needs, and (4) opportunities for public/nonprofit collaboration to enhance service delivery and/or training. To further inform the framing and focus of the study, a graduate student researcher (MSW student) developed a brief literature review to identify family stabilization training approaches, tools, and resources.

The research plan involved conducting a series of interviews with managers at multiple levels who were involved in implementing the county's family stabilization program. A list of proposed interview topics was provided to the E&SS directors and staff development managers to review and provide feedback with respect to relevance, clarity, and completeness. Thirty semistructured interviews, lasting 1 to 1½ hours were conducted over a six-month period. The topics for the E&SS Directors included: 1) Pre-existing structure/staffing; 2) All County Letter Interpretation; 3) Program Characteristics (e.g., service delivery strategy/structure changes, use of the Online CalWORKs Assessment

Tool (OCAT)); and 4) Implementation strategies and roles. Topics for the Staff Development Managers focused on describing employee characteristics as well as related training initiatives.

With the interviews and data analysis completed, a draft report was developed. In order to ensure that the analysis highlighted themes and issues directly relevant to the agencies, we worked together with the E&SS directors to develop a draft report structure that would serve as a high level guide for organizing the preliminary findings (Box 6.1). The report was shared with the county directors in order to discuss the following implications for practice: (1) increasing the skills of employment service staff, (2) increased attention to managing the program participant assessment data related to case conference and case continuity training, and (3) an exploration of training materials development. In addition, the major implications for future practice research identified by our agency partners included: (1) the current and future use of the assessment data, (2) more attention to defining and measuring the outcomes of family stabilization services, and (3) more attention to the future staffing and structuring of family stabilization services.

Building upon the report to the counties, additional data analysis was conducted by a postdoctoral fellow in order to develop a typology of implementation approaches based on the agency and county contextual factors that shaped the implementation decisions (illustrated in Figure 6.1). Her analysis, informed by the research literature on policy implementation in the field of welfare-to-work services, found that the county choices regarding different implementation approaches related closely to preexisting CalWORKs services and staffing, and to a lesser degree, to agency and county size. Smaller counties with basic preexisting CalWORKs support services used the Family Stabilization program to upgrade supports in core areas, including mental health, substance abuse, and domestic violence services. Larger counties with a richer array of preexisting services used the FS program to add specialized units of social workers and to expand services in ways allowed by the FS program—such as providing more hands-on support for participants navigating complex systems, and funding mental health services for the children of the program participants. With the exception of a connection between high-cost housing in the county and a service emphasis

Background

Legislation—What is FS?

- Background/history on legislation
- Legislative changes resulting in enhanced support services for families receiving CalWORKs—Family Stabilization (FS)
- Key elements of Family Stabilization regulations
  - Stated goals
  - Flexibility in language regarding implementation
  - Associated supports
    - Housing grants
    - Online CalWORKs Assessment Tool (OCAT)

BASSC Project

- Project overview—Interview county representatives to understand and describe:
  - How counties interpreted direction from state
  - The range of service approaches being used to implement FS
  - Staffing structure for providing FS services
  - Training and development activities to support staff doing the work
  - Implications for policy development and further research
- Initial assumptions
  - Redesigned service delivery models
  - Enhanced existing ES staff roles
  - Training and training resource needs

Findings

ACL Interpretation

- Counties' philosophical approaches
- Synthesis of county FS plans

Pre- and Post-Service Delivery Models

- Basic county structures in place prior to FS implementation
  - Services provided
  - Staffing structures
  - Partnerships
- Continuum of FS implementation strategies
  - Service enhancements
  - Structures utilized to implement FS services
    - FS services integrated into existing program/staffing structures

- New units and/or staff/positions created for FS service delivery
        - FS services being contracted out to community service providers
    - Staffing and skills
    - Partnerships
        - Intra-agency
        - Interagency
        - Community-based partners
- How/why decisions were made regarding who provides services

Assessment Tool (OCAT)
- Overview of OCAT
- Who administers?
- How is OCAT data used in service delivery transfers into and out of FS Services?
- When do cases transfer out of FS services? Why? Who decides?
- How does transfer back to regular E&SS services occur?

Staff Competencies, Development, and Training
- Identified areas of competency needed
- Existing training provided
- Identified training needs
- Training resources

Implications

Practice Implications
- Summary of relevant research literature
- Directions for future policy and program planning

Topics For Further Exploration/Research

OCAT Assessments
- How do clients experience the OCAT assessment process?
- How do clients experience FS services?
    - Service delivery
    - Transfer to and from FS services
- Is OCAT data used? If so, how?

Staff Skills / Competencies
- Are there basic competencies required of staff who do FS work? If so, what are they?
- How are employment services (ES) staff skills assessed?
- Do we have data about ES staff skill levels?

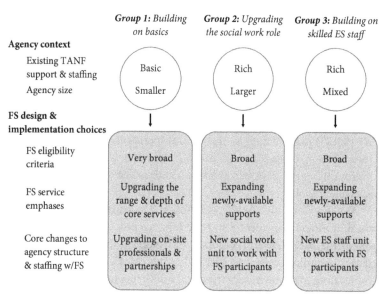

Figure 6.1. Family stabilization implementation typology.

on housing stability, the study offered little evidence of any direct connections between county economic and demographic context and FS program design and implementation choices.

This analysis of findings was shared with the county directors, presented at a national policy conference, and published in a journal (Stanczyk, Carnochan, Hengeveld-Bidmon, & Austin, 2018). The findings suggested that there are multiple routes to meeting the growing need for enhanced supports for disadvantaged CalWORKs participants and their children—and that responsiveness to agency context may be a key factor in successful implementation of such program enhancements. The findings provided a reminder of the value of local flexibility in program design and implementation.

PHASE 2: LEARNING FROM FAMILY STABILIZATION CLIENTS

The first phase of the project was aimed at understanding the perspectives of mid-level and senior managers with regard to their decisions and experiences with implementing the FS program. In order to build upon this information, the BASSC county directors requested that we develop a set of research options for a second phase of the study. In response, we presented four different study options that included: (1) analysis of participant assessment tool data (frequency and co-occurrence of barriers to participation and the relationship to case progress); (2) evaluation of the impact of services (pre/post change in client outcomes after program implementation with variation by client or program characteristic); (3) examination of agency staff perspectives on service array (including challenges and promising practices); and (4) examination of program participant perspectives (experiences with FS services and assessment tool).

The directors initially selected Option 2, consistent with their longstanding interest in identifying the effectiveness of their services, as well as the 2017 TANF (Temporary Assistance to Needy Families) legislation reauthorization discussions taking place at the national level. Responding to the interest of the county directors in pursuing Option 2, BASSC researchers began plans for a study drawing on county administrative data and records from the CA Employment Development Department to assess the impact of FS services on client case progress, employment, and earnings. We subsequently discovered, however, that a CalWORKs evaluation under a statewide contract would include many aspects of the family stabilization program. Consequently, in order to complement, rather than duplicate the statewide study, we proposed to our practice research partners a regional qualitative study aimed at providing deeper and more contextualized understanding of how FS program participants experienced the services and the assessment process, and how clients related these experiences to subsequent progress in workforce participation and gaining employment. Research questions included: (1) What challenges does this population of program participants face? What strengths do they bring? (2) What specific services do they receive through participation in FS? (3) How do clients describe their experiences with these services? (4) How do clients relate these services to their progress in CalWORKs and in finding and maintaining employment? And (5) how do these dynamics differ by client case and demographic characteristics, and by key county differences in FS design? (Examples include differences in types of services offered and whether employment services workers or social workers administer newly developed assessment tools.)

Consultations with the Employment and Self-sufficiency Directors

Following approval by the agency directors, we embarked on a series of individual conversations with the E&SS directors to refine the study aims. These conversations were carried out in the eight agencies that were considering participating in the study, based on the input from the agency director. Although many of the E&SS directors echoed the interest of their director, there were some counties in which local agency or community dynamics made participation unworkable. For example, one county declined to join the study because the E&SS division was experiencing significant staff turnover among senior and mid-level managers, leaving insufficient capacity to support the research. In another county, community advocates were arguing for access to the results of any research conducted by or for the agency, leading county legal counsel to advise against participation until the issue of dissemination was resolved. In the end, a total of six agencies joined the study. The next step was to identify agency study liaisons involved with the FS program to assist our research staff with sampling, recruiting clients, and carrying out the interviews. Depending on the size of the agency and the structure of the FS program, these liaisons held positions that included program manager and program supervisor, as well as analyst positions.

Working with Study Liaisons

The study involved particularly intensive engagement of the study liaisons in order to develop the sampling strategy, select the study samples, and communicate with program participants about the study. We sought to ensure cross-agency comparability of the samples, as well as within-agency representation of key client characteristics. In order to accomplish this, we reviewed the quarterly reports that the county agencies submitted to the California Department of Social Services to gain an understanding of the basic demographics of the respective caseloads and the data being tracked by the counties. Based on this information, we developed a sampling plan that we shared with the liaisons to confirm their approval. The next step was to obtain spreadsheets containing de-identified data for each agency's caseload, requiring that our research team make sense of the agency administrative data fields. Working with these data, we used random sampling with replacement methods to select clients for recruitment. Recruiting program participants required substantial coordination with our liaisons. While we drafted scripts and emails for staff communications with their clients about the study, agency staff made the initial invitation, helped us to understand the best times to schedule the interviews, and in one instance, played a role in the actual scheduling and transportation for the interviews.

Conducting Interviews with Clients

The interviews addressed five domains related to participant experiences of the FS program, including: needs assessment and perceptions of the OCAT, trust and relationship building with the FS client, communications about FS services, targeting FS services to client needs, and client motivation and engagement. A primary aim in the interviews related to "meeting clients where they are," consistent with core social work practice principles. In some instances, this took on literal meaning, as we interviewed individuals in their cars, in their homes, at the participating agencies, or by phone if they had moved out of county to escape the high cost of living in the Bay Area. We incorporated emerging perspectives and experiences in several revisions of the interview guide, in order to explore experiences that we had not initially expected based upon our reviews of the literature and discussions with our practice partners. Maintaining confidentiality of the interview responses while continuing to engage practitioners over the course of data collection required nuanced communications. When agency staff asked the interviewers, "How are the interviews going?" it was clear that they wanted to know whether the clients were expressing satisfaction with the services they received. The research team responded by letting them know that the interviews were going well because they were generating rich information, without disclosing the specific substance of the interview.

Preliminary Reporting

The initial reporting process was designed to engage the county agency directors as well as their E&SS directors in a joint conversation about study findings, implications, and next steps. We reported preliminary findings first to the agency directors, and asked them to extend an invitation to the E&SS directors to attend their next regional meeting. The findings highlighted the intangible and tangible assistance provided to FS program participants, as well as the services offered beyond FS by CalWORKs and community based providers (see Figure 6.2). A central theme related to the importance of the quality of the relationship between the workers and participants. We shared the same report with the E&SS directors at their monthly meeting and then facilitated a joint agency director/E&SS director meeting, which generated extensive discussion of assessment processes in the FS program, implications for future CalWORKs practice guidelines, and implications for a statewide initiative to reform California's welfare-to-work program. The discussion resulted in a decision to develop a third study phase investigating the perspectives of FS workers with respect to program challenges and improvement strategies. As with most of our research, study findings also were presented at a national conference to be followed by the development of one or more journal articles. This forum was used to narrow the focus of the analysis, providing greater depth with respect to the findings related to the bureaucratic encounter, or the relationship and interactions between FS program participants and their workers.

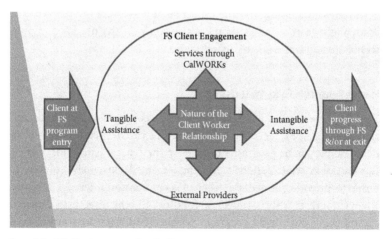

Figure 6.2. FS client perspective findings.

PHASE 3: LEARNING FROM FAMILY STABILIZATION WORKERS

As noted above, the joint meeting of the agency directors and their E&SS directors included discussion of possible next steps for the project. The group expressed an interest in examining FS worker perspectives on program services, outcomes, and improvement strategies, and we began to develop plans to carry out a third phase of the project involving worker focus groups. In order to strengthen the project's capacity to inform state welfare-to-work policy, we started by consulting with practice partners who were leading the CalWORKs 2.0 initiative. This input, along with a synthesis of the joint meeting discussion, was incorporated into a brief overview of project aims that was approved by the agency and E&SS directors. We then drafted a focus group instrument that we shared with the E&SS directors for discussion at their regional meeting. Discussion at this meeting served to refine the focus group instrument; it also raised the possibility of expanding focus group participation to staff in the CalWORKs program and at community partner agencies who engaged with the FS program. As this book is being completed, this phase of the FS study is still a work-in-progress as it enters the data-analysis phase.

PRACTICE RESEARCH LESSONS

The studies of county subsidized employment and family stabilization programs generated lessons for carrying out practice research in a number of areas, including: (1) the influence of policy, (2) the relevance of academic research and program evaluations, (3) the need for responsiveness, and (4) the role of dissemination.

Practice Research in Policy Contexts

Both of these studies demonstrate how the changing policy landscape frequently shapes the evolving practice research agenda. The subsidized employment programs funded by the federal legislation during the recession were designed and implemented extremely quickly, in order to provide immediate relief to local communities. As a result, when Congress terminated federal funding, and the directors wanted to extend these short-lived programs with state funding they anticipated would become available, they sought information about employers as key stakeholders in the program. When California enacted legislation to extend subsidized employment funding through CalWORKs, the agencies were able to incorporate study findings in order to make them more attractive to employers. In a similar vein, the FS study was initially developed in order to provide agency partners with a cross-county perspective on the array of policy implementation decisions, in the context of a policy that provided wide latitude with respect to eligibility criteria, services, and staffing structures.

Scoping the Literature: University-based Scholarship and Program Evaluation

Although it is common practice for academic researchers to search and synthesize the scholarly literature related to the topic under investigation, practice research also calls for attention to program evaluations and other forms of literature that may not be reported in journals. Familiarity with the key entities that conduct contracted program evaluations in the particular field is important, as is knowledge of any provisions in relevant policy or legislation that mandate evaluation. For the subsidized employment study, it was important to scan the publications of national research organizations (e.g., MDRC, RAND, and Mathematica Policy Research) for evaluation reports and literature summaries. In the case of the FS study, our agency partners informed us of the evaluation being conducted by RAND, which they learned of from legislative analysts at their statewide association.

Responsiveness: Flexibility and Timeliness

The process of practice research is inherently responsive; as researchers, we engage with and respond to the information needs of our practice partners. Often, this involves a lengthy process to frame a study, which includes consultation with multiple stakeholder groups that play different roles within the agency or the program (e.g., program participants, employers, managers, and supervisors). As the collaborative process unfolds, the study aims may change, requiring that we return to individuals or groups that were consulted initially in order to reaffirm their interest or approval. Agency participation decisions may change during this process, whether due to altered circumstances, or diminished interest as the research aims are refined. This reality demands flexibility with respect to study design as well as research staffing.

Dissemination and Utilization

The discussions among our practice research partners related to the FS study findings also touched more broadly on the issues of research dissemination and utilization, as well as the importance of finding ways to help transfer research findings into practical applications for use with staff at all levels. Dissemination challenges that can be synthesized from these discussions relate to the following: (1) assessing learner readiness among staff with whom study findings are shared; (2) responding to the changing nature of practice, which complicates the timing of research findings and their immediate relevance; and (3) dealing with continuous staff turnover. The recommended strategies to address these challenges include: (1) use focus groups in agencies to share findings and to gather feedback for future studies, (2) use a website portal to share/store findings for others to locate, (3) provide explicit recommendations or questions with each study to help senior staff make decisions on how to incorporate study findings in ongoing agency-based decision-making, (4) consult with agency staff responsible for planning and evaluation for recommendations about practice research dissemination and utilization, and (5) identify specific target populations for sharing the findings.

CONNECTIONS WITH PREVIOUS AND SUBSEQUENT CHAPTERS

This chapter on learning from the individuals involved in subsidized employment and family stabilization describes exploratory practice research studies that used interviews with employers, managers, workers, and clients. These examples provide an alternative form of in-depth analysis of welfare-to-work programs to complement the case studies on welfare reform implementation described in Chapter 4. In addition, the practice research lessons identified in this chapter touch upon some of the research dissemination and utilization issues shared by other research methodologies described in Chapter 8.

REFERENCES

Austin, M.J., Chow, J., Johnson, M., DeMarco, A., & Ketch, V. (2008). Delivering welfare-to-work services in county social service organizations: An exploratory study of staff perspectives. *Administration in Social Work, 32*(4), 105–126.

Carnochan, S., Taylor, S., & Austin, M.J. (2014). Employer-employee relationships in subsidized employment programs: The role of soft skills. *Families in Society, 95*(3), 187–194.

Stanczyk, A., Carnochan, S., Hengeveld-Bidmon, E., & Austin, M.J. (2018). Family-focused services for TANF participants facing acute barriers to work: Pathways to implementation. *Families in Society, 99*(3), 219–231.

Taylor, S., Carnochan, S., Pascual, G., & Austin, M.J. (2016). Engaging employers as partners in subsidized employment programs. *Journal of Sociology and Social Welfare, XLIII* (1), 149–169.

7

Learning from the Managers of Human Service Organizations

Much of the research in social work focuses on clients and service delivery, with particular attention to client characteristics, program implementation, and assessment of outcomes. In our work, we also have paid substantial attention to the experiences of managers as the individuals responsible for managing the delivery of services provided by agency staff and by community-based providers. In this chapter we describe a study that examined the experiences of public and nonprofit managers involved in human services contracting. In the context of increasingly complex human service delivery systems, the study was designed to further our understanding of the accountability and service coordination challenges that these cross-sectoral relationships pose for managers. The chapter also describes a second study that sought to inform managerial practice in the context of the growing movement toward evidence-based practice, by examining managerial perspectives and experiences related to a more broadly defined phenomenon of evidence-informed practice.

Practice Research in the Human Services. Michael J. Austin and Sarah Carnochan, Oxford University Press (2020). © Oxford University Press.
DOI: 10.1093/oso/9780197518335.001.0001

HUMAN SERVICES CONTRACTING

As has been typical in our work, the study of human services contracting progressed in multiple stages. In the first phase, we conducted a set of case studies examining performance measurement in five nonprofit human service organizations in 2011. The findings of this study pointed to the central role that external funders play in determining the performance measurement activities of nonprofit organizations, specifically as a result of the reporting demands associated with grant and contract funding (Carnochan, Samples, Myers, & Austin, 2014). Building on this study, we carried out a second set of case studies in 2014 that examined the contractual relationships between county human-service agencies and a large nonprofit agency in three Bay Area Social Service Consortium (BASSC) counties (McBeath, Carnochan, Stuart, & Austin, 2017). This study highlighted the central importance of cross-sectoral managerial relationships, informing the design of a third study phase involving a 2016 survey that examined the experiences and perspectives of county managers and nonprofit managers in five BASSC counties (Carnochan, McBeath, Chuang, & Austin, 2018; McBeath, Chuang, Carnochan, Austin, & Stuart, 2018; Chuang, McBeath, Carnochan, & Austin, 2020). In the final phase, we are analyzing the contract documents from the case study and survey counties, focusing on contract components related to accountability, measurement, and resource allocation.

Nonprofit Performance Measurement Case Studies

The Performance Measurement project grew out of a series of performance management strategy meetings related to the issue of management information system integration that we facilitated among senior managers of nonprofit human service agencies participating in our nonprofit partner consortium. The meetings identified key aims for the project from the perspectives of agency directors and senior managers. The top priority for agency directors related to modifying MIS systems to integrate agency data from programs, HR, payroll, finance & development, while for the senior managers, this issue ranked second. For senior managers, top priorities related to building/transforming major agency goals into outcome measures, technical knowledge capacity building to address fear and communication gaps, and facilitating cross-department interaction. Among the directors, the issues of outcome measure development and technical knowledge capacity building were ranked second, while cross-department communication ranked third.

Responding to the priorities articulated by our practice partners, and based on subsequent discussions with the management information system (MIS) consultant who contributed to the performance management strategy meetings, we recommended continuing the project by focusing on the MIS integration of participating agencies, while paying attention to the broader organizational issues of outcome development and agency communication needed to support integration. The proposed project was funded by a $35,000 grant from our five largest county human services agency partners to support project coordination, organizational analysis, and MIS consulting for each agency. This form of financial support for an external MIS consultant reflected a sense of responsibility assumed by the public sector for supporting their nonprofit service delivery partners. The MIS consultant worked with each participating agency to perform in-depth diagnostics of existing MIS systems for each participating agency, including: (1) infrastructure inventory, (2) data/software inventory, (3) assessment of MIS integration and a framework for mapping an integrated database for designated data (e.g., human resources, finance, programming, and development).

The broader organizational investigation sought to identify internal organizational barriers to the effective implementation of the MIS infrastructure improvement and performance management plans, particularly in the areas of: (1) service and financial outcomes development, (2) strategic planning, and (3) effective communication and dissemination of data analysis. Key aims of this component related to: (1) assessment of agency environment in relationship to achieving integration; (2) agency attitudes, awareness, and abilities in relation to use of data; and (3) agency use of logic models and defined outcomes to track service impact. Our role included facilitating and documenting ongoing quarterly meetings with a committee of senior-level managers in the areas of MIS, programming, finance, and development. The goals of these meetings were to promote cross-agency collaboration on the development of interagency performance outcomes and a sector-wide performance measurement system for agency comparisons.

Each agency was asked to designate a liaison to help coordinate the diagnostic and planning meetings. Executives were asked to continue to encourage senior managers from the agency departments of programming, finance, MIS, and development to participate in ongoing advisory discussions (e.g., via online forums) for the project, and commit staff to participating as needed in the diagnostic process, including provision of documentation where available. Four of the six agencies decided to participate in this phase of the project. All four contracted with county human services agencies to provide children and family services that included clinical, basic needs, recreational, and residential services and programs. The agencies varied in size, with budgets ranging from $5 million to $40 million. A case study of each agency was developed utilizing interviews, focus groups, and archival document review that was followed by a cross-case analysis.

CASE STUDY FINDINGS

As noted above, the case studies suggested that funders play a critical role in determining the performance measurement activities of nonprofit human service organizations (Carnochan, Samples, Myers, & Austin, 2014). In our initial reporting of preliminary findings to the nonprofit agencies in our partner consortium, we identified three broad themes: (1) challenges to defining and measuring client outcomes, (2) developing integrated systems to track data that measures client outcomes, and (3) building an organizational culture to support data informed decision-making.

Based upon these findings, we framed possible next steps for the participating agencies, which included: (1) holding individual agency meetings with research team members to discuss findings from the case study and technology assessment; (2) providing technical assistance and consultation for executive directors to support their taking a leadership role in relationship to technology; (3) organizational development consultation aimed at assessing organizational processes and defining key outcomes; (4) training for program managers and other key staff to develop staff expertise in relationship to logic models/outcomes and data systems; and (5) technical consulting services to assist in achieving data system integration. In one of the participating agencies, the management team made a number of decisions based upon study findings. First, in order to strengthen system-user voices, appropriate service outcome measures were developed under the leadership of the clinical director. Responding to the findings related to the critical roles played by people and processes, the agency redefined the role of the database coordinator so that she no longer would be the sole possessor of data expertise. Finally, they embarked on a system redesign process that included meeting with the project MIS consultant to discuss retaining their existing client data system or purchasing/developing a new system.

For an academic conference presentation and related journal article, we synthesized a set of themes as illustrated in Figure 7.1. First, the complexity of human change processes, as well as the variations among individual clients, complicate efforts to define client outcomes. Second, it was clear that organizational strategies were necessary to support performance measurement. For example, the perspectives of data users

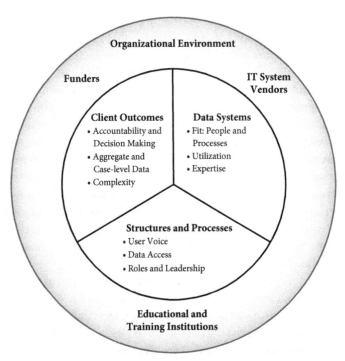

Figure 7.1. Factors influencing performance measurement systems.

(staff) were needed in system design in order to provide adequate staff access to data. Enhancing staff skills represented another organizational strategy to promote the use of data systems.

Contracting Case Studies

Over the next couple of years, continuing discussions with our county and nonprofit agency partners highlighted a number of local initiatives aimed at improving and streamlining contracting procedures. Simultaneously, we involved our graduate student research assistants in conducting literature reviews on an array of intersecting topics that included: (1) interorganizational relations; (2) public contracting; (3) performance management; (4) theories of public accountability (e.g., principal-agent theory, stewardship theory, street level bureaucrats); and (5) collaborative governance. The synthesis of the literature on interorganizational relations was presented at an international conference, where we initiated a conversation with a public administration scholar who played an important role at a later stage of the project.

Synthesizing the conceptual and practice-based questions and concepts from these simultaneous processes of inquiry, we formulated a proposal to investigate county-nonprofit human service agency contractual relationships through an initial set of dyadic case studies. We were assisted by a social work researcher with an extensive background in contracting among human service organizations. These case studies were designed to highlight the perspectives and experiences of contract managers in program and administrative roles with respect to relationships with their managerial counterparts. Three county agencies agreed to participate and went on to help identify nonprofit partner agencies in each county that were invited to participate.

The study team included a colleague at another institution along with our three doctoral and postdoctoral research assistants. The team worked together to develop the interview and focus group guides, which were shared with the members of our two partner consortia (one nonprofit sector and one public sector). There was a shared interest in identifying contractual processes that result in meaningful performance/outcome measures, given our earlier findings that performance measures were often dictated by funders and typically unrelated to the nonprofit organization's priorities or information needs. In addition, public sector agencies expressed concern with public-private contracting associated with the increasing focus on performance-based and results-based accountability, due in part to funding limitations and pressure to demonstrate meaningful accountability.

By summarizing our review of public and nonprofit research literature on interorganizational relations, collaboration, and performance measurement, we were able to note several key concepts from the literature on interorganizational relations as outlined in Figure 7.2. We had identified relevant factors from the literature related to the benefits of collaboration and factors that support collaboration in public-private contracting, as well as the contextual factors that influence the power and discretion of individual actors in the contractual process. In consultation with researchers in the field, we were reminded of the significance of individual actors and the nature of discretion in contracting. Because much of performance measurement and contract management is performed by individual actors, this perspective complemented the focus on accountability.

We then sought the input of nonprofit agency directors on the draft interview guide for nonprofit organization employees, which was structured around four key areas: (1) individual experiences and

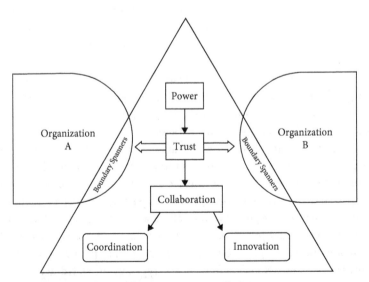

Figure 7.2. Conceptual map of interorganizational relations.

perspectives; (2) relationships (organizational and individual) between public and private sectors; (3) accountability both within and outside of the contractual environment; and (4) performance measurement. The directors noted that fostering ongoing relations between nonprofits and the county involved multiple challenges that could inform the focus of the interviews, including: (1) addressing tensions between county program and contract staff; (2) orienting new county contract staff to prevent loss of institutional memory; (3) moving beyond county focus on billing and fiscal policies and process measures of output; (4) tracking of federal and state policies and regulations affecting contracted services; (5) complying with shorter time horizons to account for contract expenditures and outcomes; (6) expanding nonprofit internal contracts staff to deal with the counties; (7) dealing with contracts that are simply viewed as "boilerplates" with little changes made from year to year; (8) responding to the increasing role of technology to manage contracts, often requiring data input into two to three systems per service program; (9) responding to county choices in database software with little attention to nonprofit-user perspectives or existing data systems; and (10) county staff appearing to be increasingly overloaded, resulting in responses that appeared to be more "head" than "heart."

Interviews and focus groups were conducted in the fall of 2013 and the spring of 2014. During this period, the study team met weekly, in person or via conference call, in order to debrief interviews, compare responses, and integrate these discussions into the evolving interview guide. In addition to individual interviews with managers, we conducted focus groups with county and nonprofit managers in the largest county. This discussion enabled us to develop an overall map of the contractual process from the initial request for a proposal (RFP) through to reporting on outcomes. It provided the interviews with a practice-based understanding of the specific context in which cross-sectoral relationships operate. Following the completion of the interviews, we sought to revisit and integrate the perspectives of scholars in the field as we engaged more intensely in data analysis by involving those of our collaborating senior researchers with a background in public administration and healthcare administration scholarship. Discussions with these researchers helped us make sense of the findings, situate them in the extant literature, and begin planning the design of the five-county survey of county and nonprofit contract managers in the next phase of the study. Our plans for the next phase included the following goals: (1) develop/expand the preliminary cross-case analysis of the dyadic case studies; (2) identify key themes to inform the design of a multiagency survey; (3) discuss design questions related to survey aims (e.g., sampling); and (4) explore alternate ways of understanding county–nonprofit relationships through intervention/observational research.

CASE STUDY FINDINGS

In our analysis of the dyadic relationships between county human service agencies and major nonprofit agencies that provide contracted services, we noted substantial shared perspectives on the overall system of services, as well as the nature of the contractual relationship (McBeath, Carnochan, Stuart, & Austin, 2017). County and nonprofit managers expressed the view that services in the county were delivered by a network of funders and providers who shared a vision, agreed about community need and role definition, and jointly determined service delivery approaches. They saw their relationships as based upon trust, while agreeing that county human services agencies possessed greater power as a result of their role as funders. With respect to service delivery, managers noted that shared case management posed challenges related to communication and referrals, service fidelity (county managers), and service expectations (nonprofit managers). Lastly, there was agreement that meaningful measurement of outcomes was sought but often not realized, due to challenges related to measurement technology, data systems, and funder mandates.

In the analysis for a related journal article, our collaborating research turned to the theoretical literature in public administration to reflect further on the findings (see Table 7.1). In this analysis, the case study findings are explored in relationship to the Managing Complex Contracts (MCC) model, a framework to understand contracting in relation to complex products and services (Brown, Potoski, & Van Slyke, 2015). This publication illustrates the opportunities available when conducting practice research for bringing the practice-based understandings possessed by practitioners together with the theoretical perspectives of university-based researchers.

Table 7.1. Main Study Findings Related to the Managing Complex Contracts (MCC) Model

MCC Model	Major Study Findings
Conditions	
Human services are complex products.	Complexity in human service delivery is heightened by: (a) unexpected and/or unclear client needs; (b) the unpredictability of the client referral process; and (c) challenges in managing the demands of multiple funders and external service partners.
Human service contracts can be incomplete.	Contracts can be incomplete in critical areas relating to clients, service delivery, and funding. Contracts may be written to allow for nonprofit discretion in implementation, and they may be amended in response to critical information that was not available prior to initial contract ratification. Contracts also may be written generically, such that different nonprofit agencies may deliver services under essentially identical contracts.
Propositions	
Governance rules may not promote performance given the complexity of human services.	Public and nonprofit managers view the governance tools most commonly in use (i.e., program monitoring through performance reporting) as irrelevant for promoting effective service delivery and client outcomes. There is a desire to incentivize outcome achievement, but it is not clear how to achieve this.
Performance is enhanced through long-lasting, successful contract-based exchanges.	The relationships between public and nonprofit agencies can be characterized as partnerships developed from successful contract-based interactions and significant cross-sector knowledge. Managers prioritize relationship management and communicate with their counterparts regularly to share information and problem solve around technical contract-based issues.
Reputational considerations promote performance.	Public managers use recent, agency-specific information as opposed to generic beliefs to develop performance expectations about nonprofit contractors. There is a general norm of commitment to partnership development as well as a general expectation that nonprofit agencies are essential for human service delivery due to their expertise in serving at-risk client populations.

Contracting Survey

We built upon the foundation laid by the contracting case studies with the development of a survey of county and nonprofit agencies engaged in cross-sectoral contracting. Over the course of a year, our study team worked on survey design, sampling design, and the institutional review board (IRB) protocol. An initial draft of the nonprofit survey instrument was shared with the consortium of nonprofit agency directors, who identified a series of key issues related to streamlining contract renewals, multi-year contracting, fiscal oversight, timely payments of contract invoices, the calculation of overhead/indirect costs, and the challenges of providing services in the absence of a final contract. There was consensus on the importance of identifying the constraints to improving the relationship, as well as the organizational factors that lead to stronger relationships. Directors expressed an interest in asking questions about desired change on both sides of the relationship, in order to identify agreement within the nonprofit community and across the two sectors.

We also engaged extensively with our five county agency study liaisons, soliciting their input on study design and implementation. We began with a day-long planning session to ensure that we fully understood their needs related to the following: (1) instrument design input, (2) final sample decisions, (3) pilot test plan and timing, (4) survey dissemination timing, and (5) communications planning. To minimize the travel demands on the study liaisons, most of the subsequent communication took place via phone and email. The meeting served to confirm our shared understanding of the following study questions related to informing effective contract development, implementation, and evaluation procedures: (1) How do public and private managers work together to resolve contract-related issues effectively? (2) What are the perceptions of public and private managers concerning their agency's use of performance monitoring tools? (3) What training and/or technical assistance needs do managers identify regarding service contracting? (4) Are there similarities and differences in the perceptions of public and private managers regarding these issues; and if so, with what implications for practice? In addition, we spent considerable time walking through the survey instrument to gather specific input related to content, format, and organization.

We pilot-tested the online survey with study liaisons in two county agencies and incorporated the feedback into the final survey instruments. We also received input from the public sector consortium partners (BASSC) related to various aspects of the survey, including: (1) format, (2) organizational structure, (3) clarity of language, (4) missing information, and (5) item-design suggestions. Feedback from the nonprofit directors was similarly rich and relevant. It focused on: (1) clarification of terms used; (2) effectiveness of content items in capturing complexity; (3) feasibility of response types; and (4) the need for additional information, such as the survey respondent's work/education.

Along with the collaborative process of study and instrument design, we were simultaneously translating these discussions and decisions into the creation of the study protocol for the university Committee for Protection of Human Subjects. This process involved five cycles of revisions and resubmissions based, in part, on concerns about the process of recruiting nonprofit agencies to participate in the study (i.e., IRB staff perceptions that the nonprofit directors might feel obligated to participate due to the invitation coming from one of their funders). Despite the fact that county directors would have no knowledge of who elected to participate in the study, the IRB required that the invitations to participate in the study come directly from the research team. We scrambled to comply with these changes regarding protections for nonprofit managers and confirmed that the county directors were able to send invitations to their own managers.

In previous projects, as well as in this study, we relied on county agency directors and study liaisons to assist us with outreach to their staff to participate in the research. This study also demanded, however, that we carry out the outreach to nonprofit agency respondents ourselves. The outreach campaign included eight days of phone calling by a team of four graduate research assistants and involved the following steps: (1) all organizations received an invitation email over a three-day period; (2) one follow-up reminder email was sent out a week later to each organization that did not yet have a 70% response rate; (3) phone calls to organizations that had not yet reached a 70% response rate; and (4) individualized emails sent to organizations for a variety of reasons. These included: (a) the agency director was no longer employed there; (b) the agency was requesting an extension due to summer vacations or heavy workload; (c) the agency description worksheet was not accessible; and (d) ongoing responses to organizations that sent us email messages (e.g., emails acknowledging receipt of the invitation, promising to finish by the due date, asking a question, or telling us they did not want to participate).

We learned a number of lessons in the outreach campaign for the first set of three study counties, and we encountered an array of challenges for which we developed strategies to increase our efficiency in the second wave of data collection in the remaining two counties. It was often hard to reach a staff member, so we left many messages. When we finally did connect, however, staff members were largely receptive and friendly. We found that sometimes the executive director (ED) was not the best contact. If we were finding the ED to be nonresponsive, we asked for his/her assistant or another contact. When we reached a staff member, the calls were personal and often quite long. Our team learned that five hours a day of calling was about all they could do, given that the calls were tiring and became less productive after about five hours. Making the calls together in the same room was important, so that we could troubleshoot problems and strategize solutions. Our sample size was small enough that we could call every organization in two days; then, we needed to take a few days off so that organizations could respond. Keeping good records about our outreach activities was important, so that follow-up communications could be personalized. All incoming calls were directed to the outreach coordinator because the graduate research assistants did not want to make themselves available to answer calls at any and all times of the day.

With respect to challenges, in our first round of calls we found that many organizations had not seen the invitation. Some recipients told us that our invitation email went to the spam, or unsolicited email, folder; others explained they deleted it because they did not know who we were. As a result, callers needed to clarify first whether the individual had received or seen the invitation email. We also recognized early on that the invitation emails were too long, and the links were too buried; as a result, few people we talked to had read the whole email. Thus, directors often did not realize they were being asked to forward the survey to staff. For the second set of counties, we shortened the emails by eliminating most of the information that was duplicated in the survey introduction. In addition, we moved the links to the top of the email message.

CONTRACTING SURVEY FINDINGS

Findings from the survey phase of the project supported multiple analyses including individual and aggregate-level reporting to our partners, as well as developing multiple journal articles focused on cross-sectoral managerial communications, service coordination experiences of county managers, and commitment to the contractual relationship among nonprofit managers.

In our initial reporting, we described findings related to the contractual relationship, performance monitoring, and perceptions of contract effectiveness. With respect to relationship activities, the findings highlighted the kinds of interactions that take place between managers, the perceptions of relationship challenges, and the levels of satisfaction among nonprofit managers with the contractual relationship. Specifically, the survey found that public and nonprofit sector managers interact at modest levels, with the greatest emphasis focused on facilitating relationships and sharing information. The contractual relationship was generally viewed as easy to manage, although participants noted some challenges involved in coordinating service referrals. Lastly, nonprofit managers reported that they were respected and understood by their public sector counterparts.

Performance measurement experiences were also fairly positive. County and nonprofit managers noted few particularly challenging aspects of performance monitoring (with the exception of information technology [IT] issues and coordinating the demands of multiple performance monitoring systems). As compared with county managers, nonprofit managers expressed more comfort with performance monitoring and greater access to and use of performance measurement data. County managers suggested that their use of performance data was primarily for monitoring nonprofit compliance and to inform future decisions about whether or not to renew existing contracts, while there was less perceived use of performance data to compare the performance of providers delivering similar services.

Finally, county and nonprofit managers shared the perception that the quality of provider performance was high. The contracting process was generally viewed as effective; contract modification was infrequent, and when it occurred, county and private managers appeared to view the process favorably. With respect to preferences for training and/or technical assistance (TA), the greatest interest among managers related to trainings, forums, and TA focused on improving the contract management process; however, county managers were more interested than nonprofit managers in these kinds of opportunities.

Managerial communications: The first theme of the research led to a paper that examined managerial communications involved in the contractual relationship (Carnochan, McBeath, Chuang, & Austin, 2018). The county and nonprofit managers who responded to open-ended questions in the survey, which were related to strategies for addressing challenges involved in contracting and performance measurement, highlighted the importance of managerial communication in facilitating the management of complex human service contracts. In particular, regular, face-to-face, two-way communications were important in building cross-sectoral relationships characterized by trust and mutual understanding. Conversely, managers also noted that strong cross-sector relationships facilitated effective contract communications.

The quality of the contractual relationship was enhanced by the quality of communications, represented by transparency, flexibility, consistency, and timeliness, as well as frequency of interaction. County and nonprofit managers articulated common perspectives on the importance of transparency and timeliness. Nonprofit managers emphasized the role of transparency regarding funding priorities and decisions in fostering trust, as well as promoting a sense of equity. County and nonprofit managers alike valued candor and accuracy with respect to performance reporting and requirements, in order to facilitate informed decision-making. The findings related to the importance of flexibility and consistency with respect to data systems, personnel, and procedures reflected a degree of variation between the sectors, with nonprofit managers somewhat more likely to emphasize the need for communication-based consistency as well as flexibility.

Service coordination: In this analysis, we examined the views of county managers with respect to the ease or difficulty of coordinating with nonprofit agency staff in regard to: (1) coordinating cross-sector service delivery; (2) addressing client referrals and determining eligibility; and (3) overseeing the use of evidence-based practices (McBeath, Chuang, Carnochan, Austin, & Stuart, 2018). Despite the complexity of service coordination, county managers reported relatively few service coordination challenges. We found further that organizational role, managerial contract involvement, and boundary spanning mattered for some aspects of contract-based service coordination. Executive-level staff generally perceived fewer challenges in coordinating services with contract providers than administrative and program staff. Interestingly, program managers noted greater challenges than executives only with respect to structuring cross-sector services. In contrast, executives and program managers had similar perceptions for the outcome measures of coordinating with contracted service providers around client referrals and eligibility as well as the oversight of contractor use of evidence-based practices (EBPs).

The number of nonprofit contract agencies for which the county manager was the primary contact was associated with fewer service coordination challenges. In contrast, the number of contracts that managers were responsible for monitoring was associated with greater service coordination challenges in structuring cross-sector service delivery and addressing issues involving client referrals and eligibility. Lastly, managerial boundary spanning (expressed in terms of the effort county managers dedicated to developing strong, collaborative partnerships with their contract counterparts) was related to fewer challenges in coordinating with contracted service providers to deliver cross-sector services including the use of EBPs.

Nonprofit commitment: We also developed a paper that focused on the perspectives of nonprofit contract managers (Chuang, McBeath, Carnochan, & Austin, 2020). We drew directly on the organizational and contracting literature to develop a conceptual framework of different relational processes and organizational factors that we hypothesized would affect outcomes related to nonprofit attitudes toward the county human service organization (HSO) and contract outcomes related to continuity and performance (see Figure 7.3).

We analyzed how these processes and factors were associated with managers' commitment to and satisfaction with the contractual relationship. The results indicated that communication quality was associated with managers feeling committed to and satisfied with the contractual relationship, but not with their specific calculation of the benefits associated with the relationship.

We also found that organizational trust was associated with the satisfaction of nonprofits with the contractual relationship, but not

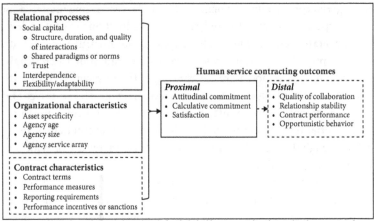

*Variables and hypothesized relationships identified with dashed lines are not directly tested in the current study.

Figure 7.3. Conceptual framework of factors affecting complex human service contracting outcomes.

necessarily with commitment. Findings also pointed to the importance of contract flexibility/adaptability for fostering nonprofit organizations' satisfaction with and commitment to the contractual relationship. In contrast, the duration of the contractual relationship was not associated with the commitment or satisfaction of nonprofit managers. Also contrary to our hypothesis, we found that sharing the same goals was not associated with levels of commitment. Given the complexity of human service delivery, where organizations may benefit from repeated cooperation in structuring service delivery and resolving common client issues, perceptions of commitment to the contractual relationship among nonprofit human service managers may be necessary for achieving such outcomes as client well-being.

Moving from Implications to Recommendations

Although practice researchers often identify practice and policy implications in collaboration with their research partners, in the past several years, our county partners have asked us to go a step further in order to translate implications into concrete recommendations that they can take to their executive team and staff for review and response. To address this request, we synthesized the findings across the multiple phases of this multi-year research project to develop the following recommendations for enhancing managerial relationships and contract management capacity:

- Build closer relationships, trust, and mutual understanding by increasing regular, face-to-face, two-way communications
- Develop shared training experiences related to collaborative contracting and program outcome achievement
- Provide technical training related to contract design, implementation, and monitoring
- Ensure contract manager capacity by assigning reasonable contract management caseloads and minimizing staff turnover
- Transform accountability-focused contract reporting systems into knowledge-sharing, decision-support systems.

We also identified organizational strategies to improve contractual processes that called for:

- Planning for regularly scheduled cross-sector meetings to identify emerging community needs and develop promising service approaches
- Improving transparency, consistency, and timeliness of communications by standardizing multiple data reporting systems
- Providing feedback to contractors regarding performance data and strengthen feedback processes to address performance issues
- Allocating resources to support contracting and contractors
- Committing resources (expertise, time, funds) needed to develop contract performance measurement systems and processes that support decision-making for county and nonprofit staff
- Funding indirect costs associated with increased performance measurement demands
- Developing contractual relationships that allow for risk-taking and failure that can inform learning and innovation.

SURVEY OF EVIDENCE-INFORMED PRACTICE

The BASSC members were increasingly intrigued by the growing emphasis among policymakers and scholars being given to evidence-informed and evidence-based practice. Based on this interest, we proposed and launched an online survey designed to identify and describe evidence-minded practitioners in the BASSC agencies, with the aim of providing information that could be used to enhance the learning capacity of their staff and organizations. The first step involved: (1) gathering their input on the online survey instrument; (2) asking them to identify the staff members they wanted to participate (e.g., all staff, selected divisions, or selected classifications); and (3) asking them to designate a staff liaison (sometimes someone we recommended) in order to facilitate the survey dissemination. Although each email message that communicated these steps to the directors contained this common set of requests, messages also were individually tailored based upon our history and relationship with the agency director.

Over the next several months, we worked to incorporate the input of the director in order to finalize the survey instrument. At the same time, we worked to make contact with the agency liaisons through emails and phone calls so as to orient them to the study background and aims. In collaboration with the liaisons, the study sample for each agency was finalized. In order to maximize the value of the survey to each agency, we engaged in extended communications regarding sampling priorities across the counties. The initial sampling choices made by the participating agencies included: (1) program managers and analysts; (2) executive team and managers; (3) executive team, senior managers, and supervisors; (4) all quality-assurance staff and a percentage of all other staff; and (5) managers, supervisors, and "lead staff" (line staff with special project or complex caseload responsibility) in all human service agency divisions. Although some liaisons had a clear sense of where to focus the survey, others were receptive to sampling all staff, or wanted to hear the choices that were being made by other agencies.

We were able to offer some flexibility with respect to the time frame for survey dissemination by each agency. This flexibility was important because it allowed the liaison to accommodate staff workload demands, including those associated with the annual budget development process of the agencies. When the opportunity arose for an in-depth discussion of the survey with senior staff involved with research, planning, and evaluation, the agenda included: (1) sampling strategies, (2) instrument feedback, and (3) potential uses of the research. The discussion of sampling strategy focused on choices related to the participation of agency divisions/units and staff classifications. For example, there was concern that including line staff or clerical staff could raise expectations that the agency intended to act in this area. Moreover, members noted that for many staff members, these ideas/practices related to evidence-informed practice would be unfamiliar, making it difficult and/or time consuming to respond. Others noted that in their agencies, surveys were used frequently, leading to a greater likelihood of survey fatigue. Lastly, there were concerns about the costs associated with broad dissemination. As one member pointed out, disseminating the survey to a 100% sample across all divisions would involve over 600 staff in one agency, with an estimated cost of approximately $15,000 in staff time.

Senior staff members also discussed the input they and their directors had provided on the pilot version of the online survey, based upon a summary that we had shared with them before the discussion. The key issues discussed included survey length, content, and language, with the primary concerns related to length. Liaisons who completed the survey reported taking at least half an hour, and they projected that for many staff, it could take 45 to 50 minutes to complete. In their view, at this length, the likelihood of people declining to take the survey or not completing it was high, given survey fatigue and workloads. It also was noted that the combination of length and a potentially inclusive sampling approach would increase county costs. Suggestions for dealing with concerns about length included: (1) deleting questions or the number of items per question; (2) providing an option to save responses and return later; (3) editing or condensing question stems; and (4) stating in the survey introduction that there would be five raffle winners per county.

Members also offered multiple suggestions relating to language clarity and specific terminology. They noted that it would be helpful to provide more explanation and definition up front for what constitutes evidence-informed practice. They also recommended providing examples of the data or evidence sources that staff might be accessing. One suggested mechanism for clarifying language and terminology was to use pop up balloons to provide definitions of specific terms, which could be helpful for staff for whom the content was unfamiliar.

The group also highlighted multiple examples where definitions would be useful, including the following terms and phrases: information system, research papers, data dashboards, online databases, literature reviews, program improvement studies, outcome studies, and evidence-gathering services.

Finally, additional valuable assistance helped to contextualize the agency setting and articulate questions related to: (1) staff roles (e.g., provide separate categories for supervisors and middle managers as these reflect quite different roles in some counties); (2) program descriptions; (3) information types (e.g., clarify dashboard—does it include paper reports, electronic data displays without live data, or just the classic dashboard definition that includes electronic, visual, live).

Following this meeting, we communicated in emails to the directors and the liaisons, finalizing the sampling decisions, requesting sample information, and outlining the timeline for disseminating the survey. We let them know know that we needed their agency's decision regarding the sample. We first asked that agency directors survey all executives and managers in order to generate comparable samples across agencies as well as adequate sample size for analysis. The goal was to provide the total number of individuals in each of these two categories who would be sent the survey link. In addition, we noted that agencies could elect whether or not to survey line staff and supervisors. Should they decide to, we needed the following information: (1) the divisions/units/programs that would be surveyed; (2) the staff classifications that would be surveyed; (3) the sampling strategy they planned to employ (e.g., percentages); and (4) total number of individuals in each category (classification + division) to be sent the survey link. Although this was relatively complex in terms of requesting specific human resources information, we deemed it important in anticipation of the planned analyses.

With respect to the timeline, we provided very specific dates for the communications sent to staff regarding the survey, on the assumption that most liaisons would have limited experience with research project management. The first email we sent was designed to clarify the process at each stage, emphasize the importance of the role the liaisons played, thank them for their assistance, and provide suggested language for the communications they would send to staff.

In subsequent emails, we also asked the liaisons to confirm that they were able to send the designated communications to staff. We reiterated that if staff had questions about the survey, we were happy to respond, but asked that they convey the questions to us without including any identifying information so that we could maintain confidentiality. In later reminder emails, we began to highlight the time-sensitive nature of the communications and staff responses, given that the survey would only be live online for two weeks. The condensed time frame was informed by research on the implementation of online surveys that indicates extended time frames do not typically generate higher response rates. An important strategy for communicating about the survey to participating agency staff involved sending advance notifications from the study team, as well as a follow-up email from the agency directors.

The email invitations were sent to 958 employees across the 11 study counties; a total of 497 people responded to the online survey, representing an overall 52% response rate. Staff participating in the survey reflected a diverse and broadly representative study sample with respect to role and division within the agencies. Respondents included staff at the frontline, supervisory, managerial, and executive levels who represented all divisions of the agencies.

Developing Findings and Disseminating Results

Agency staff were involved in the early stages of analyzing the qualitative data derived from open-ended questions in the survey. The initial phase of the analysis generated a six-category matrix of EIP activities that was reviewed and discussed by 38 supervisors and managers who were participating in the BASSC Executive Development Program (Austin, Weisner, Schrandt, Glezos, & Murtaza, 2005). Based on small group discussions, a unified perspective developed in regard to the relevance and validity of the concepts summarized in the matrix. This input, grounded in practice experience, was later used to develop a final concept map identifying four EIP process domains (see Figure 7.4).

To disseminate the findings from the study, we provided brief aggregate and individual county reports on the findings we deemed most relevant and actionable. In the introduction to the reports, we emphasized that the survey questions were not designed to evaluate staff performance but instead sought to ascertain current levels of evidence use and identify resources needed to support and enhance evidence use by practitioners. We also noted that results were organized in such a way as to highlight

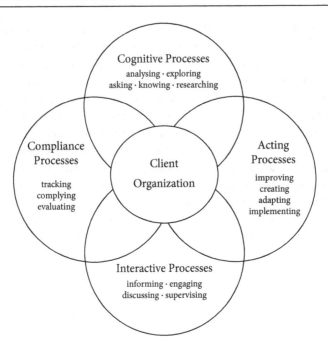

Figure 7.4. EIP Process Domains.

the strategies needed to enhance evidence use by practitioners and to support professional development through training and education.

The individual agency reports featured the specific sample and findings as well as highlighted the themes that emerged from the aggregate of findings from all agencies—displayed in a side-by-side table comparing their results to those of the aggregate of data from other counties. This allowed each agency director to note the areas where EIP experiences and perspectives were similar to and different from their own agency. Overall, reviewing agency reports, conducting literature reviews, and accessing online databases were the most common EIP activities. Practitioners reported using county information systems principally to track trends over time, make comparisons within their team, and track client status. The most preferred ways to support EIP were talking with and learning from coworkers who were knowledgeable about and already engaged in EIP work. Having time and access to evidence at work were seen as the most important elements in enhancing EIP. Lastly, respondents were interested in involving clients in planning for and evaluating programs.

We also published two journal articles based upon the survey data. Focusing on the quantitative data in one article, we sought to answer two multi-part questions (McBeath, Jolles, Carnochan, & Austin, 2015). First, we looked at the levels of evidence use by managers, as well as the purposes for which this evidence was being used. Second, we examined the organizational factors and individual attitudinal characteristics that might be associated with different levels of evidence use. We found that managers were engaged in evidence use at moderate levels, and that they were most often engaged in reviewing agency reports, searching for research literature and other evidence, and using online resources to identify promising practices. Evidence use was found to be positively associated with: (a) being an administrator, (b) being innovation-minded and responsive to organizational change, and (c) accessing performance measurement systems. Reflecting on these findings, we observed that evidence use by human service managers may be contingent on organizational resources (technology and time), organizational role (data oriented), and/or individual attitudes (curiosity, critical reflection).

The qualitative data captured by a series of open-ended questions in the survey also generated an article, focused on the daily processes involved in evidence-informed practice (Carnochan, McBeath, & Austin, 2017). Respondents described a broad array of EIP activities in which they use multiple forms of evidence to achieve multiple purposes. They reported engaging in EIP in order to respond to organizational and client needs, and carrying out EIP activities in multiple, varying sequences. The EIP activities were clustered into four domains: (1) cognitive processes; (2) interactive processes; (3) action processes; and (4) compliance processes (noted in Figure 7.4). The four EIP process domains were described as occurring in multiple, varying stages, rather than as a fixed, linear, or cyclical process. Study participants described two primary motivations for engaging in EIP—responding to client needs and addressing organizational priorities and challenges. Responding to client needs included serving individual clients as well as broader efforts to improve service quality, service targeting, and aggregate outcomes. Organizational priorities informed by EIP included: (1) increasing productivity and efficiency; (2) responding to externally imposed mandates and incentives; (3) improving staff morale; and (4) providing opportunities for staff development.

CONCLUSION

Practice Research Lessons

As with the studies described elsewhere in this volume, a number of practice research principles can be derived from the two studies noted; namely, the Evidence-informed Practice Survey and the multiphase Human Services Contracting Project. In our effort to summarize these principles, we frequently encountered challenges related to coordinating/synthesizing simultaneous design processes that integrate empirical and theoretical literature, practitioner priorities, and university bureaucratic requirements. Once the design decisions are resolved, practice research often requires extensive effort and resources to recruit busy practitioners to participate in a study, especially in the absence of an existing practice–research partnership (e.g., many of the nonprofits in the contracting study were not part of such a partnership). And finally implementing practice research calls for ensuring staff involvement in sampling decisions at the outset as well as data interpretation at later stages.

These studies also highlight lessons learned about the knowledge-building process in practice research. It is important for researchers to hear and respond to findings that were not necessarily part of the original study aims (e.g., role of external funders in performance measurement, where study aims focused on internal processes, structures, and roles). Our practice partners expressed growing interest in seeing us make concrete recommendations that they can use in senior staff discussion to generate concrete responses to the findings (acceptance/rejection/revision), rather than broader, loosely framed implications. Lastly, our experiences point to the value of multiphase studies in which knowledge builds and grows over time as all parties recognize the need for multiple perspectives when responding to the changing policy and practice environment.

Connections with Previous and Subsequent Chapters

The projects described in this chapter related to performance measurement, cross-sectoral contracting, and evidence-informed practice involve issues that appear in other chapters as well. For example, Chapter 3 describes a set of structured literature reviews examining organizational performance in child welfare agencies. Similarly, Chapter 4 examines related issues through description of a series of case studies that explore knowledge-sharing systems in county human service agencies. This current chapter also relates to the research dissemination and utilization issues noted in Chapter 8.

REFERENCES

Austin, M.J., Weisner, S., Schrandt, E., Glezos, S., &.Murtaza, N. (2005). The transfer of learning in executive development programs. *Administration in Social Work, 30*(2), 71–90.

Brown, T.L., Potoski, M., & Van Slyke, D.M. (2015). Managing complex contracts: A theoretical approach. *Journal of Public Administration Research and Theory, 26*(2), 294–308.

Carnochan, S., McBeath, B., & Austin, M.J. (2017). Managerial and frontline perspectives on the process of evidence-informed practice within human service organizations. *Human Service Organizations: Management, Leadership & Governance, 41*(4), 346–358.

Carnochan, S., McBeath, B., Chuang, E., & Austin, M.J. (2018). Perspectives of public and nonprofit managers on communications in human services contracting. *Public Performance & Management Review, 42*(3), 657–684.

Carnochan, S., Samples, M., Myers, M., & Austin, M.J. (2014). Performance measurement challenges in nonprofit human service organizations. *Nonprofit and Voluntary Sector Quarterly, 43*(6), 1014–1032.

Chuang, E., McBeath, B., Carnochan, C., & Austin, M.J. (2020). Relational mechanisms in human services contracting: Factors associated with private agency managers' satisfaction with and commitment to public agency partners. *Journal of Public Administration Research.*

McBeath, B., Carnochan, S., Stuart, M., & Austin, M.J. (2017). The managerial and relational dimensions of public-nonprofit human service contracting. *Journal of Strategic Contracting and Negotiation, 3*(2), 51–77.

McBeath, B., Chuang, E., Carnochan, S., Austin, M.J., & Stuart, M. (2018). Service coordination by public sector managers in a human service contracting environment. *Administration and Policy in Mental Health and Mental Health Services Research, 46*(2), 115–127.

McBeath, B., Jolles, M.P., Carnochan, S., & Austin, M.J. (2015). Organizational and individual determinants of evidence use by managers in public human service organizations. *Human Service Organizations: Management, Leadership & Governance, 39*(4), 267–289.

8

Emerging Principles of Practice Research

This chapter builds upon the previous chapters in order to identify some of the basic principles for implementing practice research. By reflecting upon the earlier descriptions of the various types of practice research, it is possible to see the connections between learning, knowing, and doing. As noted in Chapter 2, learning from individuals and groups of practitioners can be accomplished through the use of qualitative case study methods to provide in-depth documentation of experiences that often reflect innovative practices. Other forms of learning are noted in Chapter 3, wherein practitioner experiences take the form of data when reported in the literature, which calls upon critical thinking skills needed to conduct a literature review. Learning from the case study experiences of other organizations in the form of cross-case analysis, as noted in Chapter 4, provides another form of learning from the experiences of others.

The learning about practice research, noted in the first few chapters, can be expanded by focusing on different fields of practice. As noted in Chapter 5 on child welfare studies, two comprehensive practice research studies feature the challenges of court-based interdisciplinary practice,

Practice Research in the Human Services. Michael J. Austin and Sarah Carnochan, Oxford University Press (2020). © Oxford University Press.
DOI: 10.1093/oso/9780197518335.001.0001

as well as those found in case record qualitative data-mining. Both of these examples feature data buried deep in the culture of court proceedings as well as in complex digital data compiling systems.

Another field of practice can be seen in the operation of welfare-benefit programs designed to encourage entry into the workforce. Particular attention is given, in Chapter 6, to practice research that seeks to expand our understanding of new policies and programs related to subsidized employment and family stabilization. And finally, the practice research described in Chapter 7 features the internal organizational dynamics of incorporating evidence into administrative and program decision-making as well as the external dynamics of contractual relationship building and maintenance between public and nonprofit human service organizations.

As noted in Chapter 1, all the topics described in the previous chapters emerged from dialogue and decision-making by a group of practitioners holding leadership positions in their respective county human service organizations, as well as by university-based researchers. The practitioners and researchers participated in all phases of the practice research process from framing the research questions, providing access to the data, assisting with the data analysis and interpretation, and enabling the dissemination and utilization of the findings. The underlying theme of this participatory process is the focus on the science of the concrete (Flyvbjerg, 2001).

The process of transforming various types of practice research into a knowledge base represents an important step in preparing to carry out practice research. The 11 principles identified in this chapter serve as guides for the research implementation process. The first group of principles relates to *learning from the experiences of others* and includes the three principles of understanding the context of practice research, the role of persistent communications, and the process of disseminating results. The second group of principles focuses on *knowing how to implement practice research with regard to specialized skills*, balancing dynamics of practice with those of research, and the essential role of collaborative teamwork. The third set of principles on *anticipating and managing complexities* relates to coping with the tensions and ongoing change associated with practice research, responding to negative findings, and engaging service users. The fourth set of principles focuses on the process of *sharing practice research* with those most able to use it. All four sets of principles are illustrated in Figure 8.1 as part of an equation leading

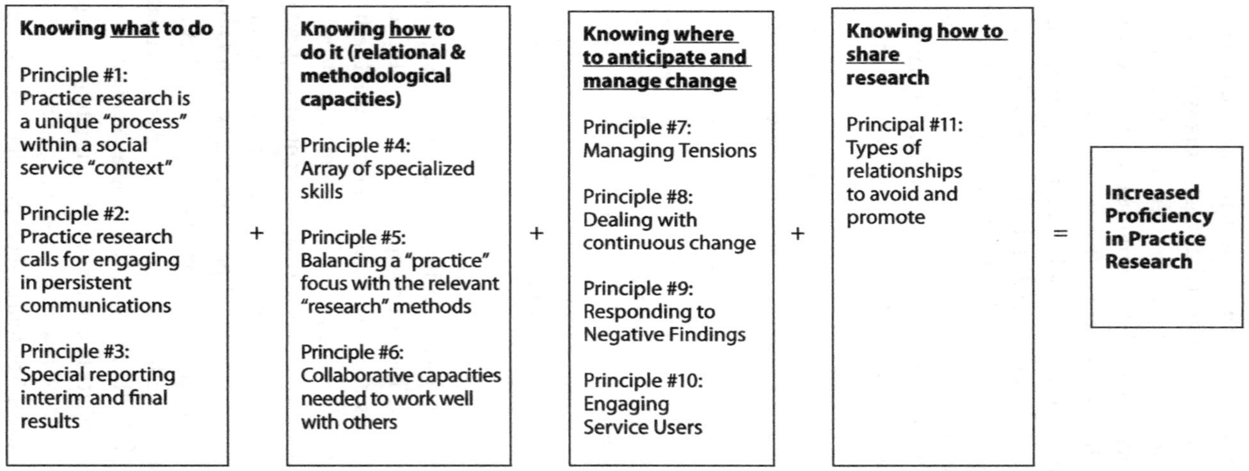

Knowing what to do

Principle #1:
Practice research is a unique "process" within a social service "context"

Principle #2:
Practice research calls for engaging in persistent communications

Principle #3:
Special reporting interim and final results

+

Knowing how to do it (relational & methodological capacities)

Principle #4:
Array of specialized skills

Principle #5:
Balancing a "practice" focus with the relevant "research" methods

Principle #6:
Collaborative capacities needed to work well with others

+

Knowing where to anticipate and manage change

Principle #7:
Managing Tensions

Principle #8:
Dealing with continuous change

Principle #9:
Responding to Negative Findings

Principle #10:
Engaging Service Users

+

Knowing how to share research

Principal #11:
Types of relationships to avoid and promote

=

Increased Proficiency in Practice Research

Figure 8.1. Principles of practice research: An evolving equation.

to framing the foundation for increasing one's proficiency in implementing practice research. In addition to the principles for conducting practice research, this chapter also focuses on the methodological challenges facing practice researchers within the context of social science research.

KNOWING WHAT TO DO

Principle #1: Understanding the Process and Context of Practice Research

The conducting of practice research needs to be viewed as a process with beginning, middle, and end phases. Forming and maintaining relationships is the foundation for the process when it comes to involving service providers, service users, researchers, and educators. Similarly, building a foundation of trust, respect, and understanding across the two very different organizational cultures found in service organizations and universities really takes time. Time is often a very limited resource in both types of organizations. It is important to anticipate the considerable amount of time needed to design a practice research study, consult with multiple stakeholders inside and outside the organization, and engage various levels of staff within the organization. The involvement of senior management in a practice research study is often an essential element in the "beginning" phase (and again at the ending phase). Similarly, involving middle managers, especially practice research study liaisons, is also an important aspect of proceeding with the "middle" phase of practice research.

The tools of agency-based practice research need to take into account the micro, mezzo, and macro levels of practice frequently characterized as "line workers," "service supervisors and program manager," and "senior management and public officials." Practice research often relates to all three levels of practice. In a similar manner, practice research is often related to the implementation of public policies that require an understanding of the research and legislative testimony underlying the development of new legislation that informs service delivery. In addition, it is important to understand the role of administrative regulations that inform the service implementation process.

The practice research process can result in many questions, including, "Why are we doing this?" Consequently, it is helpful to consider the concept of "becoming a learning organization" that seeks to promote the involvement of "research-minded" practitioners in the development of new knowledge that can improve practice and service outcomes. In addition, the organizational culture that values evidence-informed practices and services provides one more rationale for engaging in practice research.

Principle #2: Engaging in Persistent Communications

Knowing what to do in practice research includes the use of communication tools to facilitate the research process. The tools needed to create this process include persistent communications. Whether by phone, text, email, or meetings, the element of persistence is critical when engaging colleagues operating with multiple and changing workplace demands. It is important to remember that the lack of responses does not necessarily reflect no interest or investment but rather continuous workplace distractions. These communication tools are essential because the focus of the practice research may shift or evolve over time. Ongoing communications are needed to engage research partners in framing the research questions, gaining access to data (beginnings), interpreting key research and identifying practice and policy implications (middles), and designing and implementing research dissemination and utilization strategies (ends).

Delays in communication often are related to the heavy workload demands of agency practitioners, especially when being challenged to prioritize research in relationship to service delivery responsibilities. Therefore, persistent communication often includes emails, phone calls, and text messages to remind participants about the need for their assistance. The heavy demands placed on agency staff often result in reactive behaviors needed to manage the pressures of daily work life. As a result, reminders can be helpful when staff are juggling so many different workplace demands. Framing the communications with compassion and humor can lead to faster responses.

Another approach to facilitating communications, one which is used sparingly, is to involve staff up the chain of command as a way of confirming the ongoing priority of the practice research study, as well as to determine whether staff members still understand this priority. Clearly, there is some risk associated with seeking the involvement of senior staff, which may be perceived as interference by other staff. In essence, the central role of relationships and trust can facilitate this specialized form of communication.

Principle #3: Reporting Interim and Final Results

Another set of communication tools involves the use of presentation skills associated with writing reports, compiling executive summaries, constructing PowerPoint presentations, and speaking publicly to small and large groups. Some of these tools are more relevant for interim reports as opposed to final reports.

Interim reports involve checking with study liaisons and selected stakeholders with regard to the preliminary findings of the study in order to assist with the interpretation of the data. This process includes dealing with both positive and negative findings. The ultimate goal is to incorporate the practice wisdom of stakeholders in order to capture the grounded experiences emerging from everyday practice. These reports provide a tool for sharing results more quickly and promote more critical reflection as well as provide information that supports and enhances evidence-informed decision-making.

When it comes to presenting final reports of practice research to agency leadership and the broader community, it is helpful to create brief executive summaries that include the aims of the practice research study, selected key findings, and implications for practice and policy. These presentations also can be made to multiple groups of staff and provide another learning opportunity for exploring various approaches to disseminating the study results. In addition to the use of PowerPoint presentations, executive summaries provide a written form of the key aspects of the practice research study.

Study partners also may expect the development of a set of recommendations that can be shared with staff occupying a variety of roles. This step moves beyond a discussion of implications into the arena of specific recommendations for use in various types or sizes of agencies. This process is also collaborative so that the recommendations developed by the researchers are shaped by those of participating research partners. This phase of practice research can be particularly challenging when taking into account the culture of university researchers and that of agency practitioners; namely, can practice-minded researchers fully grasp the realities of research-minded practitioners when it comes to implementing research findings?

Instead of providing lengthy reports that most practitioners have limited time to read, a more complete reporting of the study can take the form of a manuscript for submission to a peer-reviewed journal. When using this form of communication to a larger national or international audience, different expectations or criteria need to be addressed. They take the form of academic writing standards that include an elaborated statement of the problem and research questions, a comprehensive review of the literature, the specification of the research methods utilized, the delineation of the findings, and a discussion of implications and future directions. The time horizons for final reports are generally quite different (e.g., one or more years to see a study published in a journal, as opposed to only a matter of weeks to finalize a report to agency practitioners).

KNOWING HOW TO DO IT: RELATIONAL AND METHODOLOGICAL CAPACITIES

Principle #4: Utilizing an Array of Specialized Skills

One of the key skills needed in practice research involves the art of negotiating among the stakeholders involved. For a practice researcher, one of the boundaries to cross is the one between the university and the agency. Given the differences in organizational culture, especially the different expectations of time needed to complete research (i.e., the slower pace of university life and the faster pace of agency life), practice researchers need to reach shared understandings in a variety of areas. One of these relates to protecting human subjects when engaging service users or service providers. Special human subject applications need to be negotiated between university staff members charged with maintaining these protections and practice researchers eager to begin the data collection process. In addition, negotiation skills are needed when seeking the support of agency administrators in order to access confidential case records or gain access to staff for the purpose of scheduling time for meetings.

A second key skill relates to critical thinking, especially needed for reviewing and assessing the current literature (Ennis, 1987; Paul, 1993). As elaborated upon in Chapter 11, the major elements of critical thinking include clarifying what is being described in the literature, analyzing its meaning, determining how it can be applied to the current research project, and owning the results of critical thinking by creating a shared interpretation of major research findings or key concepts from the theories reviewed (Gibbs & Gambrill, 1999). The same critical thinking skills are needed when searching the "gray" literature of government reports and research institutes that does not appear in peer-reviewed academic journals. In addition to consulting the literature, it is also important to consult other researchers associated with the practice research topic to learn about other relevant resources.

The third set of skills involve the capacity to collect and analyze data. These include interviewing skills (Rubin & Rubin, 2012), observational skills (Spradley, 1980), focus group facilitation skills (Krueger & Casey, 2015), and survey design skills (Fowler, 2013). An extensive research-methods literature describes each of these skill sets. The tools for coding qualitative data, triangulating data sources with one another, and extracting cross-cutting themes are also important data analysis tools (Padgett, 2017). For practice research relying on surveys, there is an extensive literature on statistical methods for data analysis (Weinbach & Grinnell, 2015) as well as an extensive literature on mixed methods (Creswell, 2015).

One of the key aspects of practice research is the capacity to articulate the limitations of the research. One major limitation includes the difficulties of generalizing from findings that are either drawn from a small sample of research participants or from a large survey sample with a low response rate. Another limitation, often difficult to detect, relates to respondent bias that may take the form of limited candor about issues facing practice or sharing information that may not be accurate. Identifying limitations, however, does not mean that other researchers, practitioners, or service users would not find the practice research results of interest. The results may yet cause others to reflect on their roles, identify service implications that might inform organizational decision-making, or stimulate more ideas worthy of further practice research.

When reflecting upon the use of case studies within the context of practice research, it is important to distinguish (as noted in Chapter 2) the differences between case studies that lead to the configuration of teaching cases (Carnochan, Molinar, Brown, Botzler, Gunderson, Henry, & Austin, 2019) and research case studies that serve as pilots for larger studies, such as the development of a survey design. The research methods associated with case studies represent another area of specialized skills for conducting practice research (Stake, 2005; Yin, 2017).

Principle #5: Balancing a "Practice" Focus with the Relevant "Research" Methods

This balancing act is best described by the metaphor of "getting caught-up in the weeds"; namely, avoid getting preoccupied by detailed practice issues (often reflected in the use of acronyms to describe changes in government policies) and detailed research issues (often reflected in the language of human-subject review procedures). In essence, maintaining a larger worldview can enrich practice research by remaining alert to larger community or policy issues that were not necessarily part of the original practice research study. For example, when a study focuses on internal organizational structures, processes, and roles, it is also helpful to take into account the role of external funders of services who are focused on assessing service outcomes.

Another form of balancing can be seen in efforts to *stay close to the data* when identifying implications for practice (e.g., not overstating the meaning of the findings) and *addressing the expectations of research audience or funders* for more specific recommendations that could be addressed inside the service agency. When called upon to make recommendations about changing something inside the agency, researchers can be reluctant to suggest ideas that relate to the findings when they perceive themselves as having limited managerial or specific organizational experience. And yet, when provocative questions or wide-ranging recommendations are suggested to senior managers, highly productive conversations and experimentation can emerge.

And finally, there is a tendency in practice research to engage in what is sometimes called "one off" or "one of a kind" studies because of the pressure to move on to other challenging situations calling for evidence to inform practice. Given the rapid pace of change in human service agencies, related in part to the changing needs of service users, it can be difficult to create a research culture that values practice research studies that "build upon one another." Multiphase studies over several months or years, however, can provide a much richer foundation for knowledge development that can inform changes in practice. These studies also can add significantly to the literature for other researchers to build upon, as well as contribute to the development of practice or interventive theory. Such contributions to theory would parallel the work of social scientists who frequently use their research findings to inform theory development.

Principle #6: Collaborative Capacities Needed to Work Well with Others

Practice research is fundamentally relational. It calls for the collaborative capacities of all of the stakeholders. Because a practice research study often represents a "work-in-progress," each stakeholder has a role to play in the design, implementation, interpretation of the findings, and development of the conclusions or recommendations. Underlying the collaborative process is the importance of understanding the backgrounds of the respective stakeholders given the cross-disciplinary nature of practice research. Although some of the stakeholders derive their expertise from professional training and work experiences, others bring expertise derived from coping/survival experiences as is common for service users. Similar issues emerge when the professional training experiences differ, as they do for nurses, teachers, social workers, lawyers, and physicians. For example, understanding how social workers and lawyers are educated can greatly enhance the collaborative process in the child welfare field of practice (Taylor, 2006; Carnochan, Taylor, Abramson-Madden, Han, Rashid, Maney, Teuwen, & Austin, 2007).

One of the biggest challenges in fostering collaboration is gaining the support and involvement of busy service providers. Given the pressures of daily work life and the minimal role that research activity plays in agency life, it can be challenging to convince participants to devote time to an interview, focus group, or survey response. As a result, considerable effort needs to be expended over time, along with reminders and updates, to communicate the nature of the research involvement. Collaboration becomes much easier when engaging well-educated, research-minded practitioners, as discussed in Chapter 12.

KNOWING WHAT TO ANTICIPATE AND MANAGE

Principle #7: Managing Tensions

One of the less visible tensions involves the standards for academic research, wherein it is common to identify the limitations of research and the conflicts of interest, or to reflect upon the validity and reliability of the data collection measures. Although these issues are important to researchers, they generally hold little interest for service providers who are more concerned with client confidentiality, negative findings that should not be shared outside the agency, or agency visibility in situations where they feel more comfortable when their data is blended with the data of other organizations. Although these tensions are manageable, they do reflect the profound cultural differences across the partnerships needed for practice research. Seeking to anticipate or manage these tensions frequently calls for cross-cultural sensitivity and skill.

Another tension relates to timeliness and relevance. The perceptions of agency practitioners about the time it takes to conduct research often differ substantially from the perceptions of researchers. Among the most common questions is, "Why does the research take so long to complete?" In the world of practice, questions are raised, and answers are pursued, in what is seen to be a timely manner. Practitioners, therefore, wonder why the research process is not equally efficient. These questions are balanced with questions from researchers, such as: "Why can't practitioners stay focused on the purpose of the research study despite the changes that have taken place in the agency since the research began?" For practitioners, the research might seem obsolete if it took too long to complete, leading to comments such as, "We've moved on," which raise questions about relevance of the findings.

In addition to timeliness, the issue of relevance emerges among practitioners on a regular basis, as in, "How are these findings relevant to our current situation?" or "What are we expected to do with these findings that seem rather esoteric within the context of our current realities?"

Although practitioners may appreciate the rigor, accuracy, and thoroughness with which the research has been conducted, there is less patience among practitioners for the nuanced approach taken by researchers with respect to implications and recommendations, given that most research contributes to some form of discovery but often calls for further research on the topic.

In addition to issues of timeliness and relevance, there can be tensions when it comes to rigor and honest reporting of both positive and negative findings. Here the tensions can be seen in the reluctance or substantial resistance among practitioners to present negative findings that may reflect badly upon practitioners or the organization. These tensions can be mediated by deleting negative findings from reports to the agency but not deleting them when reporting research in a peer-reviewed journal article. Even this solution poses difficult moral questions about the ethics of such resolutions.

Another tension can emerge when seeking to make timely progress with the implementation of a practice research study. Delays by university human-subject review boards can lead to immense frustration on the part of researchers. Similarly, delays within an agency regarding the clearance of approvals for staff participation also can frustrate those agency-based study liaisons seeking to move the study forward in a timely manner. Other forms of delay include problems with agency sampling issues (selecting case records or staff to be interviewed), getting the data coded in a timely fashion, or completing a literature review in advance of framing the research questions.

With regard to projecting the amount of time needed to complete a practice research study, both researchers and practitioners find it difficult to anticipate the multiple delays that frequently occur (e.g., when a study is projected to take 12 months to complete and turns out taking 24 to 36 months to complete). Although the multiple challenges underlying this principle of managing tensions can be addressed, they often require special skills, considerable patience, and a keen understanding of the communication issues noted in Principle #2.

Principle #8: Dealing with Continuous Change

Practice research conducted in human service organizations can be particularly challenging due to changing conditions and environments that can make it difficult to sustain the focus of a practice research study. The changes come in many forms. Given the social policy environment of service agencies, new legislation or administrative policy changes often call for new job responsibilities, new service requirements, and/or new organizational structures in order to comply with the policy changes. Beyond the issue of policy changes, the reorganization of service programs or procedures also can contribute to the change environment in which practice research is being conducted. In essence, adaptability and flexibility are essential ingredients for the implementation of practice research.

Another form of change can be seen in the discovery that ongoing research by another organization has a direct impact on a practice research study. Although there are positive aspects to such developments (e.g., data is being collected in a different study making it possible to shift some of the focus of a practice research study), this change in the environment also calls for flexibility and creativity.

The actual implementation of a practice research study can be impacted by changes within its own operation. For example, the flexibility of any researcher can be significantly affected when dealing with the following challenges: coordinating simultaneous research design processes related to the review of the literature where new findings modify the original focus of the study, shifting practitioner interests in the research, and changing university human-subject review requirements.

Although policy and organizational changes need to be taken into account, changes in the community in which the practice research study is taking place also need attention. This issue becomes readily apparent when conducting case studies related to service providers and service users where changes in the community impact respondent perceptions. Examples of these changes include housing shortages, neighborhood gang violence, local drug epidemic, toxic health exposures due to mismanaged manufacturing, job losses from the closure of businesses, and limited employability due to employer perceptions of the lack of soft job skills among service users.

And finally, changes in the expectations associated with the measurement of service delivery outcomes, as well as calls for the use of new practice skills and knowledge acquired through in-service training, also can impact the implementation of a practice research study. Whether mandated by policy changes or by the reorganization of services, dealing with change represents another dimension of knowing what to anticipate and manage in the conduct of practice research.

Principle #9: Responding to Negative Findings

One of the challenges associated with the identification and presentation of negative research findings relates to dealing with the sensitivities of various stakeholders. The most common sensitivity involves the media and elected officials. Although the internal organizational deliberations over what can be learned from negative findings can be quite informative, the external sharing of such findings can stimulate negative stories in the media and/or ongoing inquiries and investigations by elected officials. For example, when a practice research study identified an array of unmet needs shared by service users, the organization was reluctant to share the study findings because the organization's leaders were concerned about providing mothers on welfare with more latitude with regard to complying with government policies than would be allowed without penalizing the organization with reduced funding or public censure.

The suppression of negative findings can take other forms when there are organizational concerns about incurring financial penalties, political censure (e.g., review panels following a child death of a service user), other forms of negative publicity, and/or community criticism. The vulnerability of human services to criticism can create an understandably heightened sense of paranoia among staff. The suppression of negative findings can focus on external issues, but there are also internal issues facing practice research activity. For example, when those conducting practice research unintentionally engage in self-censure ("We can't say that, even though it seems true."), they may be excluding important findings that need further scrutiny. Similar processes unfold when providing far more elaboration of positive findings than is given to negative findings (e.g., overstating or understating a positive finding). These forms of self-censure represent another challenge in knowing how to manage some of the complexities of practice research.

Principle #10: Engaging Service Users

One of the most challenging aspects of conducting practice research is connected to the emergence of survivor research conducted by service users in partnership with researchers and service providers (Sweeney, Beresford, Faulkner, Nettle, & Rose, 2009). This form of research seeks to rebalance the traditional power differential between service providers and users, as well as between researchers and service users. It involves power sharing that locates the service users in leadership roles; that is, in the "driver's seat" (where researchers and service providers occupy the backseat) when it comes to framing the research questions, designing the data collection tools, analyzing the data, and framing the conclusions and recommendations. It continues the practice research tradition of promoting participation and partnerships but prominently features the "expertise of experience" that service users bring to the research enterprise as well as calling for new forms of dialogue (Natland & Celik, 2015a; Natland, 2015b).

The values that inform survivor research include: (a) partnerships with multiple stakeholders; (b) experientially based insider knowledge sharing by service users and providers; (c) holistic linkage between human behavior and the social environment; (d) appreciation of diversity and the respective intersectionality of race, gender, age, ability, and sexual orientation; and (e) linking research outcomes to empowering others, especially service users, to attain fuller social and economic participation in society, as well as acquire more informed choice with regard to the services provided or developed (Sweeney, Beresford, Faulkner, Nettle & Rose, 2009). Many of the values that guide survivor research are similar to those that inform practice research.

One of the implications of linking survivor research to practice research is to search for common ground where the attributes of both approaches can be integrated. For example, the extensive engagement in practice research as part of a major social service demonstration project in Norway provided opportunities for service providers and service users to engage in substantial shared learning opportunities (Johannessesen & Eide, 2015; Natland & Celik, 2015a; Natland, 2015b). Not only did this lead to more service user involvement in the design and implementation of practice research, it also led to employment opportunities for service users within the staffing structure of practice research projects.

KNOWING HOW TO SHARE RESEARCH

Principle #11: Types of Relationships to Avoid and Promote

The establishment of strong collaborations between practitioners and researchers has the potential to improve research dissemination and utilization. A synthesis of the literature on effective collaboration, especially among researchers and practitioners includes four core elements: (1) incentive to collaborate; (2) shared values, trust, open communication, and respect; (3) ability to collaborate: and (4) capacity to build and sustain collaboration. This section highlights the literature review findings of Lemon-Osterling and Austin (2008).

In the case of practitioner–researcher collaborations, a clear incentive for practitioners is to gain access to research and experts who can provide evidence relevant to practice. Researchers have incentives to collaborate with practitioners in order to improve the quality of the research and suggest areas of inquiry that may be new to researchers. Indeed, effective practitioner–researcher collaborations involve a high degree of reciprocity. As noted by Miles and Huberman (1994) in order for research to inform practice and practice to inform research, there needs to be a concerted effort to move away from saying "hello-goodbye," operating like two different planets, or taking standoff positions to relationships of mutual engagement and ongoing collaborative synergy (see Box 8.1).

The differing backgrounds and experiences of researchers and practitioners need to be addressed so that both parties can create an environment that reflects shared values, trust, open communication, and respect. Shared values create a willingness to collaborate and help to establish trust among collaborators. Trust is created by open communication among all parties and can lead to feelings of reciprocity in the collaboration. Correspondingly, open communication and mutual respect often are fostered by frequent contacts and communication between parties. Successful communications are characterized by both practitioners and researchers asking questions and listening to one another.

Effective collaboration between practitioners and researchers calls for advanced preparation in order for researchers to understand the practice setting and the experiences of practitioners and for practitioners to prepare for future changes in their practices and prepare researchers to work effectively with them. The shared capacities to collaborate are essential.

The building and sustaining of effective collaboration are facilitated by "conscious and continuous effort" on the part of researchers and practitioners to ensure that the collaboration is successful, especially in light of a variety of competing demands on the time and attention of both parties (Lane, Turner, & Flores, 2004). Some of the activities related to the dissemination and utilization of practice research include scheduled meetings to share findings and learn from each other, along with the use of media-related communications channels.

The gap between research and practice can be detrimental to both the quality of social service practice, as well as the quality of social

Box 8.1. Types of Relationships between Researchers and Practitioners (Miles & Huberman, 1994)

- *"Hello–Goodbye"*: No collaboration or communication between researchers and practitioners before, during, or after the study where findings were disseminated to a "passive target audience" whose priorities had not been addressed in the research, and there was no communication between the researchers and the practitioners 18 months after the study was completed.
- *"Two Planets"*: Weak collaboration between practitioners and researchers throughout and after the study reflected episodic contacts that focused on providing training or technical assistance in order to carry out the study where "largely decorative" advisory groups were involved in the research (e.g., met infrequently, lacked a concrete purpose, did not understand research findings, and engaged in few, if any, dissemination activities). Eighteen months after the study was completed both practitioners and researchers were waiting for the other to disseminate findings.
- *"Standoff"*: Moderate collaboration that remained stable throughout the study period and afterward, but that ultimately did not directly affect utilization (e.g., the researchers did not consult with the practitioners in the development of the study's focus or while the study progressed, leading practitioners to feel that the researchers were "out of touch" with their practice setting and to perceive the findings with suspicion). The dissemination strategy was simply to send the final report to the practitioners, who did little to disseminate the findings. There was no contact between researchers and practitioners 18 months after the study completion.
- *"Mutual Engagement"*: Weak initial collaboration that grew in strength throughout the course of the study based on frequent informal contacts and a series of interim reports that were concise and easily understandable. These were discussed in meetings between researchers and practitioners, which helped to neutralize power imbalances and created enthusiasm on the part of both practitioners and researchers to disseminate findings.
- *"Synergy"*: Well-established collaboration prior to the implementation of the study, and these linkages were "activated" during and after the study (e.g., regular discussions of interim reports, frequent informal contacts, meetings to discuss study findings and plan for dissemination, and efforts to use data within practitioner staff meetings and training events).

service research. Research can inform practice, just as practice can inform research. Numerous interacting factors related to individuals, organizations, the nature of research, and the nature of communication are involved in the dissemination and utilization process. In essence, effective collaborations in practice research require both practitioners and researchers to modify the ways they engage one another. For example, practitioners need to shift from such statements as, "Tell us what you found *and* what we should do differently" to "Involve us in the research process so that we can share in the data interpretation and develop our own conclusions about what we should be doing differently." In a similar fashion, researchers need to shift from such statements as, "Tell us what you want to know and we'll tell you what we found" to "How can we both use research to improve outcomes for clients and strengthen current practice?" Based on shared goals, practitioner–researcher partnerships need to focus more attention on improving the dissemination and utilization of research, if they are to reach the goals of service improvement and change.

Building upon the four categories of principles for implementing practice research (knowing what to do, knowing how to do it, knowing where to manage and anticipate change, and knowing how to share research), the next section features a discussion of specific aspects of research methodology applied to practice research. It begins with an emphasis on research rigor as related to inductive and deductive research design, the role of causality, and the relevant criteria for assessing rigor. It is followed by the central role of research relevance and its relationship to rigor (replacing validity and reliability with credibility as a test of plausibility; addressing dependability and confirmability by a focus transparency, as well as managing bias and the impact of researcher identity; and ensuring shared interpretation and participation). The section concludes by articulating the process of theorizing from practice research data with special attention to a relatively new concept of "abductive analysis" (creating a meaning-making structure to fit unexpected or unusual findings into an interpretive framework).

RIGOR, RELEVANCE, AND THEORIZING

The discussion of rigor in social science research often focuses primarily on quantitative data. In contrast, this section focuses on the role of rigor in qualitative research in relationship to the concepts of relevance and theorizing that are related to practice research. Rigor relates to practice research methodology, while relevance relates to the importance and value of the research questions and findings that serve as the foundation for practice research. Although practice research includes both quantitative and qualitative data, the key concepts for exploring the rigor and relevance of the qualitative data emerging from practice research are causal mechanisms and inductive inquiry.

This discussion begins by exploring the concept of causality. Although the evolution of mixed methods in social science research makes it clear that qualitative methods (sometimes referred to as interpretivist) complement quantitative methods (sometimes referred to as positivist), it is important to note how these complementary approaches contribute to knowledge development (Lin, 1998). In essence, the quantitative approach focuses on discovering causal *relationships* between variables, often using statistical inference in the search for plausible causes, while the qualitative approach features the discovery of causal *mechanisms* using "thick description" in the search for "how" variables relate to each other—with special attention to the context in which they operate. Although both methods rely on documented procedures for how data were collected and analyzed, the search for causality, in both cases, also calls for evaluating alternative explanations of the findings.

It often goes without saying, the use of a particular research method is directly related to the research question(s) under investigation. Does the question derive from theory-based hypothesis formulation related to a *deductive* inquiry (somewhat "top down")? Or does it derive from efforts to describe a phenomenon of interest that seeks to address "how" and "why" questions related to *inductive* inquiry (somewhat "bottom up")?

Promoting Rigor

One of the key concepts related to rigor relates to sampling; namely, how representative is the population under study when compared to other populations and how diverse is the research respondent group? When it comes to generalizing from the findings, Nowell and Albrecht (2019) note that:

> The sample of an inductive study is never purely random nor convenient. Instead, each case or participant should be purposively selected

because they represent a theoretically interesting exemplar of, or key informant about, a phenomenon of interest. In other words, by nature of being selected for inclusion in an inductive study, the scholar is making the argument that we should care about understanding the experience of this person(s) or the events of this case. Whether a pattern discerned in an inductive study is common in the general population is not the question that an inductive scholar is seeking to answer. In fact, the case may have been selected specifically because it represents something rare or unusual. (p. 353)

For example, the practice research partnership that supports the work cited in this volume offers a number of opportunities to engage in purposive sampling aimed at strengthening the design of a given study. The involvement of multiple counties allows for variation with respect to community context as well as agency and client characteristics. In our studies of cross-sectoral contracting and evidence-informed practice, agency directors and senior staff in the participating agencies played an important role in identifying and recruiting staff members to participate. The relationships that we develop with study liaisons, as in the case of the Child Welfare Qualitative Data Mining and Family Stabilization projects, enable us to draw upon agency administrative data for the client samples needed to address particular research questions.

Moving beyond the traditional criteria of generalizability and replication that are associated with deductive quantitative studies, Nowell and Albrecht (2019) call for the importance of generating new insights into causal mechanisms related to the significance and trustworthiness of the findings. Using inquiry-driven sampling, these new insights often involve findings that are unusual, typical, information-rich, or disconfirming. The wide-ranging criteria for assessing rigor are related to credible data interpretation, systematic analytical processes, and to the relevance of the research context to other settings, as illustrated in Box 8.2.

As described in other chapters, the continued engagement and communication with our agency partners also serves to strengthen the quality of our instrument design through the use of pilot surveys and interviews with study liaisons and other agency staff. In the study of cross-sectoral contracting, county and nonprofit agency partners provided valuable input on survey language, ensuring that study respondents interpreted questions in the way they were intended. Pilot testing also generated feedback on

Box 8.2. Relevant Criteria for Assessing Rigor in Qualitative Research*

In general, were the following components of the research process articulated:

Significance of the research question	• Is the phenomenon of interest important to advancing the field?
Justification of the research approach	• Does the research question address a significant gap in the literature?
Sampling	• Is the research question inductive in nature?
	• Does the research question aim to understand qualities, patterns, and mechanisms?
	• Is there a clear and compelling justification that the cases/units/ informants selected for inclusion in the study are information rich in relation to the phenomenon of interest?
	• Is the sampling approach justified within the analysis tradition utilized (e.g., grounded theory vs. ethnography)?
	• Is the number of units sampled theoretically robust in both qualitative depth as well as representing important aspects of potential variability?
	• Is the data collection protocol clearly described?
Data collection	• Do the elements of the protocol map clearly relate back to study objectives and analysis tradition?
	• Were all members of the research team trained on the study objectives and their relationship to the data collection protocol in order to ensure a high degree of fidelity in implementation?
	• Did research team members debrief regularly to review data quality in relation to study objectives and make mid-course adjustments to protocols as needed?

Data analysis	• Was the analysis approach clearly articulated and consistent with the analytic tradition employed? • Were practices to establish the trustworthiness of the analysis employed?
Reporting	• Are interpretations presented in a credible manner that offers "thick description" of the key themes or patterns identified, including inclusion of relevant examples, representative quotations, and attention to nonconforming cases? • Are sources of potential bias and alternative explanations considered and reported? • Are the interpretations insightful? Do they address the research question in such a way as to advance our understanding of a phenomenon? • Are interpretations sufficiently contextualized so as to allow the reader to consider the types of situations in which such patterns might replicate?

*Adapted from Nowell, B., & Albrecht, K. (2019). A reviewer's guide to qualitative rigor. *Journal of Public Administration Research and Theory, 29*(2), 348–363 (p. 355).

surveys that were seen to be too long, and shortening the survey proved to be an important factor in creating a strong respondent response rate. Similarly, in the data collection process, our practice partners often helped us to recruit participants who ensured adequate sample sizes.

Rigor in Relationship to Relevance

Rigor traditionally refers to accurate and systematic theory testing, often using standardized quantitative methods (Dodge, Ospina, & Foldy, 2005). In contrast, rigor related to qualitative methods involves the types and levels of data interpretation in the form of negotiated representations between the researchers and the researched. In both cases, findings are assessed with the aim of making informed decisions about important practical problems based upon a rigorous interpretation of the data collected.

In contrast to other forms of rigor, relevance refers to research questions jointly defined between the research community and its partners. The concept of relevance for practice researchers is based on closing the gap between research and practice where practitioners are viewed as "legitimate sources of knowledge" with an interest in the outcome of the research. As research sources, practitioners and service users provide their own interpretations of reality, interpreting intention and meaning in context, and they also offer an avenue for exploring causal mechanisms (i.e., the "how" and "why" behind the "what").

As noted in other chapters, the process of jointly defining research questions is central to our conduct of practice research. Each study begins with a series of conversations with agency directors, as well as their senior managers and staff involved in the areas to be investigated, in order to identify the specific issues and questions that they want addressed. For example, in the most recent phase of the Child Welfare Qualitative Data Mining Project, we engaged in discussions with the regional Child Welfare Directors group, as well as conversations with individual child welfare (CW) directors, in order to identify the topics of parental substance abuse and child mental health. Similarly, we communicated with the CW directors as we framed the preliminary and final reports in order to ensure that the analysis generated relevant information about their programs and clients.

Relevance also is related to the quality of inductive inquiry and encompasses the following major characteristics:

(1) Conveys meanings in the search for understanding intentions, beliefs, values, and emotions that reflect situated social realities
(2) Carries practical knowledge that individuals have gained through their experiences, often in the form of storytelling
(3) Is shaped by individuals for their own purposes and also represents forces that shape human beings and help give meaning to the social worlds they inhabit. (Dodge, Ospina, & Foldy, 2005, p. 291)

The process of reframing traditional research standards in terms of rigor and relevance is captured in the summary developed by Dodge, Ospina, and Foldy (2005) as illustrated in Box 8.3.

The next section builds upon this discussion of rigor and relevance to identify some of the key elements of the theorizing process with special attention to theorizing about qualitative data.

Box 8.3. Reframing Traditional Research Processes Related to the Rigor and Relevance of Qualitative Inquiry*

---

(1) *Validity and reliability* are replaced with credibility as a test of the plausibility of an argument using "thick description" of unprocessed data to back up claims by carefully:
  (a) Distinguishing between data and analysis
  (b) Distinguishing between an informant's voice and the researcher's voice in order to produce a negotiated interpretation of the informant's world
  (c) Acknowledging other informants, as in triangulation that provides for integrated, multifaceted stories
  (d) Distinguishing between the research product and the degree to which it resonates with the informants' experiences
  (e) Acknowledging the impossibility of test/retest reliability, given that narratives can change from telling to retelling due to the context dependency (place, time, and additional participants).
(2) *Dependability and confirmability* are addressed by:
  (a) The transparency of methods
  (b) The articulation of how bias has been addressed
  (c) The specification of how researcher identity (and intersectionality) influences the research context as well as data interpretations.
(3) *Interpretation and participation* in action research by:
  (a) Viewing research participants as "co-researchers"
  (b) Promoting research dissemination and utilization
  (c) Engaging in interpretive rigor by preserving, not fracturing, the participants' ways of constructing and interpreting their own meanings
  (d) Gathering the participants' experiences with the research project (both the process and outcomes)
  (e) Translating findings into policy or management insights when attending to both methodological and interpretive rigor.

*Adapted from Dodge, J., Ospina, S.M., & Foldy, E.G. (2005). Integrating rigor and relevance in public administration scholarship: The contribution of narrative inquiry. *Public Administration Review*, 65(3), 286–300.

Elements of the Theorizing Process

The process of theorizing about research findings begins when qualitative researchers start organizing a "mountain of evidence from many everyday occurrences" into a set of themes. These themes are often based on "an improvised research design to permit meaning to emerge from the data" that are drawn from "marginal, hard to study, and ambiguously defined settings, groups, and phenomena (Brower, Abolafia, & Carr, 2000, pp. 366–367).

Three key concepts that underlie the theorizing process are authenticity, plausibility, and criticality (Brower, Abolafia, & Carr, 2000). *Authenticity* refers to: (a) the existence of sufficient data to support propositions emerging from encountered experiences and (b) the quality of the description of the setting from which the data are derived. *Plausibility* involves creating face validity where conclusions seem reasonable and understandable, and the quality of the conclusions drawn from the data appear to be credible. *Criticality* relates to thoroughly examining one's own assumptions about the subject or setting under study. It is often the first step needed to begin: (a) theorizing about the meaning of the findings, (b) identifying and presenting contrasting perspectives buried in the data, and (c) exploring potential explanations. These concepts are central to reflecting upon the emergent nature of the data and its setting.

The definitions of these three concepts (authenticity, plausibility, and criticality) represent the key criteria for assessing the thoroughness of the theorizing process. The foundation for theorizing about qualitative research findings include the following elements: (1) the explanation of potential relationships using extensive data coding needed to get beneath surface explanations; (2) full description of the setting from which the data emerge that reflects rigorous data collection in order to help the reader image the nature of the setting; (3) allowing for different aspects of the data to promote theorizing rather than forcing data to comply with existing theories; and (4) capturing the "backstage" aspects of organizational life in contrast to the "frontstage" perceptions of organizational leaders (Brower, Abolafia, & Carr, 2000, pp. 390).

The next section discusses a relatively new form of analysis that links data with theory. Although practice research may not lead directly to theory development, it does provide a platform for engaging in the process of theorizing or sense-making with regard to key concepts emerging from qualitative data.

Using Abductive Analysis to Frame the Theorizing Process

This section builds upon the pioneering work of Tavory and Timmermans (2014) who define abductive analysis as the process of "inferring from observation or experience to create a structure of meaning-making that represents a speculative process that can fit unexpected or unusual findings into an interpretive framework" (p. 5). Abductive analysis is designed to complement the inductive nature of qualitative research and the deductive aspects of quantitative research by developing a pragmatist theory of meaning-making and inference development when engaged in empirical research. It involves careful attention to the generalizations emerging from qualitative data that help each research project "find its theoretical voice." Tavory and Timmermans (2014) view theorizing as a process of "joining in conversation" to learn how others view the data and as an "ongoing exercise in puzzling out the world we live in."

For example, when we engage in the process of "puzzling out the world" of human services practice, our practice partners play an essential role. They help us interpret and analyze study data, whether this involves case records documenting child welfare practice, or interviews with adults receiving Family Stabilization services. In addition, they help us make sense of simple phenomena such as program acronyms and other providers in the service system, as well as more complex dynamics involved in their efforts to engage and serve clients.

Abductive analysis involves theorizing about the relationships among data, theory, and research methods. The major steps include (Tavory & Timmermans, 2014, p. 61 & p. 124):

(a) Investing in meticulous notetaking, memo writing, and transcription wherein observations are de-familiarized (rendered unfamiliar or seen anew) by confronting our everyday experiences and gaining deeper appreciation, as well as by posing new questions

(b) Engaging in extensive open coding of data followed by axial coding (identifying promising themes by looking across data sources to account for variations and identify key concepts) that often requires further definition and operationalization of concepts, processes, and theoretical links

(c) Assessing data through different theoretical lenses (theoretical pluralism) as a process of revisiting the data

(d) Comparing observations to one another in terms of data set variation, variation over time, and variation created by different situations in order to search for patterns, processes, and similarities/differences needed to frame a grounded/logical argument

(e) Assessing data in terms of authenticity, plausibility, critical thinking, and relevance (by engaging the researchers and research subjects).

The outcome of abductive analysis relates to moving beyond the pioneering work of Glaser and Strauss (1967) related to the development of grounded theory by seeking to construct middle-range theories (rather than highly abstract theories) based on "explicit, transparent coding procedures that capture fundamental social psychological processes as they unfold" (Tavory & Timmermans, 2014, p.10). Meaning-making involves: "(a) a sign (as in a word in the data that signifies a concept); (b) an object (related to the sign in the form of an individual, word, or idea); and (c) an interpreter to make sense of the sign" (Tavory &Timmermans, p. 23). In essence, abductive analysis involves open-ended brainstorming about the potential meanings of a piece of data. The process of theorizing involves any form of generalization about observations that can lead to potentially useful insights, new questions, and/or new observations (Tavory & Timmermans, 2014).

The methods we use to analyze data represent a critical component of theory generation. The analysis and discussion of the variations located in the research findings provide a venue for seeing how research methods and theory mutually reinforce each other. As Tavory and Timmermans (2014) point out, theorizing is the result of "recursive movement back and forth between observations and theories" (p.65) and "theory construction gains momentum when we situate an observation within a broader set of phenomena by examining its similarities and differences with other members of the dataset" (p. 86).

Building upon this discussion of the theorizing process, our approach to practice research incorporates the perspective of study participants with regard to the themes emerging from the data, combined with our views as researchers and those located in existing theories. For example, in the study of evidence-informed practice, we created a conceptual matrix that we shared with a group of agency managers and supervisors in order to help us validate concepts and develop the final concept map.

In summary, the concept of causality plays a key role in abductive analysis, especially when comparing observations with one another to find similarities and differences, as well as patterns that enhance the meaning-making processes (Tavory & Timmermans, 2014). A pragmatic view of research relevance can be seen in how the development of theories provides a bridge to the practices of others as well as helps to modify or enhance thinking, especially when in dialogue with the practice community. The important role of research rigor emerges from the transparency of the research methodology, the depth and breadth of the analysis of thick description, and the exploration of the relationship between findings and meaning-making in the form of theorizing.

Transparency can be demonstrated, for example, by careful, systematic recording of the communications, decisions, problems, and solutions that arise during the course of a study. The descriptions of the research in this volume are made possible by the extensive documentation created for each project. In addition, the process of making practice research transparent emerges in the crafting of a peer-reviewed journal article that is designed to disseminate findings in order to promote their utilization. With regard to the academic standards impacting practice researchers, Wu, Wyant, and Fraser (2016) note in their guidelines for publishing qualitative research that the essence of being transparent involves providing:

(a) The background to the research questions and their relevance for practice and policy

(b) A literature review that summarized the strengths and limitations of previous studies, the current state of the knowledge base, as well as alternative theoretical perspectives where relevant

(c) A description of the data collection methods, the rationale for selecting the methods, the roles of the research project participants, and any theoretical lens used to frame the study

(d) A description of how the study participants were recruited, size of sample, and any human-subject issues

(e) Documentation of the steps in the data analysis, including a description of the thematic analysis that incorporates the criteria for theme selection, as well as the various steps and elements of the data coding process

(f) A presentation of findings (including relevant graphics) that examines the relationships among the themes emerging from the findings, notes complexities and surprises, and selectively uses quotes from the thick description of the data

(g) A discussion that links the findings to the original research questions, notes the strengths and limitations of the qualitative research methods, and fully elaborates upon the implications (and recommendations where relevant) for practice, public policy, and future research (pp. 419–423).

CONCLUSION

This chapter began with the importance of extracting lessons learned from engaging in practice research and transforming them into a set of practice research principles. Although other practice research stakeholders might identify additional or different principles, we have organized the principles into the four categories of knowing what to do when engaging in practice research, knowing how to do it by drawing upon relational and methodological capacities, knowing where to anticipate and manage change, and knowing how to share research findings.

One of the limitations of this discussion of principles is that it presumes the acquisition by researchers and others of core social science research skills related to: (a) the conduct of research-based interviews and focus groups; (b) previously acquired critical thinking skills related to reviewing literature or extracting themes from findings; and (c) exposure to an array of research methods related to both qualitative and quantitative social science research. Another limitation of these principles is that they have emerged over several decades from one research center, rather than from many, which clearly suggests an area for future research.

As noted in Figure 8.1, the combining of this array of principles should lead to an increased proficiency in the conduct of practice research. In this context, the concept of proficiency refers to becoming more skillful in carrying out practice research. As in most learning situations, multiple opportunities to apply these principles over time in a variety of practice research projects also should lead to proficiency. As noted, these principles are based on various types of practice research that are described in the preceding chapters.

In addition to extracting the principles of practice research, this chapter also included several important issues related to research methods; namely, rigor, relevance, and theorizing. These elements are common to most social science research and have special meaning for the inductive and qualitative approaches of practice research. Our descriptions of specific practice research methods and projects in previous chapters provide only highlights of our experience over the past two decades. The next set of chapters provides more in-depth discussions of some of the topics in the previous chapters.

REFERENCES

Brower, R.S., Abolafia, M.Y., & Carr, J.B. (2000). On improving qualitative methods in public administration research. *Administration & Society, 32*(4), 363–397.

Carnochan, S., Molinar, L., Brown, J., Botzler, L., Gunderson, K., Henry, C., & Austin, M.J. (2019). *Public child welfare: A casebook for learning and teaching.* San Diego, CA: Cognella Academic Publishing.

Carnochan, S., Taylor, S., Abramson-Madden, A., Han, M., Rashid, S., Maney, J., Teuwen, S., & Austin, M.J. (2007). Child welfare and the courts: An exploratory study of the relationship between two complex systems. *Journal of Public Child Welfare, 1*(1), 117–136.

Creswell, J.W. (2015). *A concise introduction to mixed methods research.* Thousand Oaks, CA: Sage.

Dodge, J. Ospina, S.M., & Foldy, E.G. (2005). Integrating rigor and relevance in public administration scholarship: The contribution of narrative inquiry. *Public Administration Review, 65*(3), 286–300.

Ennis, R.H. (1987). A taxonomy of critical thinking dispositions and abilities. In J.B. Baron & R.J. Steinberg (Eds.), *Teaching thinking skills: Theory and practice* (pp. 45–61). New York, NY: Freeman.

Flyvbjerg, B. (2001). *Making social science matter: Why social inquiry fails and how it can succeed again.* Cambridge, UK: Cambridge University Press.

Fowler, F.J. (2013). *Survey research methods: Applied social research methods* (5th ed.). Thousand Oaks, CA: Sage.

Gibbs, L., & Gambrill, E. (1999). *Critical thinking for social workers.* Thousand Oaks, CA: Pine Forge Press.

Glaser, B.G., & Strauss, A.L. (1967). *The discovery of grounded theory: Strategies for qualitative research*. Chicago, IL: Aldine.

Johannessen, A., & Eide, S.B. (2015). Evidence from social service enhancement projects: Selected cases from Norway's HUSK project. *Journal of Evidence-informed Social Work, 12*(1), 7–31.

Krueger, R.A., & Casey, M. (2015). *Focus groups: A practical guide for applied research* (5th ed.). Thousand Oaks, CA: Sage.

Lane, J., Turner, S., & Flores, C. (2004). Researcher-Practitioner Collaboration in Community Corrections: Overcoming Hurdles for Successful Partnerships. *Criminal Justice Review, 29*(1), 97–114.

Lin, A.C. (1998). Bridging positivist and interpretivist approaches to qualitative methods. *Policy Studies Journal, 26*(1), 162–180.

Miles, M.B., & Huberman, A.M. (1994). *Qualitative Data Analysis: An Expanded Sourcebook*. Thousand Oaks, CA: Sage Publications.

Natland, S. (2015b). Dialogical communications and empowering social work practice. *Journal of Evidence-informed Social Work, 12*(1), 80–91.

Natland, S., & Celik, H.D. (2015a). Service users' self narratives on their journey from shame to pride: Tales of transitions. *Journal of Evidence-informed Social Work. 12*(1), 50–63.

Nowell, B., & Albrecht, K. (2019). A reviewer's guide to qualitative rigor. *Journal of Public Administration Research and Theory. 29*(2), 348–363.

Padgett, D.K. (2017). *Qualitative methods in social work research* (3rd ed.). Thousand Oaks, CA: Sage.

Paul, R. (1993). *Critical thinking: What every person needs to survive in a rapidly changing world*. Santa Rosa, CA: Foundation for Critical Thinking.

Rubin, H.J., & Rubin, I.S. (2012). *Qualitative interviewing: The art of hearing data* (3rd ed.). Thousand Oaks, CA: Sage.

Spradley, J.P. (1980). *Participant observation*. New York, NY: Holt, Rinehart & Winston.

Stake, R.E. (2005). *Multiple case study analysis*. New York, NY: Guilford Press.

Sweeney, A., Beresford, P., Faulkner, A., Nettle, M., & Rose, D. (2009). *This is survivor research*. Ross-on-Wye, UK: PCCS Books.

Tavory, I., & Timmermans, S. (2014). *Abductive analysis: Theorizing qualitative research*. Chicago, Ill: University of Chicago Press.

Taylor, S. (2006). Educating future practitioners of social work and law: Exploring the origins of inter-professional misunderstanding. *Children and Youth Services Review, 28*(6), 638–653.

Weinbach, R.W., & Grinnell, R.M. (2015). *Statistics for social workers* (9th ed.). London, UK: Pearson.

Yin, R.K. (2017). *Case study research and applications: Design and methods*. Thousand Oaks, CA: Sage.

9

Practice Research and Related Methodologies

Describing the array of research methods is a critical element in understanding the similarities and differences between practice research and other approaches to applied research. How is practice research (PR) similar and different from the methodologies of participatory action research (PAR) or from the basic elements of program evaluation and intervention research (PEIR)? What is the role of qualitative research in each of these different approaches (Padgett, 2008)? To address these questions, this chapter includes a comparative analysis of the differences and similarities of these frameworks. The goal is to place practice research within a larger context as well as provide a rationale for its uniqueness.

COMMON RESEARCH METHODS

Based on this brief chapter overview, the focus of this analysis is the comparison of the common components of PAR, PEIR, and PR; namely, research question formulation, sources of literature and practice wisdom, data collection tools, data analysis and interpretation processes,

Practice Research in the Human Services. Michael J. Austin and Sarah Carnochan, Oxford University Press (2020). © Oxford University Press.
DOI: 10.1093/oso/9780197518335.001.0001

research dissemination processes, and knowledge development processes. With these common components in mind, this analysis of shared elements also features the key concepts of principles, process challenges, methodological challenges, and success factors.

Common Research Methods: The Research Questions

As illustrated in Table 9.1, practice research (PR) shares some common components with participatory action research (PAR) and program evaluation linked to intervention research (PEIR). All three research frameworks begin with the framing of research questions, but they proceed in different ways. In the case of PAR, the questions often relate to a community population or geographic area seeking to learn more from its constituents about the nature of shared problems (Greenwood & Levin, 2007; Israel et al., 1998, 2005; Lawson, Caringi, Pyles, Jurkowsi, & Bozlak, 2015; Minkler, 2000, Minkler & Wallerstein, 2008; Reason & Bradbury, 2006). The questions can be multiple and wide-ranging. Although research is an important component of PAR, the emphasis tends to be on the processes of "participation" and "action," both of which are informed by research.

In contrast to PAR, the research questions related to PEIR tend to be highly focused on the objectives of a particular program and are often in need of continuous refinement (Brun, 2013; Dudley, 2013; Grinnell, Gabor, & Unrau, 2019). For example, in program evaluation it is common to spend time defining or clarifying the objectives that are in operation for implementing a particular program or intervention (Patton, 2018; Smith, 2010; Wholey, Hatry, & Newcomer, 1994). This process also may require a deeper understanding of the program's theory of change; namely, what do the implementers of the program expect to happen as a result of one or more activities (e.g., learn how to apply a job-search skill or respond to multiple activities that lead to the development of a career plan) (Patton, 2011). The theory of change seeks to capture an underlying implied causal chain (e.g., "If we do this, that will occur."). The development of research questions becomes even more focused when engaging in intervention research, which often follows the research procedures of random controlled trials (RCTs) and other forms of quasi-experimental frameworks. In contrast to PAR, the focus of the PEIR framework is primarily upon new or existing programs operating inside

Table 9.1. Comparing Practice Research with Other Research Frameworks

	Frameworks		
Methods	Community-based Participant Action Research (PAR) to Address social problems	Program Evaluation (PE) & Intervention Research (IR) to Outcomes, outputs, & return on investment	Organizationally-based Practice Research (PR) to improve practices and service delivery
Framing & negotiating the development of research questions	Community population or geographic area	Decision-oriented or Objectives-oriented	Organization's service providers, service users, managers & policymakers
Identifying sources of literature & practice wisdom to inform research questions	Community members & databases	Organizational members & "Theory of Change" documents	Organizational members & documents
Specifying data collection processes	Quantitative & qualitative (borrowed/created)—Multiple study designs (interviews, focus groups, surveys, etc.)	Quantitative & qualitative (borrowed/created)—Multiple study designs (RCTs, pre/post, longitudinal, cross-sectional)	Quantitative & qualitative (borrowed/created)—Multiple study designs (interviews, focus groups, surveys, data mining, etc.)
Defining data analysis & interpretation processes	Shared analysis & interpretation with various stakeholders	Internal and/or external expert data analysis & interpretation	Shared analysis & interpretation with various stakeholders
Implementing research dissemination processes	Community problem-solving & implementation	Decision-making & funder accountability	Service & practice improvements
Articulating knowledge development processes	Sociopolitical action & community change	Service redesign & organizational planning	Practice-informed theory & theory-informed practice

an existing organization or between organizations (Fraser, Richman, & Galinsky, 2009). Intervention research also draws primarily upon the methods of random controlled trials when investigating the outcomes of specified practices (Solomon, Cavanagh, & Draine, 2009).

When comparing the "questions formulating phase" of practice research with PAR and PEIR, it becomes immediately clear that the organizational context of inquiry is critical (e.g., a human service organization designed to serve and meet the needs of vulnerable populations). In this context, the views of service providers (staff), service users (clients or participants), research authorizing personnel (senior management, policymakers, funders, etc.), and the researchers (internal or external to the organization) are critical components. The views of each of these groups regarding the framing of the research questions need to be negotiated. For example, the negotiation could involve identifying agency case records that can be used to answer questions related to substance-abusing parents caring for their children in situations of abuse or neglect in a child welfare agency. The process of framing the research questions involves the service providers who contribute to these records, the involvement of middle and senior management who assist with the sampling of case records, and the researchers engaged in case record data mining. Similarly, the views of elected officials reflected in the legislation and administrative regulations often inform practices in this situation.

In essence, each of the three research frameworks approaches the framing and negotiating of the research questions in a slightly different way. The major similarities involve the importance of identifying research questions as guides for the inquiry.

Common Research Methods: Literature and Practice Wisdom

When engaging in PAR, one of the major sources of information needed for framing the research questions comes from members of the community who have first-hand experience with the social problem needing attention. In addition, reports developed by government and nonprofit organizations often can provide historical background of the community problem as well as evidence of prior efforts to address it. Complementing the use of reports and the wisdom of community members, research question framing also can benefit from a literature review designed to learn more about the various definitions of the community problem as well as the research reports derived from the experiences of other communities.

In contrast to the more "bottom-up" approach of PAR, the PEIR framework tends to be more reflective of "top down" management in the form of requests from funders to provide evidence that the program works or that the specific interventions have been rigorously assessed (e.g., RCTs). This RCT component often relies heavily on a systematic review of existing published research literature as well as government reports on the use of specific intervention methods and their outcomes. As a result, the internal or external evaluator/researcher tends to assume a major leadership role in locating, assessing, and applying findings from previous studies.

In Practice Research, the various stakeholders are involved in a combination of bottom up and top down activities with a central focus on the activities of service providers (staff). With regard to the participation of service users who bring the *expertise of experience,* their contribution can be combined with the expertise of researchers and the expertise of service providers. This array of expertise also can be combined with that of senior management who generally reflect the legislative intent of the policymakers found in the administrative regulations that guide service delivery. Although shared expertise plays a central role in capturing and codifying relevant practice wisdom, there is an equal reliance on the literature, including government reports.

In essence, each research framework relies upon both the written and oral tradition associated with different stakeholders. This process reflects different investments in "learning from the past" or "learning from others."

Common Research Methods: Data Collection Approaches

The role of data collection tools in all forms of applied research is central to the research process. Given that all three research frameworks rely upon quantitative and qualitative tools that are either created or adapted from others, the differences emerge in the area of research tool application.

In both PAR and PR, there tends to be considerable reliance upon the tools related to interviewing, focus groups, surveys, and datamining (Epstein, 2009). Many of these tools have been refined by scholars who specialize in the use of qualitative methods. In contrast, the PEIR frameworks tend to rely more heavily on quantitative tools that support specialized research designs. They range from the most rigorous in the form of random controlled trials utilizing experimental and control groups to pre- and post-evaluation designs that make active use of baseline data. Other designs include more longitudinal approaches related to measurements at different points in time and cross-sectional surveys that reflect measurement at one point in time.

It is also important to note the growing interests among researchers in utilizing tools that reflect "mixed" methods in the form of both qualitative and quantitative designs (Creswell, 2015). It has also become clear, however, that becoming highly skilled in both approaches to research design can be a lifelong endeavor.

Common Research Methods: Data Analysis and Interpretation

Similar to the commonalities associated with data collection approaches, the tools and processes for data analysis and interpretation also can be shared among the various research methods. Qualitative data typically relies upon computer software to store, manage, retrieve, and code data. In addition, the data interpretation process relies upon the expertise of various stakeholders and calls for skills in synthesizing multiple perspectives. Data analysis may be in the hands of a few stakeholders, but interpretation of qualitative data, by design, involves a wider array of stakeholders (e.g., "What do you think the data are telling us?"). This element of research methods is a central feature of both PAR and PR, where ownership of the data is a critical ingredient of research dissemination and utilization.

The time-consuming processes associated with analyzing and interpreting qualitative data differ from the time-consuming processes related to quantitative data collection tools. For example, considerable data management and cleaning skills are needed to organize survey data in order to prepare data for analysis. Quantitative data analysis employing various statistical programs calls for both software familiarity as well as the underlying procedures involved in statistical analysis. The primary participants in quantitative data analysis tend to be researchers and possibly senior managers, policymakers, and/or funders. In some situations, preliminary interpretations of the data need to be shared with others for their input.

All three research approaches tend to rely on the expertise of the researchers to present the analysis and preliminary interpretation of the data. This may be less the case in survivor research, where service users play a central role in all aspects of the research enterprise (Sweeney, Beresford, Faulkner, Nettle, & Rose, 2009).

Common Research Methods: Research Dissemination and Utilization

Although there are similarities across the three research frameworks with regard to a commitment to disseminate research and promote utilization, there are also considerable differences. With respect to PAR, the primary focus on participatory research is action. In this case, the research needs to relate to the community issues that are in need of problem-solving so that participatory strategies can be designed to foster the utilization of the research. Similarly, educational and training programs are often essential for disseminating the research to those who could make the most use of it.

When it comes to disseminating and utilizing PEIR, different processes tend to prevail. If the research is part of a specially funded program, then it is most likely that various levels of decision-makers will be involved in the utilization process. If there is minimal evidence of impact, the dissemination process may begin and end at the senior management level with regard to expanding or contracting the program. Similarly, those involved with the external funding of the program and/or the evaluation will engage in their own decision-making processes about the future funding of a particular program.

The overall theme of research dissemination and utilization in PEIR is accountability and effectiveness; for example, did the program perform as expected? If not, why not? If so, how so? What is the return on the investment of these funds with regard to promoting the best evidence-informed practices? Given the significant role of internal or external researchers, there is an expectation for compiling an easily accessible research report (including an executive summary). There is also the potential for pursuing journal publication that involves peer review and feedback on the merits of both the methods used and the findings articulated, a level of rigor with respect to the review process rarely found in the community or agency.

Given the primary location of PR inside human service organizations, research dissemination and utilization often require organizational support and resources. This level of support ranges from providing meeting times for sharing findings to engaging senior staff, including staff development managers, in discussions about the resources needed to address the potential use of the findings. For example, if the findings point in the direction of improving specific services by modifying organizational structures or procedures, then senior management leadership is needed along with the resources to make the necessary changes and provide the related staff training needed to implement the change successfully. On the other hand, if the findings suggest, for example, that service providers need to modify their own practices in order to improve services that take into account a new role for service users, then job descriptions may need to be redesigned along with the creation of opportunities for career advancement and training for both service providers and service users.

Common Research Methods: Knowledge Development

Although each research framework provides opportunities for promoting knowledge development, the strategies that are implemented may take different forms. If there is a commitment to fostering a learning community inside an organization, as well as in the community at large, then knowledge sharing and codifying may differ. For example, given one of the major objectives of PAR that involves taking action, the knowledge derived from the research often needs to be applied, frequently in the form of sociopolitical action and community organizing. The broader goal may involve community change over time, and the results of a PAR study can provide a blueprint or pathway to inform the change process.

In contrast, PEIR tends to focus more internally on organizational change. The research could inform the process of redesigning services, provide the foundation for expanded funding, and/or stimulate more organization-wide strategic planning designed to provide the foundation for future directions. In addition to organizational change based on program evaluation, interventive research related to individual, family, or group treatment may call for a redesign of practices carried out by service providers. These practices could include organizational policies and procedures, rethinking the skill sets of service providers, and/or raising questions related to the role of "manualized" interventions built upon behavioral intervention principles.

And finally, the knowledge-development role of PR can be viewed from several perspectives. First, PR might shed new light on the role of theory in informing practice; for example, how do theories of adolescent development and behavior inform the current practices related to serving youth? Is the knowledge base sufficiently interdisciplinary? How does practice reflect the bi-directional impact of the social environment on human behavior and the impact of human behavior on the social environment? To what extent do current practices by service providers reflect policy-informed practice where an in-depth knowledge of public policies is balanced with an understanding of policy practice needed to advocate for policy change? Similar questions can be raised by the importance of research-minded practice (e.g., To what extent does research evidence on innovative practice inform current agency practice? or How does current research on the intersectionality of race, gender, sexual orientation, age, and ability inform practice?).

Second, an even more challenging aspect of knowledge development relates to the limited history of practice research informing theory, either explanatory theory (client behavior) or interventive theory (practitioner processes) (Briar & Miller, 1971). For example, does the PR related to serving isolated frail elderly suffering from neglect or abuse help us modify the explanatory theories related to human behavior and the social environment when it comes to the changing needs of the elderly? Or do our PR findings on stabilizing poor families modify our interventive theories related to practices needed to serve those suffering from problems related to housing, employment, child care, health care, and education?

All three research frameworks call for knowledge sharing and seek to inform various types of decision-making. Although the frameworks are theory-informed in a broad sense (e.g., PAR in terms of community development theory, PEIR in terms of organizational impact/outcome theory, and PR in terms of practice or interventive theory), most of them do not lead to the development of theory that is needed to advance knowledge across communities and organizations.

SHARED CHARACTERISTICS

This section describes a cross-framework assessment that identifies shared principles, challenges, and success factors related to PAR, PEIR, and PR.

Shared Principles

The three frameworks reflect an array of partnership principles that range from ensuring the informed consent of the research subjects to seeking shared involvement in the research design and implementation processes. The continuum includes the generally passive response to complying with human subject protocols (PEIR) to the active response of becoming "co-researchers" (PAR & PR). In addition to the different role that partnerships play in the three methods, there is an underlying principle of capacity-building. Each framework reflects a willingness to address complex problems that rarely include easy solutions by engaging individuals with various forms of expertise (e.g., service provider, service user, researcher). Implicit in each framework are commitments to building a capacity to support shared learning and the potential for change over time.

Another shared principle relates to promoting knowledge development related to local problem-solving and the improvement of conditions and services. The frameworks support the promotion of evidence-informed actions and practices by pursuing "actionable" knowledge to address community problems, program improvements, intervention efficacy, and organizational practices.

Shared Process Challenges

These frameworks also share similar challenges; namely, identifying collaborative partners with different perspectives to participate in the research, as well as making sure that the study participants are both diverse and representative of the larger population affected. In a similar way, the frameworks reflect the capacity to incorporate the different views of the research participants, more directly in PR and PAR and more indirectly as research respondents in PEIR.

A central process challenge relates to managing group dynamics, especially efforts to overcome the traditional power dynamics that feature the dominance of research expertise over all other participants.

Many group involvement processes include the following: (1) engaging in shared goal setting for the research; (2) building trust among the stakeholders; (3) sharing leadership roles among the stakeholders; (4) defining/utilizing conflict resolution processes (often related to specifying shared norms or rules of engagement); (5) clarifying decision-making processes as well as after-action review debriefing processes where everyone can view the research process in retrospect (Hengeveld-Bidmon, 2015); and (6) addressing the multiple issues underlying intersectionality with respect to the issues of race, gender, age, sexual orientation, and abilities.

And finally, one of the biggest process challenges relates to managing expectations. For researchers, engaging in community scholarship takes time that may conflict with gaining tenure and advancing one's career. Similarly, community participants as well as service providers often want to see results of their participation in far shorter time frames than may be feasible when carrying out applied research. In addition, the considerable investment of time needed to form and manage research partnerships may challenge the patience of most stakeholders where different expectations can lead to varying degrees of frustration.

Beyond the expectations associated with time, stakeholder expectations also may vary with regard to outcomes; namely, researchers value the final report and future publications, practitioners value the report's brief Executive Summary, senior managers and policymakers often look for specific recommendations for change, and service users look for visible examples of changed policies, procedures, and practices. The dynamics of managing the expectations associated with each of the frameworks, as well as with stakeholder groups, would benefit from more research attention.

Shared Methodological Challenges

Multiple challenges appear at the beginning and end of the research enterprise as well as throughout the process. One of the most powerful challenges relates to the process of dealing with environmental forces. These forces include: (1) changing social and political dynamics in communities that can directly impact the implementation of the research process (e.g., changes in political or organizational leadership that impact prior commitments); (2) locating broad-based support in the midst of competing institutional and community demands on time and resources (both staff time and funding); and (3) managing the expectations and demands of funding institutions, especially demonstrating how the benefits derived from the research justify the costs. Some of the internal forces include dealing with resistance to change emerging from the research findings and identifying the most effective communication tools to promote action and policy changes based on operationalizing research-based recommendations (e.g., "Just tell us what needs to change in our organization or community.").

Additional internal factors include the structuring of the research process, the limitations of data collection tools, and the challenges associated with specifying and disseminating findings. A central challenge related to determining the study design involves integrating the requirements imposed by the university's institutional review board (IRB) with agency priorities and constraints. These challenges often are heightened by the collective inability to fully specify all aspects of the research in the beginning of the process due to changes in resources and other sources of uncertainty (e.g., "We need flexibility to make adjustments if we can't locate the projected number of research subjects."). These factors internal to the research methods process are shaped by the challenges of integrating and interpreting data from multiple sources.

And finally, specifying the short-term and long-term outcomes of the research pose significant leadership challenges for those conducting applied research. In essence, the implementation of research findings often calls for additional research that can result in frustration for the various stakeholders, especially because knowledge building takes time. For example, the practice community can experience considerable frustration when they see research reports that appear equivocal (e.g., "On the one hand this finding could mean X, but on the other hand it could mean Y."). In addition, tools for effective research dissemination and utilization are needed. Beyond traditional research reporting formats, new methods are needed to transform research findings into multimedia information-sharing programs.

In summary, while many of the challenges shared by the various frameworks are viewed as common and manageable by experienced researchers, they may appear overwhelming for those with less experience. Therefore, it is important to identify the shared success factors that support the implementation of these applied research methods.

Shared Success Factors

An overview of success factors includes norms, competencies, and group decision-making. The following group process norms apply to any successful group, but they take on added significance when involving and negotiating with a diverse group of stakeholders participating in the research enterprise (Levi, 2017). Important norms for successful group functioning include: (1) active listening; (2) caring and openness to the views of others; (3) promoting inclusiveness, especially in the context of power differentials that reflect different types of expertise; (4) managing conflicts; (5) creating opportunities to participate; (6) fostering mutual respect and equality; and (7) supporting the processes of negotiating and compromising.

Many of these norms presume the existence of interpersonal competencies displayed by various stakeholders, including: (1) using understandable and respectful language (being aware of research jargon); (2) demonstrating the cultural humility required in a multicultural environment; (3) building on a prior history of effective working relationships; (4) possessing capacities to function in both formal and informal power structures; and (5) demonstrating the self-reflective capacities often needed to acknowledge mistakes (Ruch, Turney, & Ward, 2010).

Some of the core skills needed to promote the norms for successful group functioning include interpersonal competencies related to goal-setting, democratic decision-making, and community organizing. The process of identifying common goals and objectives often involves time-consuming efforts to maximize participation over time, so that participants feel engaged, rather than rushed, and are valued for their contributions to the goal-setting process. At the same time, participants need to see how democratic processes are being fostered in order to engage in shared decision-making. Many of these skills can be subsumed under effective community organizing practices for engaging internal and external stakeholders, while also assisting with the management of the research enterprise.

CONCLUSION

Multiple lessons can be learned from exploring the similarities and differences between practice research and the related methods of participatory action research and program evaluation, as well as intervention research. They share common research methods with respect to research question formulation, capturing existing literature as well as practice wisdom, data collection and analysis tools, and a focus on knowledge development.

The three research approaches also share common process challenges. These include challenges involved in developing principles related to partnership, stakeholder capacity building, systems change, problem-solving, service improvement, and the promotion of evidence-informed actions and practices. The differences are reflected in some of the research challenges related to sampling for diversity, managing power differences in groups, and managing expectations (time, outcomes, and relevance for various stakeholders). Other differences relate to the changing contexts of research in organizations and communities, managing the resistance to problematic findings, communicating the implications of findings, the limitations of funding and staff time to engage in research, and managing the expectations of research funders.

As Uggerhøj (2011a, 2011 b, 2014) has noted, PR has a specific interest in conducting research based on everyday social service issues articulated in a dialogue between researchers and practitioners/citizens and in the establishment of a collaborative process where findings are implemented into practice. The outcome of highly participatory and collaborative practice research includes the potential to increase the understanding of a specific subject, create more knowledge about practice, promote a change in practice, develop new tools and methods for practice, support a professional development learning process, and/or support a significant change in practice (Uggerhøj, Henriksen, & Andersen, 2018).

In summary, the three research approaches share common factors that contribute to success. These factors include: (1) norms for successful group functioning throughout the research process (inclusiveness, respect, negotiation, compromise, participation, active listening); (2) the array of interpersonal competencies needed to carry out the research (jargon-free language, cultural humility, relationship-building, ability to navigate power structures, and self-reflective capacity to acknowledge mistakes); and (3) the stakeholder competencies needed to complete a research project successfully (goal-setting, democratic decision-making, and community organizing).

Relationships to Other Chapters

This chapter builds upon the themes introduced in Chapter 1 by expanding the discussion of the central focus of practice research; namely, the nature of practice as viewed from the provider, service user, researcher, and policy perspectives. In a similar manner, the related research approaches (PAR and PEIR) benefit from the use of a research platform to negotiate different levels of involvement.

While this chapter builds upon previous chapters, it also informs subsequent chapters. For example, the participatory nature of service provider involvement also can be found in Chapter 10 on data-mining strategies where the worker-client issues raised by service users as well as service providers are captured in organizational case records. For those who are also research-minded practitioners, the case record provides evidence of the worker's curiosity about the service user's situation, the worker's capacities for self-reflection with regard to identifying effective strategies for intervention, and the role of critical thinking skills as described in Chapter 11.

And finally, in Chapter 12, it is possible to see the connection between educating service providers who are able to link intervention methods with research methods while also taking into account the role of service users. It includes a case vignette to demonstrate the applications of both practice principles and research methods principles as noted in this chapter.

REFERENCES

Briar, S., & Miller, H. (1971). *Problems and issues in social casework*. New York, NY: Columbia University Press.

Brun, C.F. (2013). *A practical guide to evaluation* (2nd ed.). New York, NY: Oxford University Press.

Creswell, J.W. (2015). *A concise introduction to mixed methods research*. Thousand Oaks, CA: Sage.

Dudley, J.R. (2013). *Social work evaluation* (2nd ed.). New York, NY: Oxford University Press.

Epstein, I. (2009). *Clinical data-mining: Integrating practice and research*. New York, NY: Oxford University Press.

Fraser, M.W., Richman, J.M., & Galinsky, M.J. (2009). *Intervention research: Developing social programs.* New York, NY: Oxford University Press.

Greenwood, D., & Levin, M. (2007). *Introduction to action research. Social research for social change.* Thousand Oaks, CA: Sage.

Grinnell, R.M., Gabor, P.A., & Unrau, Y.A. (2019). *Program evaluation for social workers* (8th ed.). New York, NY: Oxford University Press.

Hengeveld-Bidmon, E. (2015). *An after-action review of a research team: A teaching case.* Berkeley, CA: Mack Center on Nonprofit and Public Sector Management in the Human Services, School of Social Welfare University of California, Berkeley. Available at https://mackcenter.berkeley.edu/current-projects/guiding-organizational-change-casebook-executive-development-program-human-services

Israel, B.A., Eng, E., Schulz, A.J., & Parker, E.A. (2005). *Methods in community-based participatory research for health.* San Francisco, CA: Jossey-Bass Publishers.

Israel, B.A., Schultz, A.J., Parker, E.A., & Becker, A.B. (1998). Review of community-based research: Assessing partnership approaches to improve public health. *Annual Review of Public Health, 19,* 173–202.

Lawson, H.A., Caringi, J.C., Pyles, L., Jurkowsi, J.M., & Bozlak, C.T. (2015). *Participatory action research.* New York, NY: Oxford University Press.

Levi, D. (2017). *Group dynamics for teams* (5th ed.). Thousand Oaks, CA: Sage.

Minkler, M. (2000). Using participatory action research to build healthy communities. *Public Health Reports, 115* (2/3), 191–197.

Minkler, M., & Wallerstein, N. (2008). *Community-based participatory research for health: From processes to outcomes* (2nd ed.). San Francisco, CA: Jossey-Bass.

Padgett, D. (2008). *Qualitative methods in social work research* (2nd ed.). Thousand Oaks, CA: Sage.

Patton, M.Q. (2018). *Facilitating evaluation: Principles in practice.* Thousand Oaks, CA: Sage.

Patton, M.Q. (2011). *Developmental evaluation: Applying complexity concepts to enhance innovation and use.* New York, NY: Guilford Press.

Reason, P., & Bradbury, H. (2006). *Handbook of action research.* London: Sage.

Ruch, G., Turney, D., & Ward, A. (Eds.) (2010). *Relationship-based social work: Getting to the heart of practice.* London: Jessica Kingsley Publisher.

Smith, M.J. (2010). *Handbook of program evaluation for social work and health professionals.* New York, NY: Oxford University Press.

Solomon, B., Cavanagh, M., & Draine, J. (2009). *Random control trials: Design and implementation of community-based psychosocial interventions.* New York, NY: Oxford University Press.

Sweeney, A., Beresford, P., Faulkner, A., Nettle, M., & Rose, D. (Eds.) (2009). *This is survivor research*. Ross-on-Wye, UK: PCCS Books.

Uggerhøj, L. (2011a). What is practice research in social work & definitions, barriers and possibilities. *Social Work & Society, 9*(1), 45–59.

Uggerhøj, L. (2011b). Theorizing practice research in social work. *Social Work and Social Sciences Review, 15*(1), 49–73.

Uggerhøj, L. (2014). Learning from each other—Collaboration processes in practice research. *Nordic Social Work Research, 4*(sup 1), 44–57.

Uggerhøj, L., Henriksen, K., & Andersen, M.L. (2018). Participatory practice research and action research: Birds of a feather? *China Journal of Social Work, 11*(2), 186–201.

Wholey, J.S., Hatry, H.P., & Newcomer, K.E. (1994). *Handbook of practical program evaluation*. San Francisco, CA: Jossey-Bass Publishers.

10

Using Qualitative Data Mining for Practice Research in Child Welfare*

As practice research evolves, it incorporates increasingly complex and context-specific methods for knowledge development. As described in Chapter 5, qualitative data mining is a key example of an emerging practice research methodology. This chapter provides a more in-depth discussion of the methodology. It provides the social policy context of child welfare practice along with the role of a practice research platform described in Chapter 1. In addition to describing seven major steps for conducting practice research using case records extracted from agency databases, it maps the complex nature of child welfare practice and provides directions for using the outcome of this form of practice research.

---

* Adapted from the original: Henry, C., Carnochan, S., & Austin, M. (2014). Using qualitative data-mining for practice research in child welfare. *Child Welfare*, 93(6), 7–26.

CHILD WELFARE CONTEXT

In their daily practice, social service providers routinely collect and record large quantities of data about client characteristics, practice interventions, and client outcomes (Epstein, 2002, 2009). Although documentation of service activities is not new to child welfare (CW), over the past 30 years, federal legislation, including the Adoption Assistance and Child Welfare Act (P.L. 96-272) and the Adoption and Safe Families Act (P.L. 105-89), has promoted increased attention to documentation in CW. Consequently, administrative CW data has proliferated and administrative data systems (ADS) have made these data more accessible to researchers.

To date, the majority of studies using administrative CW data have focused on the quantitative categorical data stored in ADS (see Conn et al., 2013; Putnam-Hornstein & Needell, 2011). Quantitative data help researchers and CW administrators identify rates of reported and substantiated child maltreatment, detect corresponding risk factors, or categorize service responses. The mining of these data teaches us about the kinds of maltreatment, placements, and services experienced by children referred to CW systems; identifies the frequency of these experiences; and can be used to make predictions about which children will return home and which will remain in care. These quantitative data, however, tell us little about how CW workers define maltreatment, why children referred to CW systems are placed in specific settings, or how children and families engage in services. These latter questions are better answered through the mining and analysis of qualitative data stored in case records as part of the ADS.

Qualitative Data Mining (QDM), the mining of the narrative text contained in documents stored in ADS (e.g., risk assessments, investigative narratives, court reports, and contact notes), provides CW researchers with a unique opportunity to use existing data to examine CW practice (Epstein, 2002, 2009). Use of QDM to improve CW has received limited attention (Epstein, 2002; Tice, 1998), given that few CW studies have focused on the qualitative data stored in CW ADS or described how qualitative data is used by CW researchers (for exceptions, see Coohey, 2007; Cordero, 2004; Cross, Koh, Rolock, & Eblen-Manning, 2013; Henry, 2014). This chapter seeks to fill this gap by describing how researchers can use QDM techniques to create rich databases for qualitative CW research and answer unique questions about CW clients and practice. In a seven-step guide, the chapter summarizes QDM strategies and methods and reports on the work of a Child Welfare Qualitative Data Mining (CWQDM) Project to illustrate these methods and strategies. The chapter concludes with a discussion of how QDM can be used to enhance CW practice, research, and education.

PROJECT BACKGROUND

The CWQDM Project was developed in the context of a longstanding practice-research partnership between a university-based research center and a regional social services consortium involving the directors of 12 county social service agencies, the deans and directors of five graduate social work programs, and executive staff representing a local foundation (Austin et al., 1999). It was designed in response to agency interests in developing their capacity to engage in QDM in CW. One county agency agreed to participate as the pilot site for the project. With our agency partner, the CWQDM Project sought to: (1) create a CW database that could be used to examine CW practice, client needs, and emerging issues in the field; and (2) develop QDM techniques that could be replicated by other CW agencies and research partners.

CHILD WELFARE QUALITATIVE DATA MINING STEPS

In this section, we describe the specific actions and processes that we developed to carry out the CWQDM Project and, in seven steps, outline how CW researchers can use QDM to create retrospective databases for practice research. The description of each step includes a summary of major lessons learned and a discussion of the relevant literature.

Step 1: Build (or Build on) a University-Agency Partnership

Qualitative Data Mining requires a strong working relationship between university and agency partners. Trust, commitment, engaged leadership, and expertise are fundamental requirements, given the sensitivity and complexity of CW data and the substantial investment of time and effort required to complete a QDM project. Projects should be of mutual interest, relevant to current practice, and provide equivalent benefits to both parties.

The development and success of the CWQDM Project was enhanced by the trust fostered through the regional consortium, shared research interests, and the intersecting areas of expertise among agency and university staff. The agency had a strong research and evaluation unit with expertise in CW research, policy, and practice. Members of the university research team had significant experience conducting CW research and were familiar with the CW practice context from prior work in the field.

Step 2: Identifying Mutual Goals and Developing Practice Research Questions

University and agency partners need to identify mutual goals and work together to agree upon practice research questions. Even when there is agreement on research and practice goals, the best way to achieve these goals may be contested or limited by university and agency resources. Further, the type of qualitative data available in ADS will shape the kinds of questions that can be answered and the ability of the group to meet its identified goals. Before the university and agency can proceed with their project, the agency must provide an overview of the types of data available and the university must help the agency to understand what types of questions can be answered with these data.

Agency partners typically want to explore ways to enhance practice; increase efficiency; and meet state and federal child, safety, and permanency goals (Austin et al., 1999). University partners typically share the agency's goal of enhancing practice and improving performance outcomes, but will have the added goal of contributing to the child welfare knowledge base through presentations, publications, and academic instruction. It is essential that all goals are articulated and agreed upon at the start of the project to ensure that goals are met, and that the project maintains ongoing support from all parties.

Once mutual goals are identified, specific research questions must be developed and agreed upon. In QDM, as a form of practice research, these questions should emerge from the field. Agency partners are particularly well situated to identify research questions pertinent to the field in general and their agency specifically. University partners are particularly good at identifying what is already known, noting gaps in the literature, and helping agency partners to develop researchable questions.

As noted above, our project sought to build a CW database to examine CW practice. As an exploratory project, the research questions were framed broadly. Although the agency partners identified specific questions to pursue, such as the alignment between presenting problems and case plan development, the agency was willing to "let these data speak to us." The university partners identified research questions that were important to the national field of practice. Both partners agreed to letthe data inform an increased understanding of what QDM could teach us about CW practice.

Step 3: Identifying Practice and Research Concerns

Concerns may arise early on about agency needs related to allocation of resources, data security, confidentiality, and dissemination of research findings. These concerns need to be addressed from the outset of the project.

Balancing practice and research needs
Qualitative research in CW can be intrusive, requiring direct access to key informants for interviews, surveys, or observations in the agency or in the field. These methods can yield rich practice data, but they also can be disruptive to daily practice and divert practitioners from meeting client needs. Alternatively, QDM offers a means of examining CW in a manner less intrusive to daily practice (Epstein, 2009). QDM does require time from some CW personnel; however, this time can be fairly limited and is called for mostly at the start and finish of the projects. At the outset, agency administrators and staff are called upon to orient university researchers to the ADS, develop information-sharing agreements between the agency and the university, provide a policy and practice context for the researchers, work with university researchers to develop research questions and goals, assist with sampling, and facilitate data access.

In this project, the burden on administrators and line staff was limited, in large part because of the relationship established through the regional consortium. Members of the agency's research unit served as natural partners. Their prior work with the consortium, coupled with their own interest and expertise in CW research, ensured that there would be adequate levels of support for the project. The familiarity of the university researchers with CW policies, practices, procedures, the regional practice context, CW acronyms, and the agency's ADS also reduced the burden on agency personnel.

Confidentiality and data security

QDM raises significant concerns about client and agency confidentiality. Qualitative data contained in CW data systems are highly sensitive, often detailing personal information about vulnerable populations. In addition, qualitative data capture the daily practice of CW staff and the difficult decisions they must make. Although these data can highlight client strengths, resilience, and progress as well as skillful CW practice, these data also reveal client challenges when subjecting agencies and their practices to scrutiny. Consequently, agencies may have concerns about how researchers will: (1) protect the confidentiality of clients and staff, neither of whom have consented to participating in the research; and (2) protect the confidentiality of the agency. Given these concerns, the researcher must develop a research protocol that protects the confidentiality of all parties and ensures that data retrieved from the ADS are secure. These research protocols are reviewed and approved by institutional review boards (IRB) at the university level as well as by the agency and/or local courts.

Before beginning this project, all confidentiality and data security protocols were reviewed and approved by the university's IRB. Data security measures and confidentiality protections are described below. Data protocols also were approved by the agency's executive director and CW director, as well as by the director of the agency's research unit. Members of the university research team completed the agency's confidentiality ethics training before accessing data.

Dissemination of research

The dissemination of findings needs to balance client and agency confidentiality interests with the desire of researchers to share findings with the larger field. Although IRBs require researchers to protect the confidentiality of their subjects and to provide detailed plans about how confidentiality will be maintained (including when the findings are being disseminated), the research and agency partners need to develop their own plan about how knowledge generated from the collaboration will be shared. Issues surrounding data ownership and dissemination of findings need to be addressed early in the research process, often in an explicit protocol or memorandum of understanding. For this project, the partners agreed that the agency would play an instrumental role in deciding which analyses to pursue, and that all substantive findings emerging from the project would be reviewed by the agency before publication. Agency and university researchers agreed that whenever possible, findings would be presented together with staff and publications would be coauthored.

Step 4: Identifying Qualitative Data Sources and Assessing Data

Working with administrative CW data is often messy (Epstein, 2009). When data are collected specifically for research purposes, they need to be organized in a logical manner so that questions that researchers want answered are asked, and data are recorded and stored in a way that facilitates analysis. In contrast, administrative CW data may be stored across multiple paper files, handwritten notes may be illegible, and important pieces of data (e.g., key documents and demographic data) may be missing. Increasingly, however, CW agencies rely on ADS to document their daily practice and to organize client information (Courtney & Collins, 1994; English, Brandford, & Coghlan, 2000). Researchers can now access most records from agency computers or even offsite from university offices.

Technological advances make it easier for researchers to access administrative qualitative data and to securely export these data to the cloud for offsite analysis. However, because these agency data were not created for research, researchers must take time to assess the quality of potential data sources (e.g., CW documents). Working with the agency partner is essential; agency staff can identify the richest data in the administrative data system (ADS) as well as explain the purpose of the data (e.g., data created during the life of a case and/or mandated data that are likely to be present in all records).

Once the researcher has become familiar with the types of data available in the ADS, the researcher and agency need to work together to *map* these data onto CW practice. The specific components of CW practice differ across agencies, but most agency practice follows a similar flow. By specifying aspects of practice under study as well as the data sources in the ADS that correspond to those practices, researchers are able to determine which data sources to review. In our mapping of these data (see Figure 10.1) we were able to work with our agency partners to

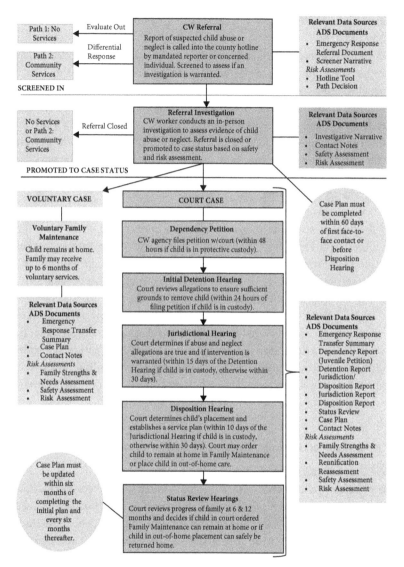

Figure 10.1. Mapping child welfare process and data sources.
Adapted with permission from Reed & Karpilow, 2009.

identify key data sources in the ADS that captured relevant aspects of CW practice.

After completing the mapping of data sources, the researcher needs to assess the quality of each source. To facilitate this review, the agency provides the researcher with access to a sample of electronic case records. In our experience, this initial review can take place over one to two days and does not require the removal or extraction of any data from the agency. It is helpful to have staff available during the review who can answer questions about how to navigate the ADS, the purpose of different data sources within the ADS, and how these data sources have changed over time.

When reviewing qualitative data, the researcher needs answers to the following questions: (1) Are data captured in narrative form (e.g., "The mother reported being struck with a closed fist.") or as checked boxes (e.g., "Domestic violence in home?—yes/no")? (2) Are there enough data to discern meaning? (3) Does data contained in one data source consistently show up in another (e.g., are narratives from the initial investigation copied into subsequent court reports?)? If so, can fewer data sources be examined? and (4) What is missing from these data sources? That is, what else does the researcher need to know about the practice context in order to accurately interpret these data? During this initial review it is important to note the format of each data source (text or image) that can affect how data are later extracted, stored, and coded.

Step 5: Secure Data Extraction, Storage, and Database Creation

Although data can be analyzed at the agency, onsite analysis can be disruptive to agency processes, taxing on limited agency resources, and may not be practical for the researcher. Instead, it may be easier to store and analyze data offsite. The extraction and migration of these data requires the development of protocols for data extraction and storage security. Electronic data can be copied, encrypted, password-protected, and securely transported on external hard drives to universities for secure storage and analysis. Alternatively, newer analytical software programs, such as Dedoose© (www.dedoose.com) allow electronic data to be exported to secure cloud-based servers that can be accessed by researchers later. These cloud-based servers typically incorporate several levels of physical and electronic security measures designed to protect data and secure IRB approval.

In an effort to minimize our impact on agency operations, we extracted and exported data to a secure cloud-based server. After working with our agency partners to select a stratified random sample of case records from the ADS, we developed an extraction manual that guided our research team through the ADS. The data extraction manual guided research team members to specific data sources (identified through our prior mapping) and provided detailed descriptions on how to extract and label each data source. This process included the assignment of unique research identification numbers to each case record and file naming conventions for each data source. The systematic labeling of case records and data sources at the time of extraction enabled researchers to organize data for later analysis. The process ensures that: (1) all data sources are tied to a specific case record and can be identified through a unique research identification number; (2) the types of data sources associated with each case record can be identified without the researcher having to review the narrative text; and (3) the data sources can be sorted chronologically to aid future analysis. For our project, file-naming conventions included a unique research identification number, the date of the data source extraction from the ADS, and an abbreviation of the types of data sources.

Over the course of five days, our research team extracted over 1,500 data sources from the agency's ADS. These qualitative data sources were linked later to the quantitative data previously provided by the agency through the research identification number assigned to each record. This created a CW database that could be used for mixed methods analyses. Just as ADS provide CW agencies with a means of organizing case records and corresponding documents for practice, our data extraction protocols and data linkages allowed us to create a CW database that organizes case records and corresponding data sources for practice research.

Step 6: Generating Practice Knowledge: Analytical Strategies

The first five steps provided the foundation for a CW database for examining CW practice, client needs, and emerging issues in the field. Equally important was the development of analytical techniques to examine and

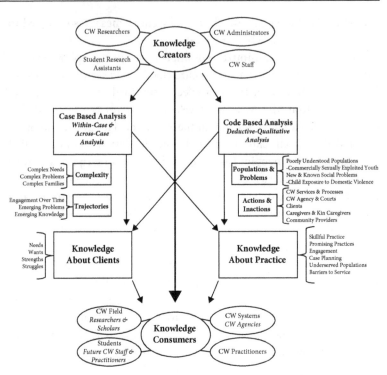

Figure 10.2. Knowledge for child welfare practice: What we can learn from QDM.

understand these data. Researchers can choose from a range of qualitative analytic approaches (Miles, Huberman, & Saldaña, 2013). The analytic approach selected should relate to the type of research questions or the overarching goal of the project.

We adopted two primary data analysis strategies, *code-based analysis* and *case-based analysis*. Both strategies were employed simultaneously, and both offered different insights into how QDM might be used to inform CW practice (see Figure 10.2).

Code-based analysis

Code-based analysis was employed to gain a better understanding of the types of phenomena that were captured in the CW database. Although grounded theory suggests that researchers enter the field, or approach the text, with "an open mind" and let problems and themes emerge through open-coding (Glaser, 1992, p. 23), Gilgun (2005, p. 42) argues that researchers and practitioners should not have to "forsake well-formulated conceptual models" when engaging in qualitative research.

Instead, Gilgun (2005) suggests that researchers employ what she has coined, "deductive-qualitative analysis," which encourages researchers to develop preliminary deductive codes based on their preexisting knowledge or conceptual models and then develop additional inductive codes through open-coding of data. Using this analytic approach, our research team developed a preliminary deductive codebook based on Belsky's (1980) ecological framework for child maltreatment. This framework conceptualizes child maltreatment as a "social-psychological phenomenon" that is determined by forces at work in the individual, the family, the community, and the culture (Belsky, 1980, p. 320).

The research team piloted the preliminary codebook through review of the data sources for a small sample of case records. Consensus was reached among the research group members that the codes included in the codebook reflected phenomena observed in the data. During this initial review and subsequent reviews, new codes were identified through inductive open-coding. These codes captured CW services and processes, actions and inactions, unique social problems (e.g., child exposure to domestic violence) and information about the experiences of poorly understood populations (e.g., commercially sexually exploited youth) (see Figure 10.2). During a four-month period the codebook was revised through an iterative process that generated over 65 unique codes nested under 12 broad themes.

The coding of these data mapped the types of phenomena captured in the CW database. Each code can be used as an entry point into the database for future in-depth analyses. For example, in our coding we identified and labeled all narrative data related to the experiences of kin caregivers. Additional analyses could examine how CW staff collaborate with kin caregivers to support children and birth families and the role this cooperation plays in establishing permanency for youth. These types of code-based analyses enable us to identify patterns that are common within a subset or across all CW cases. Building on these patterns, we can develop hypotheses for later testing. In addition, where categorical quantitative data are not available, code-based analyses can be used to estimate the prevalence of a specific phenomenon. This is particularly useful for capturing emerging social problems.

Case-based analysis

While coding these data, our research team simultaneously engaged in case-based analysis. We used a within-case analysis approach, the goal of which is to "describe, understand, and explain what has happened in a single, bounded context" (i.e., the case or site) (Miles et al., 2013, p. 100). We used a prestructured case outline to summarize key aspects of each case in the database. The close reading required for our code-based analysis ensured that case summaries captured more consistent and accurate data across all cases. We began by reviewing all qualitative data sources associated with a single case. From this review we then developed a summary of the case that included: (1) a description of child and family characteristics; (2) an overview of key stakeholders, their relationship to the child, and initial and emerging problems; and (3) a summary of case events. In addition, the summary included a detailed timeline of significant events and the reviewer's critical reflections on the case.

Cross-case analysis

A cross-case form of analysis (Miles et al., 2013) also can be employed to explore the inherent complexity of CW practice and the common and divergent trajectories of cases over time (see Figure 10.2). Cross-case analyses "increase generalizability" and ensure that "events and processes in one well-described setting are not wholly idiosyncratic" (Miles et al., 2013, p. 101). Analyses of similarities and differences within and across cases can expand our understanding of client needs and the ways that individual CW practice is shaped by the local, state, and federal contexts.

Analysis and review

After a multi-day training on the qualitative analytic software, codebook structure and application, and case summaries, each member of the research team was assigned a unique set of CW cases to code and summarize. Initial coding and summarizing were carried out in a conference room space in order for the research leaders to be available to respond to coding and summary questions as they arose. Throughout the duration of the project each member of the research team was encouraged to conduct analysis in a space shared with other team members to facilitate ongoing discussion of code application and enhance intercoder reliability (MacQueen, McLellan, Kay, & Milsten, 1998). Throughout the analytic process the project leaders reviewed and edited case summaries for completeness and clarity.

Qualitative methodologists suggest that researchers check their preliminary findings with key informants during the research process (Guba & Lincoln, 1989). Throughout our project we discussed our research process and analytical frameworks with members of the regional consortium and agency partners. Agency research staff reviewed preliminary codebooks, provided policy insights, clarified the meaning of local terminology and acronyms, and encouraged team members to further analyze themes that were of particular importance to agency practice. We provided interim reports and presentations to agency staff to gain their feedback on (1) the patterns and themes we had identified, (2) the case summaries we had generated, and (3) their relevance and utility for practice. This "member-checking" (Guba & Lincoln, 1989) served to validate the findings and also helped to identify emerging practice research directions worth pursuing given the available data in the CW database and the CW needs in the region.

Step 7: Generating Practice Knowledge: Dissemination of Findings

Dissemination of the knowledge generated through QDM can be accomplished in several ways. Dissemination to CW agencies may involve internal reports, conversations with CW administrators, or presentations to staff. Dissemination to the field of child welfare includes academic instruction, government reports, conference presentations, and publication in academic or professional journals.

Child welfare databases and the qualitative analyses that emerge from these databases also can serve as valuable training tools for CW staff. CW staff rarely have the opportunity to read an entire case record; notable exceptions include rare critical incident reviews and periodic case record review processes conducted for compliance purposes (Carnochan, Samples, Lawson, & Austin, 2013; Douglas & McCarthy, 2011; The Children's Services Outcomes and Accountability Bureau & The Office of Child Abuse Prevention, 2014). Generation of case summaries and cross-case analyses from CW databases allow CW staff to examine how other staff meet client needs and how cases unfold over time. Review of these summaries can help staff to identify promising practices and areas for improvement. In addition, researchers can make CW databases available to partner agencies or other CW agencies so they can conduct their own analyses or use the data for training purposes.

QDM and CW database creation also can be used to educate future CW staff or others in the helping professions. For example, by recruiting and training graduate social work student research assistants to help with the extraction, organization, and analysis of qualitative CW data, our project served to familiarize future social workers with QDM, ADS, client needs, promising practices, and the complexity of CW. Many students used the database and case summaries generated by the CWQDM Project to carry out their own master's-level research projects (see Figure 10.2). The high level of student interest in reviewing extensive case records led to the development of a casebook of teaching cases for pre-service university education programs and in-service agency staff development programs (Carnochan, Molinar, Brown, Botzler, Gunderson, Henry, & Austin, 2019).

Discussion

Qualitative data mining offers CW researchers and agencies a relatively nonintrusive means of examining CW practices and services. It generates new knowledge about CW clients and practice that cannot be gleaned from quantitative data alone. Unlike other qualitative methods (e.g., surveys, interviews, and participant observation that only capture data from selected research participants), QDM offers researchers the potential to capture the practice experiences of a wide range of CW staff and clients (Epstein, 2009). With respect to clients, QDM allows us to gain a more nuanced understanding of CW populations, particularly the prevalence of new and known social problems, poorly understood subpopulations, and complex client needs. Regarding practice, QDM provides new insights into: (1) promising practices, (2) case trajectories, (3) case planning; (4) defining and responding to parental acts and omissions; and (5) the enhancement of child safety, permanency, and well-being in daily practice (see Figure 10.2).

Despite its utility, QDM also raises critical challenges with respect to the complexity, trustworthiness, volume, and sensitivity of the qualitative data contained in ADS. The complexity and trustworthiness of these data relate in part to the presence and absence of multiple perspectives captured in data sources over time, as well as missing data. The data for each case are entered into ADS by multiple CW staff members over time, resulting in a case record that reflects multiple perspectives. When these perspectives identify similar client strengths and needs or effective interventions, the trustworthiness of the data may be enhanced (Creswell & Clark, 2006). However, all data contained in ADS are filtered through the CW staff perspective. Data stored in ADS describe maltreating behaviors, client needs and wants, and services rendered. And yet all of these data, even when recorded in the client's voice, reflect what CW staff saw, heard, or were told and may not accurately represent events or the perspectives of those outside the agency. Although similar narratives by CW staff may not point to a full picture of a client, the case descriptions may illustrate how client identities are similarly constructed by staff (Swift, 1995; Tice, 1998). In addition, important data may not be recorded in the ADS; as a result, critical knowledge about practice and clients may be missing.

The complexity of these data is intensified by their sheer volume. Data often capture CW practice across years; narrative text recorded in one data source is often copied into another; and data are often not recorded by staff in-vivo, making it difficult for the researcher to piece together a linear account. Coding these data in a reliable manner presents challenges for research teams. Although codebooks, consensus-based coding, qualitative analytic software (e.g., Dedoose©, Atlas TI©), and automated text analysis (e.g., Python©) help to improve intercoder reliability (Miles et al., 2013), the volume of these data poses significant challenges.

Data contained in ADS are highly sensitive, and the use of these data for research purposes presents threats to confidentiality. Although data can highlight promising CW practices, the practices and experiences recorded in ADS could place agencies at risk of community censure, legal liability, or fiscal sanctions and could serve to stigmatize both CW workers and clients. The strategies to protect confidentiality through the use of de-identification include algorithmic methods used in conjunction with researcher review to locate and modify identifying data.

Despite these challenges, QDM offers substantial knowledge building opportunities for CW agencies, researchers, and future CW staff. Through engagement in QDM, CW staff become both producers and consumers of practice knowledge (see Figure 10.2). Participation in this process and familiarity with these data may decrease staff resistance to the use of data reported in some studies and may enhance the importance that staff give to the documentation of practice (DeFraia, 2015; Hutson & Lichtiger, 2002). QDM, when done in partnership with CW agencies, provides researchers with an opportunity to utilize existing data to enhance agency practice and share new CW knowledge through publications seen by a national audience. QDM also offers future CW staff (i.e., students) an opportunity to better understand and generate CW knowledge. Engagement in QDM and qualitative analysis provide both current and future CW staff new skills to make meaning of complex data. Finally, QDM and the CW databases that can be constructed with these data offer CW researchers and agencies the ability to look beyond the quantitative data that describe basic caseload characteristics and performance outcomes in order to examine how CW agencies work to meet the complex needs of clients within the boundaries of daily practice.

REFERENCES

Austin, M.J., Martin, M., Carnochan, S., Goldberg, S., Duerr Berrick, J., Weiss, B., & Kelley, J. (1999). Building a comprehensive agency-university partnership. *Journal of Community Practice*, *6*(3), 89–106. http://doi.org/10.1300/J125v06n03_05

Belsky, J. (1980). Child maltreatment: An ecological integration. *American Psychologist*, *35*(4), 320–335. http://doi.org/10.1037/0003-066X.35.4.320

Carnochan, S., Molinar, L, Brown, J., Botzler, L., Gunderson, K., Henry, C., & Austin, M.J. (2019). *Public child welfare: A casebook for learning and teaching*. San Diego, CA: Cognella Academic Publishing.

Carnochan, S., Samples, M., Lawson, J., & Austin, M.J. (2013). The context of child welfare performance measures. *Journal of Evidence-Based Social Work*, *10*(3), 147–160. http://doi.org/10.1080/15433714.2013.788946

Conn, A., Szilagyi, M., Franke, T., Albertin, C., Blumkin, A., & Szilagyi, P. (2013). Trends in child protection and out-of-home care. *Pediatrics*, *132*(4), 712–719. http://doi.org/10.1542/peds.2013-0969

Coohey, C. (2007). What criteria do child protective services investigators use to substantiate exposure to domestic violence? *Child Welfare*, *86*(4), 93–122.

Cordero, A. (2004). When family reunification workers: Data-mining foster care records. *Families in Society*, *85*(4), 571–580.

Courtney, M.E., & Collins, R.C. (1994). New challenges and opportunities in child welfare outcomes and information technologies. *Child Welfare, 73*(5), 359–378.

Creswell, J.W., & Clark, D.V.L.P. (2006). *Designing and conducting mixed methods research* (1st ed.). Thousand Oaks, CA: Sage Publications.

Cross, T.P., Koh, E., Rolock, N., & Eblen-Manning, J. (2013). Why do children experience multiple placement changes in foster care? Content analysis on reasons for instability. *Journal of Public Child Welfare, 7*(1), 39–58. http://doi.org/10.1080/15548732.2013.751300

DeFraia, G.S. (2015). Knowledge consumption to knowledge generation: Traveling the road of practitioner-conducted research. *Social Work in Mental Health, 13*(6), 515–531. http://doi.org/10.1080/15332985.2014.966883

Douglas, E.M., & McCarthy, S.C. (2011). Child fatality review teams: A content analysis of social policy. *Child Welfare, 90*(3), 91–110.

English, D.J., Brandford, C.C., & Coghlan, L. (2000). Data-based organizational change: The use of administrative data to improve child welfare programs and policy. *Child Welfare, 79*(5), 499–515.

Epstein, I. (2002). Using available clinical information in practice-based research. *Social Work in Health Care, 33*(3-4), 15–32. http://doi.org/10.1300/J010v33n03_03

Epstein, I. (2009). *Clinical data-mining: Integrating practice and research* (1st ed.). New York, NY: Oxford University Press.

Gilgun, J.F. (2005). Qualitative research and family psychology. *Journal of Family Psychology, 19*(1), 40–50. http://doi.org/10.1037/0893-3200.19.1.40

Glaser, B.G. (1992). *Basics of grounded theory analysis: Emergence vs. forcing.* Mill Valley, CA: Sociology Press.

Guba, E.G., & Lincoln, Y.S. (1989). *Fourth generation evaluation* (1st ed.). Newbury Park, CA: Sage Publications.

Henry, C. (2014). *Constructing maltreatment: An urban child welfare agency's response to child exposure to domestic violence* (Unpublished doctoral dissertation). University of California, Berkeley, CA.

Hutson, C., & Lichtiger, E. (2002). Mining clinical information in the utilization of social services. *Social Work in Health Care, 33*(3-4), 153–161. http://doi.org/10.1300/J010v33n03_10

MacQueen, K., McLellan, E., Kay, K., & Milsten, B. (1998). Codebook development for team-based qualitative analysis. *Field Methods, 10*(2), 31–36.

Miles, M.B., Huberman, A.M., & Saldaña, J. (2013). *Qualitative data analysis: A methods sourcebook* (3rd ed.). Thousand Oaks, CA: Sage Publications.

Putnam-Hornstein, E., & Needell, B. (2011). Predictors of child protective service contact between birth and age five: An examination of California's 2002 birth cohort. *Children and Youth Services Review, 33*(11), 2400–2407. http://doi.org/10.1016/j.childyouth.2011.07.010

Reed, D., & Karpilow, K. (2009). *Understanding the child welfare system in California: A primer for service providers and policymakers* (2nd ed.). Berkeley, CA: California Center for Research on Women and Families, a program of the Public Health Institute. Retrieved from http://phi.org

Swift, K. (1995). *Manufacturing "bad mothers": A critical perspective on child neglect*. Toronto, ON: University of Toronto Press.

The Children's Services Outcomes and Accountability Bureau, & The Office of Child Abuse Prevention. (2014). *California: Child and Family Services Review instruction manual. California Department of Social Services*. Retrieved from http://www.childsworld.ca.gov/res/pdf/CCFSRInstructionManual.pdf

Tice, K.W. (1998). *Tales of wayward girls and immoral women: Case records and the professionalization of social work*. Champaign: University of Illinois Press.

11

Building Organizational Supports for Research-minded Practitioners*

There are two major assumptions underlying the previous chapters that need more attention. First, since not all practitioners are interested in practice research, it is important to conceptualize the role of a "research-minded" practitioner who might be interested in participating in the process of practice research. Second, practitioners often expect organizational support for participating in something new and therefore it is helpful to identify the nature of such support. A third assumption relates to the aspirations of human service organizations to become learning organizations by building knowledge sharing systems within their structures that support the efforts of practitioners to engage in evidence-informed practice (Austin, Claassen, Vu, & Mizrahi, 2008).

This chapter addresses this new challenge by describing: (1) the emerging organizational context for evidence-informed practice, (2) an

* Adapted from the original: Austin, M.J., Dal Santo, T., & Lee, C. (2012). Building organizational supports for research-minded practitioners [Special issue]. *Journal of Evidence-based Social Work, 9*(1/2), 174–211.

evolving definition of the critical elements of a research-minded practitioner, (3) a beginning framework for conceptualizing relevant organizational supports, and (4) case examples of organizational supports provided by national organizations in the United Kingdom. The chapter concludes with an emerging set of lessons learned and questions to guide future practice research.

ORGANIZATIONAL CONTEXT

In this age of service accountability in the United States and the United Kingdom, increased attention is being given to measuring and assessing outcomes. This development has placed new pressures on managers and practitioners to specify service objectives and invest time and resources in measuring the outcomes of these objectives. The efforts to establish, expand, update, and refine information systems have been at the heart of this recent development. Although there has been considerable investment in this type of managerial infrastructure, there has been much less attention given to the presentation, dissemination, and utilization of the results coming out of these information systems. Monthly or quarterly reports on services have focused over time on outputs (e.g., how many clients served) and less on outcomes (e.g., level of change or improvement in client conditions). Even when outcome data is available, it is rarely presented in a form that practitioners can either understand or utilize to improve their practice.

At the same time that outcome measurement is being stressed, practitioners are being called upon to identify how evidence, either administrative data emerging from their agency information systems or evidence emerging from research centers, is being used to inform their practice. For some staff, the language of evidence-informed practice is viewed as another mandate from top management that needs to be accommodated. For others, the elements of evidence-informed practice have challenged them to look for new ways and promising practices that they might assess and incorporate into their own practice. In addition to these internal organizational dynamics, there is a growing interest (especially in the United Kingdom) to incorporate the voices of service users and care providers into the process of promoting evidence-informed practice. All of these new developments are creating a new climate in which to reassess organizational-staff relations as well as organizational-client relations (Hasenfeld, 1983).

One of the biggest challenges facing human service organizations is the proliferation of information from inside and outside the agency that needs to be managed if it is to be of use. The for-profit sector has the most experience in the area of knowledge management, and the application of this experience to the public sector is captured in the concept of knowledge sharing and knowledge transfer (Austin et al., 2008). The essential elements of knowledge sharing are the use of tacit and explicit knowledge; namely, the tacit knowledge stored in the minds of practitioners (often called practice wisdom) and the explicit knowledge reflected in organizational procedure manuals and the textbooks developed to prepare practitioners.

The concept of knowledge transfer relates to the substantial investment made by organizations in the on-the-job training of staff and the capacity to transfer new learning back to the workplace. Both knowledge sharing and knowledge transfer rely upon the capacities of intermediary organizations (e.g., universities, institutes, consortia) or intermediary units within organizations (e.g., research, policy, evaluation staff, or link officers) to effectively disseminate knowledge and promote utilization (Anthony & Austin, 2008; Graaf, McBeath, Lwin, Holmes, & Austin, 2017). In the light of the challenges presented by knowledge management, it is clear that very few of them can be addressed until human service organizations adopt the principles of a learning organization and reflect them in their mission, future directions, and practices modeled by senior management (Austin & Hopkins, 2004).

DEFINING THE RESEARCH-MINDED PRACTITIONER

The definition of the research-minded practitioner depends on who does the defining. If educators do the defining, it usually focuses on becoming knowledgeable research consumers (sometimes referred to as appraisal training in the context of agency training programs) and/or becoming a beginning social science researcher. If practitioners do the defining, the definition often includes aspects of the following as essential practitioner attributes: (1) a capacity to critically reflect on practice to develop researchable questions, (2) a capacity to be informed by knowledge and research related to social work values, and (3) a capacity to understand research designs and related methodologies in order to theorize about practice (Harrison & Humphreys, 1998).

The growth and support of a research-minded practitioner is often assumed to emerge as a result of attending research courses while pursuing professional education at the undergraduate and/or graduate level of a college or university where practitioners gain an overview of research methods and are encouraged to conduct research projects. Given the fact, however, that most research courses are taught without much attention to practice, many practitioners acquire either a limited appreciation of research or a negative perception of its relevance to practice. As a result, it often falls to the workplace and on-the-job learning experiences for practitioners to begin to value the use of data and see the value of research within an organizational practice context.

An example of a career trajectory of a research-minded practitioner is presented in Box 11.1. There are several important processes buried within such a trajectory, one of which is *curiosity* or *interest* in finding explanations for practice dilemmas:

> " . . . I increasingly found myself in a process of exploring research and thinking about methodological issues that were interesting, stimulating and empowering . . . the movement from being concrete to identifying patterns that are informed by previous knowledge and theories were very enlightening . . . my mind had been opened up and I was seeing practice and service delivery in a new light . . . "

Having a capacity to engage in *critical reflection* of one's practice also emerged as an important process:

> " . . . My feeling is that this intellectual work, required for evidence-informed practice can be very challenging for practitioners as it requires time and support to reflect and make judgments. Perhaps most challenging, the process raises questions about what you are doing and why (this uncertainty, in the first instance, can be quite overwhelming but it is part of the learning process that many practitioners are not exposed to) . . . "

In line with critically reflecting on one's practice, having a capacity to engage in *critical thinking* about available knowledge usually reflected

Box 11.1. A Case Vignette of Organizational Career Development Supports for On-the-Job Continuing Professional Education*

(1) Learning on the job following completion of professional education
   • Learning from other professionals through case conferences
   • Learning from a supervisor who encourages practitioners to be reflective about their practices in order to identify future learning needs
   • Being given assistance in making conscious the impact of one's professional knowledge and practice experience on service users
   • Learning from other members of a service team
   • Being made aware of learning opportunities, formal and informal, that could be pursued or self-directed
(2) Working in an organization that fosters learning by
   • Scheduling weekly staff development events in the form of an afternoon journal club, case discussion, in-house learning event, or research presentation
   • Promoting links with local university research centers
   • Using case scenarios that simulate real cases and provide staff a safe place to unpack the service issues
   • Receiving special assignments to develop a program and search out resources electronically and through networks (small-scale literature reviews)
   • Receiving support for conducting a needs assessment related to a client population or participating in a program evaluation
   • Given opportunities to consult with researchers to find resources related to a client population
(3) Providing support for pursuing further education (certificate or degree programs)
   • For example: "We were encouraged and coached to apply for a study fellowship through contacts with an academic researcher. I considered it because it was an exciting opportunity to work with researchers on a practice problem that I felt was important to our clients and for the opportunity to design a service that facilitated better client outcomes. Intellectually it was a huge opportunity and challenge as I increasingly found myself in a process of exploring research and thinking about methodological issues that were interesting, stimulating and empowering. I think it is interesting to reflect back on the links between my own intellectual curiosity, my practice concerns, the need for service design, my previous work experience, and exposure to critical and reflective thinking and the supportive organizational

systems and structures. I am not sure that if any of these elements were missing whether or not I would have found my way into the research arena. It was a very non-linear process that included a mix of several facilitative factors."

- Reviewing literature fosters increased opportunities to reflect on one's own practice.
- The process of analyzing data in which one moves from concrete description to analysis of aggregated data can be challenging and provide for much learning.
- Making the transition from viewing individual clients as unique to seeing common patterns in their behaviors and searching for similarities and differences and speculating on the reasons why these patterns occurred.
- For example: "This movement from the individual to the collective and the movement from being concrete to identifying patterns that are informed by previous knowledge and theories were very enlightening. My feeling is that this intellectual work, required for evidence-informed practice can be very challenging for practitioners as it requires time and support to reflect and make judgments. Perhaps most challenging, the process raises questions about what you are doing and why (this uncertainty, in the first instance, can be quite overwhelming but it is part of the learning process that many practitioners are not exposed to)."
- Pursuing doctoral education does not mean a commitment to an academic career when there are numerous opportunities in an agency to promote evidence-informed practice.
- For example: " I was totally inspired by my academic supervisor but I never for a moment thought I would be able intellectually, practically or financially to pursue a PhD. The issues of confidence and identity were pertinent here. In my mind at the time, someone who pursued a PhD was clever, had done well at the university, and was a good student prior to university enrollment. When I got the "research bug," my mind had been opened up and I was seeing practice and service delivery in a new light. I was questioning pretty much everything and my efforts to challenge common practices probably threatened some of my colleagues. I wanted my work to impact on practice—directly and immediately—but of course the relationship between evidence and practice is not straight forward and implementing research findings is most challenging."
- For example: "After my PhD, which I found to the most stimulating and challenging of processes, I was driven to undertake research that had a relevance to and currency with

practice. I took a job as a researcher in a social work research centre and worked there for four years as a contract researcher. However it continued to frustrate me that not enough of the research focused on practice. So when this position came up I saw it as a an opportunity to promote evidence-informed practice at strategic and operational levels by encouraging government to fund practitioners and managers to use research in a way that benefits their services and service users as well as expanding the use of technologies to increase access to knowledge and working with managers to see the value in it."

*Developed with the assistance of Dr. Rhoda MacRae, Institute for Research and Innovation in Social Services, Dundee, Scotland.

explicitly in the research literature is another important element of research-minded practice:

" . . . Making the transition from viewing individual clients as unique to seeing common patterns in their behaviors and searching for similarities and differences and speculating on the reasons why these patterns occurred . . . I was questioning pretty much everything and my efforts to challenge common practices probably threatened some of my colleagues . . . of course the relationship between evidence and practice is not straight forward and implementing research findings is most challenging."

These three elements of curiosity, reflection, and critical thinking are the focus of the next section, where they are examined further, especially in relationship to facilitating research-informed practice.

Exploring Curiosity and Interest

Curiosity is a mindset associated with asking questions, examining/manipulating interesting images/objects, reading exhaustively, and/or persisting on challenging tasks. The function of curiosity is to learn, explore, and immerse oneself in an interesting topic/event. Curiosity also serves a broader function of building knowledge and competence.

In the process of defining curiosity, Kashdan and Silvia (2008) note that curiosity can include the recognition, pursuit, and intense desire to explore novel, challenging, and uncertain events. It is an innate characteristic of humans that varies in its level of intensity but is always present to some degree (Harvey, Novicevic, Leonard, & Payne, 2007). To truly appreciate the importance of curiosity in nearly every area of human activity, it is important to examine its fundamental attributes. According to Loewenstein (1994), curiosity is voluntary, intense, transient, immediate, stimulus-bound, and varying in satisfaction. It is caused when focusing on a gap in one's knowledge. Curiosity also can result from a motivation to increase one's competence related to mastering one's environment (Deci, 1975).

Over a century of psychological study has resulted in several different models of curiosity. New, complex, and surprising things can activate a reward system related to exploring novel things (externally stimulated). There are at least four approaches to understanding curiosity: (1) *epistemic curiosity* (desire for knowledge); (2) *perceptual curiosity* (aroused by novel stimuli); (3) *specific curiosity* (desire for a particular piece of information); and (4) *diverse curiosity* (general seeking of stimulation) (Silvia, 2006, p. 33). Different situations can arouse curiosity as complex, novel, uncertain, and conflict-laden phenomena (Silvia, 2006, p.180).

Curiosity and interest also have been placed within the category of knowledge emotions (Keltner & Shiota, 2003) that are associated with learning and thinking as well as the building of knowledge, skills, relationships, and well-being (Kashdan & Steger, 2007). By connecting curiosity to interests, an appraisal model of curiosity can help to explain why people do not find the same things interesting, why interest changes dynamically over time, and why feelings of curiosity vary in response to similar events.

Kashdan, Rose, and Fincham (2004) further elaborated on curiosity as a knowledge emotion, proposing that curiosity is a "positive emotional-motivational system associated with the recognitions, pursuit, self-regulation of novel and challenging opportunities" (p. 291). This personal growth model of curiosity differs from motivation or cognitive models in that it assumes that curiosity stems from a person's interest in self-development. In this area of research, Litman and Jimerson (2004) have proposed that individual differences in curiosity can reflect either curiosity as a feeling of interest or as a frustration about not knowing something. As an emotional-motivational state, curiosity is complex in that its arousal can involve positive feelings of interest associated with the anticipation of learning something new, as well as relatively unpleasant feelings of uncertainty due to a lack of knowledge (Litman & Jimerson, 2004). Curiosity is aroused by novel questions, complex ideas, ambiguous statements, and unsolved problems, all of which may point to a "gap" in one's knowledge and reveal a discrepancy between that which one knows and desires to know (Litman & Spielberger, 2003, Loewenstein, 1994). It has become increasingly clear that curiosity is influenced by both situation and disposition where situational interventions can stimulate a disposition to satisfy one's curiosity.

The model of situational and individual curiosity includes three types of curiosity: (1) individual interest is a *dispositional tendency* to be curious about a certain domain (individual differences in what people find interesting); (2) when someone with an individual interest encounters an activity relevant to the interest, *actualized interest* arises; and (3) *curiosity* is caused by external aspects of activities and objects that may involve complexity, novelty, uncertainty, conflict and/or inherently emotional content (Hidi, 1990).

Lowenstein (1994) offers an intriguing theory of curiosity based on information theory. He proposes an information gap theory, which "views curiosity as arising when attention becomes focused on a gap in one's knowledge." Such information gaps produce the feeling of deprivation and can be labeled curiosity. He notes, "The curious individual is motivated to obtain the missing information needed to reduce or eliminate the feelings of deprivation" (p.87). Thereby, nurturing the curiosity of practitioners also may facilitate the development of research-minded practice, with the following implications for the development of staff:

1. Curiosity requires a preexisting knowledge base and the need to "prime the pump" to stimulate information acquisition in the initial absence of curiosity.
2. To stimulate curiosity, it is important to recognize/increase staff awareness of manageable gaps in their knowledge, helping staff "know what they don't know."
3. As staff gain knowledge in a particular area, they are not only likely to perceive gaps in their knowledge, but those gaps will become smaller relative to what they already know. Staff

members are likely to become progressively more curious about the topics that they know the most about.

4. The intriguing intersections of cognition and emotion suggest that interests promote learning (Schiefele, 1999; Son & Metcalf, 2000).

5. Curiosity-induced behaviors, such as information seeking, can play a meaningful role in workplace learning as well as in job performance (Reio & Wiswell, 2000).

Ultimately, staff members who are curious are able to challenge their views of self, others, and the world around them as they seek out information, knowledge, and skills. This process can provide a pathway to the building of a meaningful work life that is supported by a focus on the present (mindful engagement, sense of meaningfulness) and the future (continuous search for meaning with minimal concern about obstacles).

Critical Reflection

One of the specific contributions of workplace learning is the emphasis on informal and socially situated learning that focuses on the everyday ways that people learn within specific work situations (Argote, 2005). Hager (2004) argues that we need to view learning as a reflection process in which learners construct their learning in interaction with their environments. In this sense, reflection is more about the processes by which individuals think about their experience and learn about this in an organizational context (Fook, 2008, p.10). The process includes the recapturing, noticing, and re-evaluating of their experiences and "to work with their experiences to turn it into learning" (Boud, 2006).

Reflection refers broadly to the intellectual and emotional processes by which individuals change their thinking in order to make meaning of and thus learn from experience (Fook, 2008, p.33). This may involve many different activities and processes. According to Fook (2008), learning from experience is not prompted by the existence of experience per se, but by the disquiet or discomfort that some experiences entail; reflection is the key element in response to this disquiet. For example, reflection can lead to discrepancies between professional practice as enacted and the need to expose the tacit assumptions inherent in enacted practice to resolve the discrepancies. Reflective practice therefore involves the unearthing of implicit assumptions by professionals in their own work (Heath, 1998).

Although critical reflection refers to general thinking processes in order to make meaning from experience, there are several specific theories that differentiate those processes and changes. For example, "Transformative learning refers to the process by which we transform our taken-for-granted frames of reference. . . .to make them more inclusive. . . . and reflective as they may generate beliefs and opinions that will prove more true or justified to take action" (Mezirow, 2000, pp. 7–8 cited in Fook, 2008, p. 35). Transformative learning is linked to critical reflection when it transforms "frames of reference within the scope of one's awareness through critical reflection on assumptions" (Mezirow, 1998, p. 190 cited in Fook, 2008, p. 35).

By recognizing and allowing the expression of the disquieted or emotional elements of professional practice, critical reflection may provide invaluable support in sustaining workers in difficult or anxiety-producing work situations. It also may assist in managing some of the organizational dynamics that are shaped by emotions. For example, by understanding how power works (implicitly and explicitly) in an organization, critical reflection may help workers gain a sense of their own power and see different ways in which to create organizational changes (Fook, 2008, p. 39). For instance, critical reflection may be used as a form of dialogue that "involves learning how to learn from one's own experiences and learning how to learn from the experiences of others" (Schon, 1983, p. 82).

Critical reflection is a process that may be used to mine tacit knowledge and make it more assessable so it can be more organizationally acknowledged and changed. According to Fook (2008), the essential elements of the learning process involve critical reflection processes that include cognitive, emotional, and action elements throughout based on some of the following: (1) initial discrepant experience; (2) examination of discrepancy with regard to both past experiences and cultural contexts; (3) re-examination of past experiences/interpretations; (4) reconstruction of past and present experiences in this light; and (5) testing the resulting interpretations (in action). Critical reflection in a learning organization is a process where people are continually discovering how they create their reality and how they can change it (Senge, 1990).

Steps in the Critical Reflections Process

The reflective process includes several different stages or levels. Williams (2001) identified the following key stages: (1) awareness of an event or situation that creates puzzlement, surprise, or discomfort; (2) an analysis of the situation leads to an examination of current knowledge, perceptions, and assumptions; and (3) revised assumptions that lead to a new sense of balance.

Step #1—Creating Awareness: Identifying the discomfort that some experiences entail is a key element of critical reflection. Reflective practice involves staff in exploring the implicit assumptions in their own work based on perceived discrepancies between a practitioner's beliefs, values, or assumptions and new information, knowledge, understanding, or insight. According to Stein (2000), the learning strategies designed to create awareness in individuals and work groups include dialogue journals and diaries, action learning groups, autobiographical stories (Brookfield, 1995), and sketching (Willis, 1999).

Three additional techniques often used in critical reflection include critical incidents, diaries, and small group processes. Critical incidents are used in teaching critical reflection (Stein, 2000) as a way to critically examine one's beliefs and positive or negative experiences. Creating a safe and structured climate can increase the willingness to share difficult experiences (Stein, 2000). Diary keeping or journaling involves recording events and reactions to events for later reflection (Orem, 1997; Williamson, 1997). The limitations of this approach may include the lack of writing skills and expressive skills, or the inability to confront comfortable assumptions (Stein, 2000). Using a small group process to share experiences, personal insights, and ideas among practitioners is another reflective strategy to develop ways of improving professional practice (Stein, 2000). Using the concept of "externalization," Nonaka and Takeuchi (1995) place reflection in a process of social interaction between individuals devoted to the development of new explicit knowledge out of tacit knowledge.

Step #2—Analyses: Questioning is an essential component of critical reflection and is needed to make assumptions explicit and to validate underlying premises. Brookfield (1988) identified four processes for analyzing critical reflections:

- Assumption analysis—activity engaged in to bring awareness of beliefs, values, cultural practices, and social structures that regulate behavior in order to assess their impact on daily activities (making explicit the "taken-for-granted" notions of reality).
- Contextual awareness—identify how assumptions are created within specific historical and cultural contexts.
- Imaginative speculation –opportunities to challenge prevailing ways of knowing and acting by imagining alternative ways of thinking.
- Reflective skepticism—represents the combination of assumption analysis, contextual awareness, and imaginative speculation needed to question claims of universal truths or unexamined patterns of interaction.

Step # 3—Action: The primary outcome of critical reflection is an increased ability to reflect and act on newly formed knowledge understandings based on reconstructing experiences in the light of new interpretations or areas for further elaboration (Stein, 2000). At the individual level, critical reflection can increase a practitioner's understanding of the need for change, the complexity of personal or interpersonal dynamics, and the prospects for future action by:

- Identifying and constructing shared meanings from critical reflection experiences
- Identifying and developing ways in which this shared meaning can be supported at the colleague, group, and organizational levels
- Identifying new ways to make tacit knowledge more explicit in the form of new organizational processes that link organizational learning with the development of a culture of learning that is essential for the growth of learning organizations

Critical reflection provides an opportunity for managers and practitioners to learn from their own experiences as well as the experiences of others. Critical reflection contributes to a learning organization where staff can continuously discover how they create reality and how they can change it. Engaging colleagues in critical reflection allow practitioners and managers to examine views different from their own. Understanding the views of practitioners is essential for building the trust that is critical for developing the creative tension need to encourage learning.

When it comes to organizational supports for critical reflection, it is clear that management needs to provide a safe space where practitioners/managers have the freedom to build their understanding of how their own experiences shape, and are shaped by, social conditions (Stein, 2000). This process is based on the following assumptions:

- Power is both personal and organizational
- Practitioners/managers participate in their own sense of being dominated
- Organizational change is both personal and collective
- Evidence is both empirical and constructed
- Dialogue and communication are essential in critical reflection

In summary, with the appropriate organizational supports, the use of the steps in critical reflection (creating awareness, conducting analysis, and action) can lead to the following outcomes (Fook, 2008, p.41):

- Increased understanding of the connections between individual and organizational identity (and ways of preserving individual integrity)
- Increased understanding of the need to acknowledge, express, and accept emotion in individual work and organizational dynamics, to both support workers and improve organizational processes and practices
- Increased capacity to use an awareness of power (both personal and organizational) in helping staff to see different possibilities for change
- Increased capacity to make sense of organizational issues
- Increased capacity to "mine" the tacit knowledge (about both being and doing) related to individual and group/ organizational practices in order to make these explicit and allow reformulation.

Critical Thinking and Decision-making

Decision making is at the heart of social service practice (e.g., making and using client assessments for service planning and evaluation) (Gambrill, 2006). The quality of well-reasoned practice decisions depends precisely on the quality of the thought involved. If we want to think effectively, we need to understand the rudiments of a thought process (Elder & Paul, 2007). Several structures can be used to describe the critical thinking process. The eight-part structure developed by Elder and Paul (2007) is illustrated in Figure 11.1 and the process explained as follows:

> When we think, we think for a purpose within a point of view based on assumptions leading to implications and consequences. We use concepts, ideas, and theories to interpret data, facts and experiences in order to answer questions, solve problems, and resolve issues. These elements are interrelated. If you change your purpose or agenda, you change your questions and problems. If you change your questions and problems, you are forced to seek new information and data. (Elder & Paul, 2007, p.5)

This eight-part structure developed by Elder and Paul (2007) provides the outline for this section, along with considerable expansion from the pioneering work of Gambrill (2005).

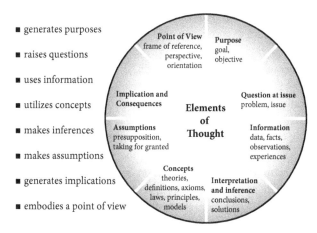

Figure 11.1. Eight basic structures of critical thinking (Elder & Paul, 2007).

1. Identify Fundamental Purpose

Several questions can be used to help determine the fundamental purpose of the social services practice decision. What exactly is the issue or pattern of behaviors that you want to understand or what data or information have you received or want to receive? What context can be used to clarify the issue (program changes or big picture concerns related to connecting personal trouble with social issues)? What am I trying to accomplish?

2. Develop Questions

A key step in critical thinking is translating practice and policy issues or concerns into specific, answerable questions and stating them as clearly and precisely as possible (Gambrill, 2005, p. 287). Different kinds of questions elicit different types of information and require different forms of analysis. Examples of different types of questions include the following (Gibbs 2003; Sacket Rosenberg, Gray, Haynes, & Richardson 1996): (1) For people recently exposed to a catastrophic event, what evidence exists to support brief psychological debriefing or doing nothing in order to avoid or minimize the likelihood of post-traumatic stress disorder? (2) For adolescents in foster care, what is the evidence that early home visitation programs reduce the frequency of delinquency?

Although experience may be a valuable source of information about what may be true, experience needs to be continuously and critically appraised in terms of "what works, for what client, in what circumstances, and to what effect?" (Gambrill, 2005, p. 80). Are there other studies that support the findings? Do the findings apply across populations or only for certain populations? Also, some suggest that answerable questions need to be posed as part of critical thinking: (1) How can the population be described? (2) What interventions are relevant to address the need of the population? (3) How can the interventions be compared? and (4) what are the outcomes? (Sackett & Strauss, 1998). Gibbs (2003) referred to these as client-centered questions that have practical importance and can be used to search the literature as well as used to identify outcomes.

3. Point of View

Critical thinking includes the search for the big picture to identify and make explicit underlying or opposing points of view. In everyday practice, it is often easy to forget about economic, political, and social context in which personal and social problems are defined (Gambrill, 2005, p.31). Therefore, when thinking critically, it is important to clarify the influence of values and standards used in decision-making. Values can be defined as the social principles, goals, or standards held by an individual, group, or society. Values reflect preferences regarding certain goals and how to attain them. They are used to support decisions at many different levels.

Although problems are often socially constructed and defined differently at different times and receive more or less attention, the resources available to address personal and social problems are related to larger structural factors. These factors that influence decision-making include large caseloads, lack of clear policy priorities, contradictory demands from diverse sources, availability of resources, social and time pressures, perceived value of task, goals pursued, access to information, and agency culture (Gambrill, 2005, p. 42).

4. Operating Assumptions

A key element of Gambrill's (2005) approach to critical thinking is the clarification of operating assumptions, which she defines as either an assertion that we believe to be true in spite of a lack of evidence of its truth or an assertion that we are willing to accept as true for purposes of debate or discussion (p. 69). A recommended question for checking for assumptions is—What am I taking for granted? As Gambrill notes, the identification of bias is central to critically appraising the quality of research and decision-making. Bias is a systematic "leaning to one side" that distorts the accuracy of thinking. For example, we tend to seek and overweigh evidence that supports our beliefs and ignore or underweigh contrary evidence (i.e., we try to justify [confirm] assumptions rather than to question them) (Gambrill, 2005, p. 227).

Oversimplifications can be based on biases about certain groups, individuals, or behaviors that influence our judgments (Gambrill, 2005, p. 209). Generalizations influence what we do and what we believe. They are quick and easy; and we do not have to think about all the ways in which a client, for example, may not fit preconceptions. If the degree of variability is underestimated, however, a chance is lost to identify clues about what a person is like or may do in certain situations. If we search only for evidence that supports a stereotype, we may miss more accurate alternative accounts (Gambrill, 2005, p. 209).

5. Implications and Consequences

Different ways of defining problems have different consequences. Critical thinking requires an *evaluation of options*, taking into account the advantages and disadvantages of possible decisions before acting. What consequences are likely to follow from this or that decision?

6. Essential Concepts

Gambrill (2005) points out the importance of clarifying and analyzing the meanings of words and phrases. Practitioners use words to describe people and events, to describe relationships between behavior and events and to express evaluations. Language is used in posing and "thinking" about practice questions. At the same time, language may compromise the quality of decisions through carelessness, lack of skill in writing and thinking, and deliberate intent. Some common errors in clarifying and analyzing the meaning of words and phrases include: (1) incorrectly applying labels, (2) assuming that a word has one meaning when words have different meanings in different contexts, and (3) using vague terms (Gambrill, 2005, p. 131). If terms are not clarified, different meanings may be derived.

7. What Information is Needed?

Observation is always selective and is influenced by our theories and related concepts. We are influenced by our own evolutionary history in how we see and react to the world as well as by the culture in which we have grown up. According to Gambrill (2005, p. 103), because we see what we expect to see, we need to collect information carefully by asking such questions as (Gambrill 2005, p. 466):

- What data is most helpful in making evidence-informed decisions?
- How can such data be obtained?

- When has enough information been collected?
- How should contradictory data be handled?
- What criteria should be used to check the accuracy of data?
- How can inaccurate and incomplete accounts be avoided?
- Does the measure reflect the characteristic it is supposed to measure?

8. What Does it Mean? Interpretation and Inference

Basic to deriving meaning is the critical discussion and testing of theories (eliminating errors through criticism). As Gambrill (2005) observes, what is called scientific objectivity is simply the fact that no scientific theory is accepted as dogma, and that all theories are tentative and are continuously open to rational, critical discussion aimed at the elimination of errors. Scientists are often wrong and find out that they are wrong by testing their predictions. In this way, better theories (those that can account for more findings) replace earlier ones. Unexamined speculation may result in acceptance of incomplete or incorrect accounts of problems. Untested speculation can get in the way of translating problems into outcomes that, if achieved, would resolve problems (Gambrill, 2005, p. 328). The kinds of inferences questioned in an evidence-informed assessment include the following: (1) frequency of a problem, (2) contextual factors, (3) accuracy of assessment measures, and (4) accuracy of different practice frameworks.

Additional analytic techniques used in critical thinking include: (a) identifying significant similarities and differences, (b) recognizing contradictions and inconsistencies, and (c) analyzing and evaluating arguments, interpretations, beliefs, or theories. Evaluating an argument is a classic critical thinking technique to understand a problem. An argument is a group of statements one or more of which (the premises) support or provide evidence for another (conclusion). An argument is aimed at suggesting the truth (or demonstrating the falsity) of a claim. A good argument offers reasons and evidence so that other people can make up their own minds. Argument is an essential form of inquiry. It provides a way to evaluate the accuracy of different views. Steps to analyze an incomplete argument include the following from Gambrill (2005, p. 74):

(1) Identify the conclusion or key assertion
(2) List all the other explicit assertions that make up the argument as given
(3) Add any unstated assertions that are necessary to make the argument complete (Put them in parentheses to distinguish them from assertions that are explicit in the argument as given.)
(4) Order the premises (or supporting assertions) and conclusion (or key assertion) so as to show the structure of the argument

In summary, critical thinking involves the careful examination and evaluation of beliefs, arguments, and actions by considering alternative views to arrive at well-reasoned decisions, such as "paying attention to the process of how we think, not just the outcome" (Gambrill, 2005, p. 253).

In an effort to integrate all three elements of a research-minded practitioner, Figure 11.2 summarizes the elements and provides the conceptual foundation for the construction of training and course curricula.

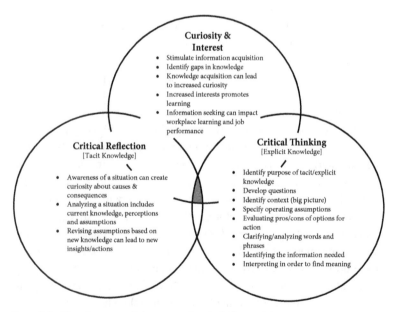

Figure 11.2. Key elements of the research-minded practitioner.

Defining Organizational Support

The traditional forms of organizational supports are usually located in a range of professional development activities for practitioners. They include taking an educational leave to complete a degree program or more time-limited workplace learning (e.g., derived from a performance evaluation, participating in induction or specialized training, effective supervision, and/or given a special assignment that involves new learning).

The newer forms of organizational support can be found in an array of examples from the United Kingdom related to the implementation of evidence-informed practice. The examples noted in this section include the role of top management, the use of link officers, the use of an evidence request service, the use of agency-based research and development units, the role of service standards (and accreditation), and the sharing/learning from other organizations.

Commitment of top management
Given that the design and management of organizational support systems are often the responsibility of senior management, it is logical to start with the role of top management in supporting evidence-informed practice. According to Research in Practice (2006) in their publication titled *Firm Foundations: A Practical Guide to Organizational Support for the Use of Evidence-informed Practice*, organizational support includes: (1) providing strategic leadership, (2) setting expectations, (3) supporting local research, (4) improving access to research, and (5) encouraging learning from research. Setting directions and expectations involves bringing together and consulting with any staff interested in evidence-informed practice, often led by one or more senior staff members who can demonstrate how evidence-informed practice can be linked to both planning and review processes.

A second dimension of organizational support involves increasing staff competence related to evidence-informed practice through training and ongoing support. The support could include outcome measurement, opportunities to use data-based websites, conducting focus groups with service users, and involving student interns. The roles of senior management related to research (modeling critical thinking; incorporating evidence into agency documents; and maintaining research partnerships with universities, institutes, and consultants) are identified in Box 11.2.

Box 11.2. Role of Senior Management in Promoting Evidence-informed
Practice (EiP)—Barnardo's Northern Ireland

I. Supporting and enabling critical thinking about practice and
   applying evidence to improve services for users
   • Exercises in critical thinking built into EiP training related to
     Research in Practice materials and searching electronic databases
   • Working with staff to define models of service user assessment and
     engagement
   • Evaluating services using surveys and focus groups of service users
     and service referral sources
   • Helping staff use appropriate research methods in evaluating
     service outcomes
   • Sharing logic modeling with staff

II. Generating and sharing evidence
   • Encouraging staff to write-up and share their evaluation results at
     conferences and online
   • Help staff prepare briefings for senior management and other staff
   • Encourage staff to participate in larger, multi-country studies

III. Modeling appropriate behaviors
   • Making sure that evidence is incorporated into annual reports,
     business plans, communication tools, and communications with
     funders

IV. Creating strategic partnerships
   • Maintain relationships with other EiP organizations
   • Maintain university partnerships

Another approach for senior management is to identify the role of
evidence-informed practice in the organization's mission statement. For
example, Barnardo's in the United Kingdom has developed the following
component for their agency's mission statement related to:

• Improving outcomes for children based on evidence-informed
  decision-making: Service development and design are driven by
  evidence drawn from performance evaluation data derived from
  existing services and/or external research evidence
• Basing practice decisions on the best available evidence
  (external research, views of service users, government service

audits, program evaluations, and expertise of managers and practitioners)

- Promoting a form of practice that is monitored, evaluated, and inclusive of performance data generated to ensure that intended outcomes are being achieved and are not causing harm
- Using evaluated pilot efforts before full-scale implementation if staff is unsure about the effectiveness of an approach or intervention

Although there are multiple staff barriers to achieving this mission (e.g., work pressures and lack of time, lack of research knowledge, lack of practical supports and resources, relevance of current research to practice), it is also recognized that senior management can help to address these barriers by:

- Demonstrating a clear commitment to the mission
- Investing organizational resources in staff training and senior staff facilitation as well as Internet access
- Building evidence-informed practice into ongoing organizational processes (e.g., supervision, team meetings, reading opportunities, Internet searching)
- Increasing communications devoted to sharing practice knowledge up and down as well as across the organization
- Managing and sharing in-house (administrative) data and ensuring that information reaches the people who need it
- Using evidence to inform (influence) public policy
- Modeling reflective practice as an organizational norm by creating a learning organization that values curiosity, inquiry, and lifelong learning
- Supporting communities of practice that bring practitioners in similar areas together on a regular basis to work on similar issues and share resources

Link Officers

Another approach to creating organizational support for evidence-informed practice features the role and functions of staff members who serve as Link Officers (Research in Practice, 2007). The role can be carried out by a staff member or a group of staff working as part of a knowledge-sharing team. Although each organization can shape the role to meet its own needs, the link officer role often includes one or more of the following:

- Fostering relationships between agency and research organizations (e.g., universities)
- Helping staff use service evaluation research to improve services and outcomes
- Identifying opportunities for special projects and partnerships
- Contributing to the integration of evidence-informed practice in the agency
- Participating in multi-county knowledge-sharing projects when they benefit the agency
- Coordinating learning events, disseminating materials, and encouraging the use of relevant websites

The implementation of the link officer concept can include a wide variety of activities. If the role is shared with a group of key managers, it could include monthly meetings that involve: (1) sharing external reports with specific staff along with an overview of key findings and possible relevance for practice; (2) assessing the transfer of learning from various learning events; (3) sharing information on agency intranet site; (4) coordinating student research projects by including relevant staff members; (5) assisting staff with the conduct of small evaluation projects; (6) supporting staff with the presentation of in-house or outside research at staff meetings; (7) promoting research collaboration with local universities; (8) fostering greater service user involvement in evaluating services; (9) including content on evidence-informed practice in staff induction programs; and (10) promoting more staff training related to becoming a more research-minded practitioner. There are multiple opportunities and challenges associated with promoting the link officer concept (Graaf, McBeath, Lwin, Holmes, & Austin, 2017).

Evidence Request Service

Although senior management frequently has access to analysts or evaluators who have the skills and resources to engage in quick literature searches, this is often not the case for middle-management and line staff. It is clear that the research interests of top management are often different from those of line staff. As a result, the search for evidence is different. Senior management tends to focus more on the issues facing populations being serviced (e.g., Why are there so many children of color entering the child welfare system?) while line staff tend to be more interested in learning about interventions or "what works" with specific types of clients.

One approach to address this dilemma is the development of an Evidence Request Service (ERS) by Barnardo's in the United Kingdom. Building upon the publications from a nationally funded project (*What Works for Children*, Economic and Social Research Council, 2001–2005), the ERS was launched in 2004 to improve staff access to relevant and reliable research evidence and to increase the use of research evidence in service planning and delivery. Based on specific requests from staff that are refined for database searching, the ERS operation (one full-time researcher and an assistant) informs staff about existing research and information inside and outside the organization through the use of a comprehensive online search for the most rigorous and relevant research related to the topic under investigation. Staff members are then provided with a clear and easy-to-read summary (three to five pages) that identifies some preliminary implications so that staff can meet to develop their own implications for practice. With a sufficiently refined search topic, the literature review summaries can be produced in up to eight weeks at a modest cost.

Some of the topics researched in the first several years of operation included:

- What is the best way to involve young fathers with children on the child protection register?
- What are the best counseling interventions for sexually abused children?
- What are the effects of abuse and neglect on brain functioning and cognitive development?
- What are the risk factors associated with sibling sexual abuse?
- What works with children of parents who abuse substances?
- What works in emergency and short-term foster placements?

Research and Development Unit

One of the most innovative forms of organizational support can be found in the local public social service agency in Helsinki, Finland. When staff members were unable to find relevant research related to their practice concerns, they needed a venue for engaging in small-scale studies to build their own foundation for evidence-informed practice. When staff defined the research questions (in contrast to those developed by academics, policy analysts, and/or senior management), a form of practice research was begun and needed a place to thrive. When the Helsinki department established an agency-based Practice Research & Development Unit (R&D), it was created to help staff explore client and service delivery issues emerging from their practice.

The R&D Unit has the following unique operating features: (1) staff can submit a plan for conducting a piece of exploratory research, provided that it relates to the strategic directions of the department; (2) if the topic is selected, they can be reassigned to the R&D Unit for a period of time (a year or more) along with a small number of other staff working on different topics; (3) staff are supervised by part-time researchers from the faculty of a local university social work department who rotate through the unit for a period of time (a year or more); (4) most approved research projects include multiple perspectives (staff, administration, service users, and faculty researchers); and (5) the research process includes weekly case presentations (internal staff or external experts), weekly journal clubs, involvement of students currently placed in the agency, and annual senior staff presentations. The outcomes of the R&D Unit include:

- Expanded number of research-minded practitioners
- Increased faculty involvement in practice research
- Increased agency capacity to identify and disseminate promising practices
- Increased agency capacity to focus on service outcomes and improve service effectiveness
- Increased opportunity to elicit service user perspectives
- Expanded venue for agency-university collaborative research
- Enhanced in-house think tank capacity to engage in policy-relevant research

Service Standards

As noted earlier, one of the strongest rationales for providing organizational support for evidence-informed practice can be found in the current pressure on social service agencies for increased accountability in the form of measuring outcomes. These new pressures often require a change in the culture of an organization that has been more concerned with serving as many clients as possible than with measuring service outcomes. As a result, senior management often finds itself searching for tools to use in communicating the importance of outcomes with staff. However, Research in Practice (UK) has developed a promising communications tool called Performance Pointers (www.rip.org.uk) noted in Chapter 3. These publications are designed for dissemination to staff and combine the following critical ingredients of outcome assessment:

- A full explanation of a service standard in terms of its policy origins and rationale (e.g., stability of placements of foster children in terms of number of moves related to: [a] increasing choice of placements; [b] developing/supporting foster caregivers; [c] using multidisciplinary treatments; [d] stabilizing placements of older children; and [e] stabilizing residential care)
- A synthesis of relevant research (selected, not comprehensive)
- An identification of promising practices related to the service standard (selected, not comprehensive)
- An identification of key questions for staff to explore in staff meetings
- A selected list of references for further inquiry

LESSONS LEARNED

Implications for Practice: Identifying the Research-minded Practitioner

This chapter provides an opportunity to explore the processes of identifying research-minded practitioners and the types of organizational supports needed to promote evidence-informed practice. As noted in Figure 11.2, the activities of a research-minded practitioner might include: the search for promising practices (curiosity) to address practice dilemmas, integrating critical reflection into one's daily practice, and regularly engaging in critical thinking about the available knowledge and research related to one's practice. One approach to identifying research-minded practitioners and enhancing their professional development is to locate practitioners who display considerable curiosity about the services provided, critically reflect on their practice, and critically think about the impact of research on their practice. Supervisors and administrators are often in a position to identify critically thinking practitioners who use organizational data and knowledge to inform their practice as well as request or seek out specific research to increase their understanding of specific practice questions.

Conversely, senior-level administrators may find less interest in research-mindedness where practitioners are resistant to learning how to use data, to reading reports, or to seeking out practice relevant research. It may be that the previous attempts of staff members to pursue their curiosities and interests were met with organizational challenges and barriers. In a similar way, the tools being used to convey knowledge and research may be incomprehensible and confusing for practitioners (e.g., complicated graphs and reports with little clarification).

Supporting research-minded practitioners, once identified, often requires the development of organizational supports to promote evidence-informed practice. These include focusing on staff and career development, revising job definitions to include research learning, incorporating evidence into ongoing managerial decision-making, and creating an organizational culture of curiosity that creates the link between organizational supports and nurturing the growth of research-minded practitioners.

Organizational Supports Promoting Evidence-informed Practice

Culture of Curiosity: The organizational culture of curiosity can be described in terms of goals, processes, and supports. The goals of such a culture could include efforts to create an organizational climate where there is room to be creative, where it is safe to question decisions and those in authority, and where there is a consistent message about pursuing new or better ways of doing business. The processes that would need to be visible in an organizational culture of curiosity include: (1) creating a sense of wonder about how things might be done better; (2) encouraging staff to ask the "why" questions and to value the pursuit of more information; (3) encouraging the search for input from others at all levels of the organizations; and (4) clarifying boundaries for question-raising related to the rationale for various work procedures and ways to improve them as they might relate to client outcomes. And finally, the organizational supports for a culture of curiosity might include: (1) increased recognition for those who develop new approaches; (2) encouragement of those who innovate by acknowledging their contributions; (3) increased attention to opening doors for staff to pursue ideas; and (4) providing resources for staff to search for alternatives and thereby cultivate individual and situational sources of curiosity.

Staff Development and Career Development: The second crossover area between the research-minded practitioner and organizational supports relates to staff development in the form of learning/training events and career development in the form of project-based learning as noted in Box 11.1. At least three core skills are needed to promote evidence-informed practice in an organizational environment of outcome assessment: (1) cultivating curiosity, (2) critical reflection, and (3) critical thinking. These three competency areas need to be reflected in training programs and project learning opportunities irrespective of their content.

Three primary connections are needed in order to incorporate these areas into all practice learning opportunities. The first connection is between the *tacit knowledge* (stored in the head/experiences of all staff) and *the capacity to critically reflect* on their practice. Critical reflection capacities grow over time if they are nurtured and supported by peers, supervisors, and managers as part of lifelong learning. The second connection is between *explicit knowledge and critical thinking*. Analyzing new social policies or recent research articles/reports involves critical thinking skills that are needed for evidence-informed practice. Although it is often assumed that these critical thinking skills are acquired in undergraduate and graduate programs, it is not clear that these skills are well developed and/or effectively transferred to the workplace. For many staff members, years of experience with trial and error efforts have contributed to their own skill development in critical thinking.

The third connection that needs far more attention in the workplace as well as on campus involves the *relationship between practice skills and research skills*. Until staff and students fully recognize that engaging in practice is a form of research, it will be difficult to make this connection apparent to all. It means that practice and research need to be taught as two sides of the same coin and integrated on campus and in field work education. For example, efforts to assess client outcomes need to be integrated into all phases of case management practice. The challenges associated with this level of integration are captured in Chapter 12.

Job Redefinition and Research Learning: In addition to the focus on a culture of curiosity, there are many implications for prioritizing organizational supports. For example, in the area of job descriptions, the definition of practice performed by line staff from worker-client facilitator and worker-supervisor facilitator could be expanded to include new collaborator roles "worker-evaluator" and "worker-policy analyst." Such changes can help staff connect what they see in their caseloads with the broad policy dialogue about how policies need to be changed, enhanced, or created (Harris et al., 2009). Although some have noted that these multiple roles are part and parcel of generalist practice, they need to be identified for students on campus or called for in agency practice.

Both agency senior management and university educators need to be able to articulate the theories of change that underlie practice and demonstrate how logic modeling can inform research on practice. This capacity can equip practitioners in the conduct of exploratory pilot studies of practice issues. This often requires an in-house research and development capability. In a similar way, senior management needs to find ways to support the career trajectories of their most research-minded practitioners through in-house research opportunities and outside learning opportunities at universities and elsewhere.

Managerial Leadership and Organizational Support Mechanisms: And finally, organizational supports for evidence-informed practice need to be mainstreamed into ongoing managerial decision-making. As noted in Table 11.1, systems of organizational support need to be built in the four areas of evidence requesting, evidence linking, evidence generating, and evidence monitoring. Each of these can be described in terms of their relationship to tacit knowledge (practice wisdom) and explicit knowledge (published research).

First, the process of requesting evidence involves the capacity to continuously scan the local, regional, national, and international

Table 11.1. Systems of Organizational Support for Evidence-informed Practice

	Practice Wisdom (tacit knowledge)	Published Research (explicit knowledge)
Evidence Requesting	Survey Promising Practices	Search Existing Literature
Evidence Linking	Convening Staff to Share	Routing & Discussing Relevant Sources/ Citations
Evidence Generating	Critical Reflection for Research Questions	In-house Research & Development Units (R&D)
Evidence Monitoring	Case Record Review, Case Conferencing, and Administrative After-Action Reviews	Administrative Data & Reports Linked to National Service Standards

environment for promising practice related to human service delivery. The same scanning is needed in the area of explicit knowledge through in-house and national databases, most frequently aided by experts in the field and at universities.

Second, evidence linking involves continuous efforts to convene staff to share in their questions and curiosity, critically reflect upon recent practice experiences, and critical think about recently published articles (e.g., possibly raised in a Journal Club), as well as to learn from each other by the sharing of tacit knowledge and related practice wisdom. From the perspective of explicit knowledge, systems need to be created by senior management to enhance the routing, sharing, and discussing of relevant research publications, policy analyses, and other citations.

Third, the process of evidence generating involves efforts to support the translation of critical reflection questions emerging from staff into research questions to be addressed inside or outside the organization. In addition, the explicit knowledge generated by senior staff in the form of administrative data needs to be effectively disseminated in a form that all levels of staff can understand and ultimately utilize as part of service delivery decision-making. Densely filled tables of numbers with little attention to the principles of effective communication are generally not effective evidence-sharing activities.

And finally, the fourth dimension of organizational supports relates to evidence monitoring. The tacit knowledge dimensions of monitoring can be found in the processes of case record review, case conferencing, and after-action reviews, wherein the tacit knowledge of staff can be shared, organized, and disseminated for future decision-making.

In summary, developing a culture of curiosity involves special attention to staff/career development, job redefinition and research learning, and managerial leadership related to organizational support mechanisms. There are many challenges facing research-minded practitioners and senior managers engaged in creating organizational supports for evidence-informed practice. There are unlimited opportunities, however, to transform human service organizations into learning organizations that engage in data-based decision-making at all levels of the organization.

CONCLUSION

Evidence-informed practice continues to gain momentum as a framework for linking research and practice in human service organizations. Despite the offerings of university research courses and the interest in evidence-informed and evidence-based practice in the field, the integration of data and research into daily practice remains an elusive goal for human service organizations. Although many factors are at play, it is critical to nurture the curiosity, critical reflection, and critical thinking in front-line practitioners who are often responsible for implementing evidence-informed practice. They also may be more capable of seeking out, consuming, and applying the knowledge needed to support evidence-informed practice with clients. Simultaneously, the process of putting in place organizational supports that promote the pursuit and application of information and knowledge is needed for the research-minded practitioner to succeed. With administrators and managers leading the way, working to develop a culture of curiosity within their organizations, research-mindedness and evidence-informed practice can become the new norm needed to promote excellence in human service organizations.

REFERENCES

Anthony, E.K., & Austin, M.J. (2008). The role of an intermediary organization in promoting research in schools of social work: The case of the Bay Area Social Services Consortium. *Social Work Research, 32*(4), 287–293.

Argote, L. (2005). Reflections on two views of managing learning and knowledge in organizations. *Journal of Management Inquiry, 14*(1), 43–48.

Austin, M.J., Claassen, J.B., Vu, C.M., & Mizrahi, P (2008). Knowledge management: Implications for the human services. *Journal of Evidence-based Social Work, 5*(1), 361–389.

Austin, M.J., & Hopkins, K. (2004). *Supervision as collaboration in the human services: Building a learning culture.* Thousand Oaks, CA: Sage Publications.

Boud, D. (2006). Creating the space for reflection. In P. Cressey, D. Boud, & P. Docherty (Eds.), *Productive reflection at work: Learning for changing organizations* (pp. 158–169). London: Routledge.

Brookfield, S. (1995). *Becoming a critically reflective teacher.* San Francisco, CA: Jossey-Bass Publishers.

Brookfield, S. (1998). Critical reflective practice. *Journal of Continuing Education in the Health Professions, 18*(4), 162–184.

Deci, E. (1975). *Intrinsic motivation.* New York, NY: Plenum.

Elder, L., & Paul, R. (2007). *The thinker's guide to analytic thinking.* The Foundation for Critical Thinking: Dillon Beach, CA. Retrieved from http://www.criticalthinking.org/

Fook, J. (2008). *Developing model(s) of critical reflection to contribute to organizational learning via case reviews in children's services: A scoping review of relevant concepts and frameworks.* London: Social Care Institute for Excellence.

Gambrill, E. (2006). Evidence-based practice and policy: Choices ahead. *Research on Social Work Practice, 16*(3), 338–357.

Gambrill, E. (2005). *Critical thinking in clinical practice: Improving the quality of judgments and decisions* (2nd ed.). Hoboken, NJ: John Wiley Sons.

Gibbs, L. (2003). *Evidence-based practice for the helping professions.* Pacific Grove, CA: Brooks/Cole.

Graaf, G., McBeath, B., Lwin, K., Holmes, D., & Austin, M.J. (2017). Supporting evidence-informed practice in human service organizations: An exploratory study of link officers. *Human Service Organizations, 41*(1), 58–75.

Hager, P. (2004). Conceptions of learning and understanding learning at work. *Studies in Continuing Education, 26*(1), 3–17.

Harris, J., Scott, S., & Skidmore, P. (2009). *Child sexual exploitation: A Barnardo's teaching case on the integration of practice, research, and policy.* Barkingside, UK: Barnardo's.

Harrison, C., & Humphreys, C. (1998). *Keeping research in mind.* London: Central Council for Education & Training in Social Work.

Harvey, M., Novicevic, M., Leonard, N., & Payne, D. (2007). The role of curiosity in global managers' decision-making. *The Journal of Leadership Studies,* *13*(3), 43–58.

Hasenfeld, Y. (1893). *Human Service Organizations.* London, UK: Pearson.

Heath, H. (1998). Keeping a reflective practice diary: A practical guide. *Nurse Education Today, 18*(7), 592–598.

Hidi, S. (1990). Interest and Its Contribution as a Mental Resource for Learning. *Review of Educational Research, 60,* 549–571.

Kashdan, T., Rose, P., & Fincham F. (2004). Curiosity and exploration: Facilitating positive subjective experiences and personal growth opportunities. *Journal of Personality Assessment, 82*(3), 291–305.

Kashdan, T., & Silvia, P. (2008) Curiosity and interest: The benefits of thriving on novelty and challenge. In S.J. Lopez (Ed.), *Handbook of positive psychology* (2nd ed., pp. 210–227). Oxford, UK: Oxford University Press.

Kashdan, T., & Steger, M. (2007). Curiosity and pathways to well-being and meaning in life: Traits, states, and everyday behaviors. *Motivation and Emotion, 31,* 159–173.

Keltner D., & Shiota, M. (2003). New displays and new emotions: A commentary on Rozin and Cohen (2003). *Emotion, 3*(1), 86–91.

Litman, J., & Spielberger, C. (2003). Measuring epistemic curiosity and its diversive and specific components. *Journal of Personality Assessment, 80*(1), 75–86.

Litman, J., & Jimerson, T. (2004). The measurement of curiosity as a feeling of deprivation. *Journal of Personality Assessment, 82*(2), 147–157.

Loewenstein, G. (1994). The psychology of curiosity: A review and reinterpretation. *Psychological Bulletin, 116*(1), 75–98.

Mezirow, J. (1998). On critical reflection. *Adult Education Quarterly, 48*(3), 185–198.

Mezirow, J. (Ed.) (2000). *Learning as transformation: Critical perspectives on a theory in progress.* San Francisco, CA: Jossey Bass.

Orem, R. (1997). Journal writing as a form of professional development. In S.J. Levine (Ed.), *Proceedings of the 16th Annual Midwest Research-to-Practice Conference in Adult, Continuing, and Community Education.* East Lansing: Michigan State University.

Nonaka, I., & Takeuchi, H. (1995). *The knowledge creating company. How Japanese companies create the dynamics of innovation.* New York, NY: Oxford University Press.

Reio, T., & Wiswell, A. (2000). Field investigation of the relationship among adult curiosity, workplace learning, and job performance. *Human Resource Development Quarterly, 11*(1), 5–30.

Research in Practice. (2006). *Firm foundations: A practical guide to organizational support for the use of evidence-informed practice.* Dartington, Tones, UK: Research in Practice.

Sackett, D.L., Rosenberg, W.M.C., Gray, J.A.M., Haynes, R.B., & Richardson, W.S. (1996). Evidence based medicine: What it is and what it isn't. *British Medical Journal, 312,* 71–72.

Sackett, D.L., & Strauss, S.E. (1998). Finding and applying evidence during clinical rounds. The "evidence cart." *Journal of the American Medical Association, 280,* 1336–1338.

Schiefele, U. (1999). Interest and learning from text. *Scientific Studies of Reading, 3,* 257–279.

Schon, D. (1983). *The reflective practitioner: How professionals think in action.* New York, NY: Basic Books.

Senge, P. (1990). *The fifth discipline: The art and practice of the learning organisation.* New York, NY: Random House.

Silvia, P.J. (2006). *Exploring the psychology of interest.* New York, NY: Oxford University Press.

Son, L.K., & Metcalfe, J. (2000). Metacognitive and control strategies in study-time allocation. *Journal of Experimental Psychology: Learning, Memory, and Cognition. 26,* 204–221.

Stein, D. (2000). *Teaching critical reflection: Myths and realities No.7.* ERIC Clearinghouse on Adult, Career, and Vocational Education, Columbus, OH. Retrieved from http://www.ericacve.org/fulltext.asp.

Williams, B. (2001). Developing critical reflection for professional practice through problem-based learning. *Journal of Advanced Nursing, 34*(1), 27–34.

Williamson, A. (1997). Reflection in adult learning with particular reference to learning-in-action. *Australian Journal of Adult and Community Education, 37*(2), 93–99.

Willis, P. (1999). Looking for what it's really like: Phenomenology in reflective practice. *Studies in Continuing Education, 21*(1), 91–112.

12

A Framework for Teaching Practice-based Research*

As noted in the previous chapter, practice research involves curiosity about finding evidence to improve practice. It is about identifying promising ways to help people as well as critically examining practice in search of new ideas emerging from experience. When practitioners are working in partnership with researchers, they both have much to learn from each other. The development of professional knowledge involves understanding the complexity of practice along with a commitment to improve practice. Practice research involves the generation of knowledge of direct relevance to professional practice and therefore involves knowledge generated directly from practice itself in a grounded way (Salisbury Forum Group, 2011, p. 5).

---

* Adapted from the original: Austin, M.J., & Isokuortti, N. (2016). A framework for teaching practice-based research with a focus on service users. *Journal of Teaching in Social Work, Special Issue, 36*(1), 11–32.

As noted in Chapter 1, there is a growing international interest in defining and utilizing practice research. The issues range from a focus on identifying models of practice research (the practitioner oriented, the method oriented, the democratic model, and the generative model) (Julkunen, 2011; Marthinsen & Julkunen, 2012) to exploring the process of negotiating relationships between research and practice (Uggerhøj, 2011) to using data-mining methods with the administrative and case records of human service organizations (Epstein, 2009; Epstein, 2010; Epstein, 2011) to the changing relationship between university and practice-based research and the need to raise standards in practice research (Shaw, 2005; Shaw & Lunt, 2012; Shaw & Lunt, 2011). In addition, as noted in the previous chapter, there is also a call for more thinking about the role of human service organizations in building knowledge-sharing systems to support evidence-informed practice and promoting practice-based research (Austin, Del Santo, & Lee, 2012).

As the art and science of practice research evolves, equal attention needs to be paid to educating the next generation of social work practitioners about different ways to incorporate practice research into their daily work. Not only are students expected to integrate their understanding of practice methods with their understanding of research methods, they are also increasingly expected to integrate the service user involvement perspective. This chapter begins with an exploration of the implications of practice research focused on service delivery with special attention to service users as a foundation for building a framework to guide the teaching/learning of practice research. The chapter concludes with a teaching case that illustrates an application of the framework as well as the implications for practice and future research.

EMERGING DEFINITION OF PRACTICE RESEARCH

As noted in the first chapter, practice research involves "the science of the concrete" as defined by Flyvbjerg (2001), in which research: (1) needs to be carried out close to the phenomenon being studied; (2) seeks to surface the minor details in the context of major events or processes; (3) focuses on practical activities that can generate knowledge about everyday practices; (4) involves building upon case examples and their contexts; (5) represents a linkage between people and/or processes and their organizational contexts; and (6) generates and interprets findings through a fundamentally dialogical process whereby multiple voices and perspectives are honored without giving special privilege to one voice.

As noted in Chapter 8, practice-based research faces a unique challenge with regard to its level of robustness. Nowotny (2003) helps us understand the challenge by focusing on the social context of knowledge production where validity is tested within the nature of the practice itself as well as in the broader networks of the community. Her emphasis on "socially robust" knowledge features both the research process and the proposed changes emerging from knowledge production. Given the inductive, bottom-up nature of practice research, the dissemination and utilization of knowledge are directly linked to the involvement of those practitioners and service users who can make the most use of the research. It is this perspective on knowledge development that gives practice-based research its socially robust rigor.

Practice research can be seen as a shared enterprise that values the science of the concrete by taking into account the organizational and policy contexts of producing and using research. For example, a considerable amount of service-related data is buried in an organization's information system in the form of administrative and case record data as well as in the tacit knowledge and practice wisdom of both service providers and service users.

Julkunen (2015) reminds us that practice research in social work is primarily relational (both conversational and perspective sharing) where different actors are invited to participate and share their different ways that contribute to diverse processes and outcomes. She notes that by focusing on the nature of practice it is possible to see how change processes are influenced by practices that direct our thinking and action. She calls for building upon study and analysis in order to implement improvements that can affect all the actors. For example, service user participation "is not a phenomenon with a given content (but rather) . . . a relational phenomenon that takes place in interactions between people that must be subject to interpretation" (p. 14).

SERVICE IMPLICATIONS OF PRACTICE RESEARCH

The evolution of practice research methods within the context of providing social services has been receiving increased attention over the past decade. In some cases, the focus has been on the power dynamics of the worker-client relationship (Carnochan & Austin, 2015). In other cases, the focus has been on redefining the core concepts underlying practice methods (Ruch, 2010). And in still other cases, the focus has been on expanding the research-method processes (Epstein, 2010).

One of the critical issues emerging from the implementation and development of practice research is the changing nature of practice itself. For example, there has been a slow but steady process of relabeling the populations being served by social service organizations; namely, "client" to "customer" to "consumer" to "service user." The most recent use of the term "service user" helps us reframe the worker-client relationship as a way to restructure the power-dependence relationship between practitioners and those they seek to serve. Another example of the changing nature of practice can be seen in the Nordic countries, where the term "client problems" is less useful than the concept of "shared worries" between the service provider and the service user (Seikkula, Arnkil, & Eriksson, 2003). Given that all people have worries and the terminology is both normative and generally not stigmatizing, there is a potential here to reduce the power differential between service providers and users by sharing their respective worries in order to engage in shared problem-solving. This shift in terminology also represents a different understanding of the service user based on the growing realization by service providers that service users are "experts" within the context of their own experiences and that this form of expertise needs to be combined with the "expertise" of the service provider.

This shift in language accompanies a shift in service provision, from the traditional authorized service (in the form of governmental or nonprofit service delivery) to a shared process of "co-constructed and co-implemented" services. For example, if a traditional service provider is unable to provide a specific service, the generally accepted response is to refer the service user is to another organization, assuming the needed service is actually provided someplace in the community. As an alternative, the "co-construction" approach to service delivery actively engages service users in making use of their own expertise derived from experience by building upon the personal resources and strengths of the service user as well as resources in the service user's community. Resource mobilization provides an example of co-construction; namely, the individual human behaviors of both the service provider and service user are combined to impact the social environment related to developing or modifying services and thereby enhance service outcomes.

Service providers rely heavily on both the network of local services and the resources and strengths of the service user. This high level of inter-dependence provides further support for the co-construction and co-implementation of services.

This shift in service orientation also has implications for how human service organizations collect data to evaluate services. If service users function as co-constructors and co-implementers of services, then it also important to engage service users in a more active role in service moni-toring and evaluation. This would involve rebalancing the evaluation criteria from primarily policy implementation and financial accountabil-ity to include co-constructed data collection processes that feature the perspectives/interests of both service users and providers. While service user satisfaction surveys represent a traditional method used by service providers, more service user involvement would be needed to promote co-construction of tools to assess service outcomes. Similarly, traditional service user advisory committees attached to human service organiza-tions also would need restructuring with respect to shared agenda devel-opment, shared facilitation, shared debriefing, and shared reporting (inside and outside the organization). A somewhat similar process exists in most universities, for example, where the service users (students) are asked to evaluate a course and the service provider (faculty) are thereby evaluated at least twice or more times per year with the results publicly reported for the student community to access. To date, however, students rarely have been involved in the co-construction of the course evaluation surveys nor are they involved in a shared process of evaluating the results.

In the light of these shifts in practice related to service user involve-ment, it seems timely to explore the reconceptualization of practice meth-ods. It is often difficult for service providers to fully comprehend how they are perceived by service users and to understand the depth and breadth of the perceived power they hold over the service user. As Lipsky (1980) has noted in his classic study of street-level bureaucrats, human service providers possess considerable power in the form of discretion when it comes to helping others. They can bend or interpret rules in favor of the service user, and they can significantly misinterpret service user behaviors without sufficient grounding in cultural competency or humility.

Service providers are in a position to exercise different forms of power in their relationships with service users. As defined by French and Raven (1959) and Raven (1990), these multiple forms of power include: (a) coercive power (used by service providers to gain service user compliance with policy-based rules and regulations); (b) reward power (used by service providers to incentivize service user behaviors by providing pathways for change or removing barriers to change through various forms of acceptance); (c) positional power (used by service providers to promote their authority over others inside and outside the organization); (d) referent power (demonstrated by service providers when seeking personal acceptance or approval from the service user, as in the role of counselor or coach); (e) expert power (used by service providers to demonstrate the knowledge or skills needed to engage service users in a relationship-building process, wherein the service user frequently defers to the service provider); and (f) informational power (demonstrated by both service providers and service users when using information, often based on experience, to persuade, convince, and/or manipulate).

Building effective helping relationships with service users requires a wide-ranging understanding of the power of the service provider, a topic that tends to receive little attention in pre-service social work education or in-service training. Service user involvement calls for a more collective form of engagement with service providers that includes: (1) the shared search for resources within the community of the service user and service provider; (2) the involvement of service users in all aspects of decision-making that affect their lives by drawing upon their "expertise of experience"; and (3) the search for ways to engage the service users using multiple points of view to support empowerment and self-sufficiency. Particular attention is needed in the education of service providers to the role of power in relationship-building, the cultural diversity of service user populations, the importance of using the strengths-based perspective to capture the service user's "expertise of experience," and the capacities of service providers to effectively manage the tension and stress created by the policies of the service organization and the unique needs of service providers.

Practice also can be viewed as a cross-cultural experience; namely, the culture of the service user and the culture of the service provider. This distinction becomes important when seeking to identify the theory of change (e.g., "If we do this, then the following should occur . . .") that underlies any of the interventions used to address the needs of service users. The process of exploring the theory of change that underlies various service interventions calls for sharing the practice processes of engagement and assessment between the service user and service provider. By articulating a theory of change, practice expertise can be conceived as the capacity to articulate various mental models that capture current research and service user experience related to social problems (poverty, substance abuse, homelessness, mental/physical disabilities, crime/delinquency, violence, etc.) and help service users to recognize and utilize their expertise of experience within the context of family, friends, neighbors, and community. In addition, practice expertise includes the capacity to create the space and time for critical reflection about the experiences of service users, the co-construction and implementation of interventions, the nature of dialogue between service provider and service user, and what it means for service providers to make effective use of self by using their discretion to promote service effectiveness/outcomes as co-defined with service users.

Another dimension of practice relates to the parallel process between the mental map of a service provider and the mental map of a service evaluator or researcher. Although skilled service providers are able to engage in active listening in order to understand the perspectives and needs of service users, more attention may be needed in the area of documentation, wherein researcher-minded service providers engage in data gathering, data clarifying, and data documenting when listening to an "expert in experience" as well as sharing the data analysis process with the service user. A parallel process between the way practitioners think and the way researchers think can be integrated into daily practice if the service user is to be viewed as a viable and important partner in data-collecting and analysis. Practice methods and research methods (when seen as part of a whole) clearly overlap, but their integration into the minds of practitioners can be difficult to articulate (Fisher, 2013; Sheppard, 1995).

AN EVOLVING FRAMEWORK FOR INTEGRATING PRACTICE, RESEARCH, AND SERVICE USER INVOLVEMENT

As Landsman (2013) notes, "the days in which research and practice were taught as mutually exclusive activities are long past; evidence-based practice demands that researchers understand practice and that the service providers understand research" (p. 72). By adding the active involvement of service users to this challenge of integrating research and practice, the complexity increases considerably. Table 12.1

Table 12.1. Parallel and Integrated Processes between Practice, Research, and Service User Involvement

Practice Processes Used to Engage Service Users	Service User Involvement	Research Processes Used to Inform Practice
1. Engagement Relationship formation through shared worries Information and referral searching Identifying how theory might inform practice	1. Recognition Hearing and seeing the service user as a person with resources Hearing and promoting service users' voice Moving from "hard to serve" to "hard to hear" Sharing worries	1. Problem formulation Curiosity and question-formulation using key-informant probes Identifying key literature and concepts
2. Assessment & service planning Specifying service-user goals and objectives Designing and specifying interventions Engaging service user in shared dialogue about issues emerging from exploring shared worries	2. Participation Service users as co-participants in assessment process Co-learning	2. Developing hypotheses & research plan Evidence-collection methods Specifying research questions Sampling Using critical thinking skills
3. Service implementation Delivering services Using existing agency data gathering tools Monitoring the process Consulting and collaborating with others	3. Collaboration Service users as active resource contributors Drawing upon service user expertise of experience	3. Shared data collection and processing Multiple sources Measurement
4. Service outcome assessment Using service-user goals and objectives Using existing agency evaluation or outcome measurement tools	4. Shared analysis Service users as independent and competent persons in assessing findings and recommending practices, policies, and more research	4. Shared data analysis and interpretation Use of critical reflection Utilizing knowledge base Reassessment of shared worries/research questions
5. Service transition/termination Consulting and referring Designing follow-up strategies	5. Self-advocacy Managing, defining, and framing services, research, and education Organizing Modeling success	5. Reporting Drawing conclusions Disseminating and promoting the utilization of the findings

illustrates the elements of this complexity when specifying how the traditional phases of practice intervention and research methods reflect a parallel process impacted by the power-sharing role of the service user.

It is important to identify how the knowledge and expertise of service users can inform the process of integrating practice and research. The service users are in a unique position to inform the service providers about the usefulness of the services, thereby informing both the practice and research processes by sharing their expertise of experience. As noted in Table 12.1, there are potentially three parallel processes that need to be integrated when capturing the various processes operating between practice, research, and service-user involvement; namely, (1) engagement, recognition, and problem formulation; (2) assessment and service planning, participation, and study planning; (3) service implementation, collaboration, and shared data collection; (4) service outcome assessment and shared data analyzing; and (5) service transition/termination, self-advocacy, and reporting. First, the traditional *practice processes* used to engage service users include engagement, assessment and service planning, service implementation, service outcome assessment, and service transition/termination. Second, these phases can operate in parallel fashion with the traditional *research methods* phases of research problem formulation, hypothesis development, data collection and processing, data analysis and interpretation, and reporting. And third, inserted into this parallel process are the *phases of service user involvement* in the form of recognition, shared participation, collaboration, shared analysis, and self-advocacy. An example of the contribution of the three elements is noted in Table 12.1, which features engagement, recognition, and problem formulation:

In Phase 1, research-minded service providers in collaboration with experience-minded service users create a platform for relationship-building. As Carnochan and Austin (2015) note, hearing and seeing the service user as a human being is a significant aspect of the relationship between the service user and the service provider. The engagement process calls for the service providers and service users to draw upon different expertise acquired in different cultures. In order to engage in the first-phase intervention process, the service providers and users need to identify and share their worries within the context of assessing the situation (Seikkula, Arnkil, & Eriksson, 2003).

As noted in Table 12.1, the second phase of practice intervention calls for continued dialogue in order to formulate a shared understanding of the situation and define the service objectives and outcomes. The dialogical approach to engaging the service users with the service providers involves balancing the traditional expertise of the service provider with the expertise of experience possessed by the service user. In this second phase, the service providers and the service users work together to specify the needs of the service user in order to formulate a service plan, as well as identify questions needed to evaluate the implementation and assessment of the service plan.

The third phase focuses on collaboration and the identification of multiple sources of data in order to capture different perspectives. In order to achieve mutual goals, both the service users and the providers contribute to the service planning, implementation, and gathering of evidence. While the service providers share responsibility for the delivery of services to the service users, they also share the monitoring of service implementation in order to gather data.

The fourth phase involves a shared process of assessing service outcomes in order to identify progress toward meeting service goals. In this phase, the service providers and the users might ask the following questions: Did we focus on the right issues? Did we identify the appropriate criteria for assessing service outcomes? How does the assessing of progress inform next steps? What additional data should be collected?

The final phase includes the shared process of defining the next steps in order to promote service user self-sufficiency and service provider accountability for service delivery. Within the context of service transition/termination, the shared findings are designed to equip service users with the capacities to advocate for themselves. At the same time, service providers engage in follow-up strategies relevant to the service user as well as report on case termination and referral options. In essence, both the service provider and the service user contribute to the dissemination process and the design of next steps. Each of the phases of the parallel process noted in Table 12.1 is illustrated in a teaching case vignette located in Appendix A.

IMPLICATIONS FOR RESEARCH METHODS

The unique configuration of the relationship between the service user and service providers also calls for a reconceptualization of research methods as tools for knowledge development. There is a growing need to expand the various ways that key stakeholders in a human service organization learn about how they engage one another, identify relevant sources of information that informs practice, and how such information is used to inform the decision-making capacities of both service providers and service users. In defining a learning organization, Garvin (2000) notes the following key functions: information gathering and problem-solving, experimentation, learning from the past, learning from best practices, and transferring knowledge. In this context, human service organizations often find it challenging to demonstrate their capacities to become learning organizations as they seek to build knowledge-sharing systems to support evidence-informed practice *and* service-user informed capacity building.

Practice research, in essence, can be viewed as a form of "knowledge testing" designed to explicate both the tacit knowledge and explicit knowledge found in the perspectives of service users and service providers. If one of the primary goals of practice research is to maximize the potential for the generalization of findings and to promote the dissemination and utilization of new practice knowledge, then it is critical to address the complexities of the interpersonal and contextual dimensions of knowledge development. These complexities include the considerable time and effort needed to engage frequently overloaded service providers and sometimes reticent service users in the research process "from the beginning" with respect to: (1) defining the shared questions and worries by building on existing knowledge (found in both electronic databases *and* in the "expertise of experience" located in the tacit knowledge of service providers *and* users); (2) sharing data collection and interpretation; and (3) sharing information dissemination and utilization. In essence, there is a parallel process between engaging in practice and engaging in research as highlighted in Table 12.1.

ORGANIZATIONAL SUPPORTS FOR PRACTICE RESEARCH

One approach to illustrating the implementation of practice research can be seen in the research produced in the Helsinki, Finland, Department of Social Services, serving both Swedish and Finnish populations for over a decade (Martinsen & Julkunen, 2012). At the height of this initiative, there was significant senior management and funding support in the form of two institutes (Mathilda Wrede and Heikki Waris), where research social workers were given either release time (50% to100% for two years) or were employed (frequently part-time while engaged in part-time doctoral studies) to conduct practice research while engaging in university graduate courses. Examples of the studies undertaken provide findings of direct relevance to practice and the processes of knowledge development (see Appendix B). These examples illustrate the potential for practice-based research *inside* a social service organization where service delivery issues receive considerable research attention within a context of informal research collaboration with local university researchers. For many of the research social workers, practice research offers an opportunity to study a practice issue based on a long-standing interest, while enjoying the support of senior management, as well an opportunity to engage in part-time doctoral studies. This model has significant implications for social workers in other countries.

If innovation is to receive higher priority in the delivery of human services, then service settings will need to include "design labs" where practice research and new practice approaches are identified and supported over time (Cohen, 2011). It is increasingly clear that the production of practice knowledge calls for boundary-crossing behaviors spanning the world of practice and the world of research for practitioners to produce and disseminate new knowledge. A similar process is needed to make sure that service user perspectives are incorporated into this process, especially when they are supported in the form of service user-led "survivor research" (Sweeney, Beresford, Faulkner, Nettle, & Rose, 2009). In essence, practice research calls for the involvement of all levels of staff in a human service organization as well as service users. Gaining the trust and support of colleagues for new forms of practice research involves power-sharing with service users.

For service providers, becoming a research-minded practitioner involves the formation of a new identity that balances the intense demands of service delivery with the time needed for critical self-reflection in order to engage in practice research. This process can be supported and enabled when the part-time research social worker role is supported by part-time doctoral education.

And finally, the ultimate test of practice research is its impact on improved service delivery processes and outcomes for service users. The credibility of the research outcomes is based on: (1) the rigorousness of the research methods used, (2) the clarity and transparency of the research questions under study, and (3) the explicitness of the research methods used. One of the tests of the robustness of practice research can be found in the application of the findings in other practice settings.

CONCLUDING WITH LINGERING QUESTIONS

The expansion of efforts to engage in practice research will most likely need to address one or more of the following questions:

1. *If practice research is to be informed by theory (explanatory theory related to the behaviors of service-user populations and/ or interventive theory related to service delivery processes used to assist service users) then how will practice research inform future theory development?*

This question emerges from some of the unique differences between educating social workers in European countries and in the United States. In Europe there appears to be a stronger tradition of expecting social work students to acquire an understanding of major theories that can contribute to theory-informed practice and thereby guide the intervention process. In the United States, however, there is a greater interest in empirical research and how findings derived from research can contribute to evidence-informed practice. In either case, we have externally derived theory or research driving practice with little attention to how practice research can inform theory development and frame research questions relevant to practice. We need to find ways to balance the "outside-in" influence of theory and research methods with the "inside-out" influence of practice experience. The emergence of Cultural Historical Activity Theory in Europe (Engeström, 2009) holds considerable promise as mid-range theory that can inform practice as well as research.

2. *How will practice innovations, supported by practice research, be disseminated and utilized by current and future practitioners?*

Although dissemination and utilization of new knowledge has been greatly enhanced by the use of Internet communications, there are still insufficient venues for disseminating peer-reviewed practice research and even fewer opportunities inside our human service agencies to either access publications (due to publisher's proprietary interests) or create the time and safe space for staff to convene seminar-style discussions on the latest research or the discovery of promising practices. Building organizational supports to promote evidence-informed practice continues to be a challenge hampered by limited resources and increased service demands (McBeath & Austin, 2014).

3. *What form of learning networks will be needed to support practice research that continues to engage practitioners in dialogue with each other and serve users?*

Similar to the role of science writers/journalists in the field of medicine, a parallel development could be used to condense and highlight research findings in online versions that provide easy access for both service providers and service users who may not have the time, access, or inclination to read traditional publications. The outcomes of practice-based research call for new approaches to sharing information through in-person discussions with members of the practice community.

4. *How do we keep social work practitioners up-to-date with practice research when they find so much disconnection between practice and research courses in their formal education programs?*

The old adage went something like this: "Social work education follows practice when it comes to teaching new innovative or promising practices, while social work research leads practice when it comes to increasing our understanding of client populations and/or the validity and reliability of interventive methods." If this old adage is to be updated, it will need to account for service user voice and participation. It will also call for more "research-minded practice" and more "practice-minded research." These issues may take decades to address and/or resolve.

5. *Once social work practitioners graduate from a social work education program, how can we identify practitioners who ponder major questions on an ongoing basis? (Am I having any effect on my clients? Why is poverty such a dominant theme in my*

caseload? What role does the environment play in impacting my
client's behaviors?) And how are these questions translated into
learner readiness for new academic challenges/degrees?

The process of transforming human service organizations into learning organizations is a major challenge. It can begin with senior management fostering the development and utilization of practice research in order to enhance/redesign service delivery systems as well as improve evidence-informed managerial decision-making. Finding and supporting service providers who bring researchable questions to staff meetings and other venues may call for new processes to create safe space to explore ideas within a demanding and frequently over-loaded and overextended work environment. Although not every staff member may be interested in practice research, there is probably a small group of potential champions who could be identified and sup-ported over time, especially when linked to part-time graduate studies. Opportunities to acquire both qualitative and quantitative research skills could enable human service staff to play more of a leadership role in public policy development, especially when the administrative and case record data are mined for practice and policy implications.

Although the issues raised by these questions are complex, they pro-vide a beginning blueprint for future action when it comes to promoting practice research that is co-constructed and co-implemented by service users and providers.

APPENDIX A
TEACHING CASE ON INTEGRATING RESEARCH INTO PRACTICE USING A CHILD WELFARE CASE VIGNETTE

This teaching case illustrates the connection between practice and research within the context of service user involvement as illustrated in Table 12.1 by focusing on the interactions between a child welfare worker and a service user (both parent and child). Each section of the case reflects the five phases in the research and practice processes along with relevant references located in Note #1. The bold parentheses refer to **(research)** and the italicized parentheses refer to *(practice)* whereas brackets are used to capture the [practitioner self-reflections].

Engagement and Problem Formulation

Anna is 5 years old and lives with her 27-year-old mother, Maria, in a rental apartment in a large urban U.S. city. Anna is an active and playful girl and attends local day care. Occasionally, Anna suffers from anxiety and has displayed some behavior problems at home and in day care. Maria has been unemployed for four months, and therefore, is currently experiencing an economically challenging situation. After receiving her high school diploma, Maria has held several temporary jobs but not continued her education. Maria has an alcohol abuse problem and currently she does not receive substance abuse treatment. To prevent eviction from her apartment, Maria receives emergency rental assistance from a local nonprofit organization (*baseline intake information*). Anna is referred to Tina, an experienced child welfare worker at the local Child Welfare Services (CWS) by Maria's brother who called the Child Abuse Hotline, where he expressed his concern about Anna's well-being because he had seen Maria drunk at home several times.

Tina begins an in-person investigation to assess potential child abuse or neglect. During the investigation, Tina finds evidence of child neglect and begins to consider out-of-home placement. Maria opposes Anna's possible out-of-home placement and seems highly motivated to keep Anna at home. During the investigation process, Maria has not used any alcohol and is determined to begin a substance abuse treatment program. In addition, she has been participating consistently in a job training program (*baseline information from intake*).

Tina concludes that Maria appears to be able to provide a safe and secure environment for Anna, but she is still worried about Anna's safety and initiates 30-day emergency response services to monitor the situation in order to avoid child removal (**problem formulation;** *assessment; service transition*). In addition to reflecting on her similar prior cases, Tina draws upon the existing literature of substance abuse problems in families, theories of mother-child relationships, multiproblem casework practice, and the role of child participation in social work practice by referring to previous social work course materials and checking online sources (**review literature;** *critical self-reflection; practice wisdom*).

From the beginning of the case, Tina worked actively to gain Maria's trust to form a relationship based on *shared worries* related to the mutual goal of ensuring a safe and nurturing home environment for Anna that draws upon both Maria's and Tina's expertise. Tina utilizes her social work skills whereas Maria's expertise and capabilities are based on her own life experiences, parenting experiences, and personal strengths (**involving others in problem formulation; inclusive knowledge sharing;** *service user involvement; collaboration; balancing power in the service user–service provider relationship; practice wisdom; tacit knowledge*). They both recognize the shared responsibility of protecting and safeguarding the well-being of children (*duty to protect*). Tina believes in learning from service users and vice versa (*co-learning*). Tina continuously seeks to increase the participation of family members in order to gain their commitment to achieving service objectives that can lead to service effectiveness (*service user involvement*). In essence, she aims to sustain their relationship, not only as a vehicle to offer support and a necessary element of social control, but also in the hope that the experience of this continuing and persistent personal commitment can empower Maria to take control of her life.

Assessment and Hypothesis Formulation

Tina's next step is to develop a preliminary assessment (**working hypothesis about the underlying causes of child neglect**). If Maria can stay alcohol-free and effectively parent Anna, then Anna would be able to remain in her familiar home environment with her biological and custodial mother to whom she is attached. On the other hand, if Maria cannot stay alcohol-free, Anna's safety could be threatened and thereby undermine her developmental processes. In this scenario, out-of-home placement could be a viable option. Tina focuses primarily on identifying the best interests of the child by assessing risks regarding Anna's safety and finding ways to expand Maria's parenting skills (**problem identification as a form of risk assessment; formulating questions and probes as a form of key-informant dialogue;** *co-constructing service objectives*). In particular, she assesses Maria's strengths and commitment to Anna's safety as a form of problem identification in order to design service objectives. [Tina begins to identify the following **research questions**: What actions serve the best interests of Anna? What risks does Anna face and how can they be reduced? What services are relevant for supporting Maria's parenting efforts?] Tina continuously reflects upon the support and control aspects of her work. She recognizes prevailing power relations between her and Maria and how it impacts their work (*use of critical reflection*). In order to maintain transparency in client-centered decision-making, Tina shares her worries with Maria and seeks her perceptions about Anna's situation (**inclusive knowledge sharing; informed consent;** *engaging service-user in shared exploration of worries; a shared assessment process to promote service-user self-determination; shared specifying of service user goals and objectives*).

Through her observations and discussions with Maria, Tina begins to organize her thinking (**in the form of developing a hypothesis about the risk factors associated with this case through the use of single subject case design thinking about creating baselines to assess progress over time**). Tina suspects that Maria's alcohol abuse underlies Maria's parenting problems and Anna's anxiety and affects her ability to consistently meet Anna's needs. Based on her work experience and a review of the literature, Tina acknowledges that substance-abusing parents are at increased risk for abusing and neglecting their children (**searching/ utilizing knowledge base; validity;** *tacit knowledge; identifying risks*). She notes that children of parents who have a substance abuse problem are more likely to suffer from psychiatric, behavior, mood, and eating disorders as well as anxiety, aggression, and attention deficit/hyperactivity. In addition, she finds that children of substance-abusing parents tend to have poorer educational achievement than their peers (**problem identification; searching/utilizing knowledge base;** *tacit knowledge; identifying risks*). Because Maria's alcohol abuse creates risks to Anna's safety, Tina determines that their situation calls for continuing observation and assessment (**problem statement**). In addition to identifying risk factors, Tina searches for information about protective factors for children exposed to substance abuse (**using critical thinking skills related to existing social problem and intervention evidence;** *designing interventions*). She notes that key supportive factors include parental participation in substance abuse treatment, multiprofessional support for children and parents, regular preschool attendance that provides safe daily routines and supportive peer relationships, adequate income support, and the maintenance of a clean and safe home (**searching/utilizing knowledge base**). Tina and Maria develop a shared understanding of the situation and together *design a service plan* (**constructing a shared conceptualization of reality; specifying research objectives**). In accordance with the service plan, Tina explores the need and availability of community services provided by nonprofits (**exploring research methods**; *designing interventions*). Tina refers Maria to a substance abuse treatment program as well as Anna and Maria to child/parent therapy program (**defining research methods**; *specifying interventions*). Tina's case documentation includes updates from Maria's substance abuse therapist and employment specialist, as well as Anna's kindergarten teacher. Maria's family, friends, neighbors, and the parents of Anna's friends also provide updates (**sampling**; *service monitoring*). If these services are not adequate, Tina will consider petitioning the court to place Anna in out-of-home care.

Service Implementation and Data Collection

In addition to maintaining regular contact with the substance abuse counselor, the employment service counselor, family therapists and Anna's kindergarten teacher (**data gathering; triangulation; sampling;** *multi-professional collaboration; monitoring*), Tina makes several home visits in order to assess whether the home environment is supportive of Anna's development (**home survey; participant observation**). In addition, Tina explores Anna's connection with members of her extended family (**network survey; sampling**) and learns that Maria has no contact with her father, has lost contact with her mother and grandparents, and is in frequent contact with her brother. Tina organizes a meeting with Maria's brother, as a way of connecting with a consistent caring adult who has been involved in Anna's life and represents a safe adult to Anna (**specifying data collection;** *specifying interventions*).

In addition to the network of agency supports and her colleagues, Tina meets regularly with Anna and Maria (**data gathering;** *service user involvement*). Committed to a child-centric approach, Tina perceives children as individuals with opinions and viewpoints that need to be expressed and considered (**inclusive knowledge sharing;** *promoting children's participation*). To understand Anna's opinions and perspectives, Tina uses various methods (e.g., drawing with Anna as well as playing with cards and pictures to facilitate interaction) (**participant observation**). Furthermore, Tina frequently talks with Maria about Anna's well-being, Maria's future plans, and her parenting responsibilities (**interviewing**). In their discussion, Tina continuously focuses on their mutual goal of enhancing Anna's safety and well-being. She also visits Anna and Maria to observe their interaction and level of attachment (**interaction analysis; participant observation: use of attachment theory to inform practice**).

Assessing Service Outcomes by Analyzing Data

Tina often steps back from this case in order to consult with her supervisor and colleagues and reflect upon the progress being made (**analyzing data; triangulating different sources of data; guarding against false positives and negatives; searching/utilizing feedback;** *managing confidentiality; maintaining relationships with supervisor and peers; member checking*). As Tina seeks to acquire a deeper understanding of her own practice, she decides to use the Client Mirror case conferencing technique (Yliruka, 2011) that includes the following components: (1) documenting the client's evaluation of her situation and the work to be done, (2) conducting a self-evaluation of one's own work in preparation for a peer evaluation meeting, (3) facilitating a peer evaluation discussion within the social service team and the assessment of further work, (4) following-up with formative or summative evaluation meetings, and (5) concluding with the team's identification and analysis of the specific themes that require monitoring or follow-up (*using existing agency evaluation and outcome measurement tools*).

With regard to assessing service outcomes in an organizational environment of change and stress as well as the policy directives to promote family preservation, Tina acknowledges that the increased pressure for accountability and limited resources pushes her to take on more and more work in order to promote the "best interests" of service-users in addition to the need to engage in critical reflection in order to ensure her own well-being (*use of critical reflection*). To monitor the environmental aspects of her practice, Tina constantly searches for information on the current trends in child welfare practice (**searching/utilizing knowledge base;** *use of critical reflection*). The nature of her reflective practice is to continuously raise questions about her own practice. This process feeds her curiosity about the knowledge and expertise needed to provide effective and supportive services (**searching/utilizing knowledge base; comparing research findings to previous research**). Tina recognizes the importance of informed self-reflection and open communication with service users and others, especially in terms of how her personal and professional experiences influence the work and how the work impacts on her. In her analysis of current cases, she draws upon her prior experience and accumulated practice wisdom along with searching for promising practices emerging from related research (**searching/utilizing knowledge base; comparing research findings to previous research**).

By working together, Tina and Maria identify services that support Maria in her parenting efforts (**analyzing and interpreting data; comparing research findings to previous research;** *service user involvement; mutuality in an assessment process; monitoring; evaluating outcome and efficiency*). [When analyzing the data, Tina seeks to identify multiple factors that could help her interpret the data needed to measure outcomes. She also uses previous research to interpret the findings.] In order to monitor Maria's service plan and assesses the effectiveness of the services (**analyzing and interpreting data;** *monitoring; evaluating outcome and efficiency*), Tina examines the data that she has collected from Anna, Maria, collaborative agencies, her supervisor and colleagues as well as the observation data on Anna's and Maria's relationships with others (**analyzing and interpreting data; triangulation; reliability; construct and concurrent validity; promoting a holistic perspective**). She takes into account the perceptions of all those involved in this case in order to identify and assess service outcomes (**triangulation; developing a synthesis;** *measuring service outcomes and interventions*).

Termination and Reporting

After reflecting on the data as well as her tacit knowledge that reflects her practice wisdom, Tina concludes with Maria that Anna's best interests include remaining at home with Maria (**synthesis; drawing conclusions**). As part of the process of sharing her assessment with Maria, she ultimately closes the case (*service termination*). Based on her experience with this case, Tina continues participating in ongoing professional development by attending a regional social work conference where they promote the use of the Mirror technique in the child welfare services (**disseminating and promoting the utilization of the research findings; reporting**).

Note 1:
Research methods – concepts and principles
Rubin & Babbie (2011), pp. 28–36; .37–38; 66–68; 83; 136–138; 138–142; 142–143; 143–147; 158; 166–168; 172; 176–179; 198–203; 209–212; 294–296; 298–304; 318–348; 351–380; 437–438; 442–445; 445–448; 455–476; 477–497; 499–570; 587–595
Vonk, Tripodi, & Epstein (2007), pp. 7–9; 10; 15–31; 70–105, 111; 135–138; 142; 155–173; 98–105, 135–136; 138–145, 147–153, 210–234.
Child welfare services
Reed & Karpilow (2002), pp. 9–11.
Hogan, Myers & Elswick, (2006).
Milner, (1995).
Girling, Huakau, Casswell, & Conway (2006).
Cleaver, Unell & Aldgate (2011).
Aldgate and Jones (2006).
Pösö (2011), 125.
Skivenes (2011), 170.
Ervast and Tulensalo (2006), 58–60.
Muukkonen (2008), 151.
Bowlby (1977).
Practice principles
Eriksson & Arnkil (2009).
Seikkula, Arnkil, & Eriksson (2003).
Ruch (2010), pp. 15; 117
Doel (2010), pp. 202, 208–209.
Fook and Gardner (2007).
Yliruka (2011).
Brookfield (2009).
Karvinen-Niinikoski (2009).
Case vignette construction
Bisman & Hardcastle (1999), pp. 55–60; 67; 151–162.

APPENDIX B
HEIKKI WARIS AND MATHILDA WREDE INSTITUTES

The Heikki Waris Institute (HWI) and Mathilda Wrede Institute (MWI) are located in Helsinki, Finland and operate as research and development units that combine research, practice, and education. The primary focus of the institutes is social work knowledge production based on collaboration between the welfare agencies within the region, the University of Helsinki, and local colleges. Founded in 2001, the Finnish-speaking HWI is a part of Socca, the Centre of Expertise on Social Welfare in the Helsinki Metropolitan Area. Socca was recently moved to the auspices of the Hospital District of Helsinki and Uusimaa following a major national government reorganization that combines health and social services. The organizational reform has shaped the collaborative relationships and redirected research to the needs of local service practices. In contrast, the Swedish-speaking MWI was founded in 2002 and engaged in contracts with the local municipalities, the University of Helsinki, various polytechnics, and FSKC, the regional Centre of Expertise within Welfare Services. The research context extends to local municipalities in Uusimaa.

Previous practice research themes in both institutes focus on child and youth welfare, elder care, mental health services, and diversity. In addition to a focus on service users, research also addresses practitioner issues (critical reflective practice) and organizational issues (accountability for service outcomes). Current practice research themes include the well-being of young adults, disability, multiprofessional collaboration, participatory approaches, theory-driven supervision, trans-generational social exclusion, assessment of intervention methods, social reporting, and exploratory research. The vast majority of projects reflect collaboration between researchers, educators, practitioners, and service users.

The ongoing current research projects reflect the challenges facing Finnish social work practice, especially the impact of the national social and health service reform on the increased need for multiprofessional collaboration and coordinated services.

ILLUSTRATIVE EXAMPLES OF PRACTICE RESEARCH (2016–2019)**

Heikki Waris Institute

- The art of practice research
- The coping of Finnish young adults after out-of-home care and aftercare services: A document-based analysis.
- Trans-generational problems and prevention within child and youth welfare

- Complex client situations in social work
- From relationship-based practice in social work and family support services to co-production with families
- Students as researchers of social work practices: From the obscurity of practice research to brilliant insights
- Integrating theory and practice: An intervention with practitioners in Finland
- The Mirror method as an approach for critical evaluation and reflective structure within social work
- Inspiring collaborative learning in child welfare

Mathilda Wrede Institute

- The art of practice research
- Biographical agency in health social work
- Pre-adoption services and user perspectives
- Systemic child welfare
- Social work in digital transfer
- Participatory approaches within child and youth welfare
- Multiprofessional practices, mental health, and young people's involvement.
- New perspectives on family mediation: Perceptions, models, and assessments
- Collaborative learning in changing multiprofessional service user environments

**SOURCES

Heikki Waris Institute, http://www.socca.fi/in_english
Heikki Waris Institute publications, http://www.socca.fi/julkaisut/heikki_waris_-instituutin_julkaisuja
https://blogs.helsinki.fi/heikkiwaris/kaytantotutkimus/julkaisut/
Mathilda Wrede Institute, https://fskc.fi/mathilda_wrede_institutet/in_english/
Mathilda Wrede Institute publications, https://fskc.fi/publikationer/forskningsrapporter/
https://fskc.fi/publikationer/projektrapporter/

REFERENCES

Aldgate, J., & Jones, D. (2006). The place of attachment in children's development. In J. Aldgate, D. Jones, W. Rose, & C. Jeffery (Eds.). *The developing world of the child* (pp. 67–96). London, UK: Jessica Kingsley Publishers.

Austin, M.J., Dal Santo, T., & Lee, C. (2012). Building organizational supports for research-minded practitioners. *Journal of Evidenced-based Social Work, 9*, 1–39.

Bisman, C., & Hardcastle, D. (1999). *Integrating research into practice: A model for effective social work.* Belmont, CA: Wadsworth Publishing Company.

Bowlby, J. (1977). The making and breaking of affectional bonds. *British Journal of Psychiatry, 130*, 201–210.

Brookfield, S. (2009). The concept of critical reflection: Promises and contradictions. *European Journal of Social Work, 12*(3), 293–304.

Carnochan, S., & Austin, M.J. (2015) Redefining the bureaucratic encounter between service providers and service users: Evidence from the Norwegian HUSK projects. *Journal of Evidence-based Social Work, 12*(1), 64–79.

Cleaver, H., Unell, I., & Aldgate, J. (2011). *Children's needs—parenting capacity. Child abuse: Parental mental illness, learning disability, substance misuse and domestic violence.* London, UK: The Stationery Office Publications. https://www.gov.uk/government/uploads/system/uploads/attachment_data/file/182095/DFE-00108-2011-Childrens_Needs_Parenting_Capacity.pdf.

Cohen, B.J. (2011). Design-based practice: A new perspective for social work. *Social Work, 56*(4), 337–346.

Doel, M. (2010). Service-user perspectives on relationships. In G. Ruch, D. Turney, & A. Ward, (Eds.). *Relationship-based social work: Getting to the heart of practice* (pp. 199–213). London, UK: Jessica Kingsley Publisher.

Epstein, I. (2009) Promoting harmony where there is commonly conflict: Evidence-informed practice as an integrative strategy. *Social Work in Health Care, 48*(3), 216–231.

Epstein, I. (2010). *Clinical data-mining: Integrating practice and research.* New York, NY: Oxford University Press.

Epstein, I. (2011). Reconciling evidence-based practice, evidence-informed practice, and practice-based research: The role of clinical data-mining. *Social Work, 56*(3), 284–288.

Ervast, S-A., & Tulensalo, H. (2006). *Sosiaalityötä lapsen kanssa. Kokemuksia lapsikeskeisen tilannearvion kehittämisestä* [Social work with a child. Experiences of developing a child-centric child welfare assessment]. Helsinki, Finland: Heikki Waris Institute, no. 8.

Fisher, M. (2013). Beyond evidence-based policy and practice: Reshaping the relationship between research and practice. *Social Work and Social Sciences Review,16*(2), 20–36.

Flyvbjerg, B. (2001) *Making social science matter: Why social inquiry fails and how it can succeed again.* New York, NY: Cambridge University Press.

French, J.R.P., & Raven, B. (1959). The bases of social power. In D. Cartwright & A. Zander (Eds.), *Group dynamics* (pp. 150–167). New York, NY: Harper & Row.

Fook, J., & Gardner, F. (2007). *Practicing critical reflection. A resource handbook.* Maidenhead, UK: Open University Press.

Girling, M., Huakau, J., Casswell, S., & Conway, K. (2006). *Families and heavy drinking: Impacts on children's wellbeing.* Wellington, NZ: Centre for Social and Health Outcomes Research and Evaluation and Te Ropu Whariki Massey University.

Hogan, T., Smarsh, B., & Elswick R.K. Jr. (2006). Child abuse potential among mothers of substance-exposed and nonexposed infants and toddlers. *Child Abuse & Neglect, 30*(2), 145–156.

Karvinen-Niinikoski, S. (2009). Premises and pressures of critical reflection for social work coping in change. *European Journal of Social Work, 12*(3), 333–348.

Julkunen, I. (2011). Knowledge-production processes in practice research: Outcomes and critical elements. *Social Work & Society, 9*(1), 60–75.

Julkunen, I. (2015). Practice-based research: The role of HUSK in knowledge development. *Journal of Evidence-informed Social Work, 12*(1), 102–111.

Landsman, M. (2013). Family-centered practice. In K. Briar-Lawson, M. McCarthy, & N. Dickinson (Eds.). *The children's bureau: Shaping a century of child welfare practices, programs, and policies* (pp. 59–78). Washington, DC: NASW Press.

Marthinsen, E., & Julkunen, I. (2012). *Practice research in Nordic social work: Knowledge production in transition.* London, UK: Whiting & Birch.

McBeath, B., & Austin, M.J. (2014). The organizational context of research-minded practitioners: Challenges and opportunities. *Research on Social Work Practice, 25*(4), 446–459.

Milner, J. (1995). Physical child abuse assessment: Perpetrator evaluation. In J. Campbell (Ed.), *Assessing for dangerousness: Violence by sexual offenders, batterers, and child abusers* (pp. 41–67). Thousand Oaks, CA: Sage.

Muukkonen, T. (2008). Suunnitelmallinen sosiaalityö lapsen kanssa [Planning based social work with a child]. Helsinki, Finland: Heikki Waris Institute, no 17. http://www.socca.fi/files/1031/Planning_based_social_work_with_a_child.pdf

Nowotny, H. (2003). Democratizing expertise and socially robust knowledge. *Science and Public Policy, 30*(2), 151–156.

Pösö, T. (2011). Combatting child abuse in Finland: From family to child-centered orientation. In N. Gilbert, N. Parton, & M. Skivenes (Eds.). *Child protection systems. International trends and orientations* (pp. 112–130). New York, NY: Oxford University Press.

Raven, B.H. (1990). Political applications of the psychology of interpersonal influence and social power. *Political Psychology, 11,* 493–520.

Reed, D., & Karpilow, K. (2002). *Understanding the child welfare system in California: A primer for service providers and policymakers.* Berkeley, CA: California Center for Research on Women and Families.

Rubin, A., & Babbie, E. (1997). *Research methods for social work.* Pacific Grove, CA: Brooks/Cole Publishing Company.

Ruch, G. (2005). Relationship-based practice and reflective practice: Holistic approaches to contemporary child care social work. *Child and Family Social Work, 10*(2), 111–123.

Ruch, G. (2010). The contemporary context of relationship-based practice. In G. Ruch, D. Turney, & A. Ward (Eds.). *Relationship-based social work: Getting to the heart of practice* (pp. 13–28). London, UK: Jessica Kingsley Publisher.

Salisbury Forum Group. (2011). The Salisbury Statement. *Social Work & Society, 9*(1), 4–9 (2011).

Skivenes, M. (2011). Norway: Toward a child-centric perspective. In: N. Gilbert, N. Parton, & M. Skivenes (Eds.). *Child protection systems. International trends and orientations* (pp. 154–179). New York, NY: Oxford University Press.

Seikkula, J., Arnkil, T.E., & Eriksson, E. (2003). Postmodern society and social networks: Open and anticipation dialogues in network meetings. *Family Process, 42*(2), 185–203.

Shaw, I. (2005). Practitioner research: Evidence or critique? *British Journal of Social Work, 35*(8), 1231–1248.

Shaw, I. (2012). *Practice and research.* Aldershot, UK: Ashgate Publications.

Shaw, I., & Lunt, N. (2011). Navigating practitioner research. *British Journal of Social Work, 41*(8), 1548–1565.

Shaw, I., & Lunt, N. (2012). Constructing practitioner research. *Social Work Research, 36*(3), 197–208.

Sheppard, M. (1995). Social work, social science and practice wisdom. *British Journal of Social Work, 25,* 265–293.

Sweeney, A., Beresford, P., Faulkner, A., Nettle, M., & Rose, D. (Eds.) (2009). *This is survivor research.* Manchester, UK: PCCS Books.

Uggerhøj, L. (2011). What is practice research in social work: Definitions, barriers and possibilities. *Social Work & Society, 9*(1), 45–59.

Uggerhøj, L. (2011). Theorizing practice research in social work. *Social Work and Social Sciences Review, 14*(2), 49–73.

Vonk, E., Tripodi, T., & Epstein, I. (2007). *Research techniques for clinical social workers*. New York, NY: Columbia University Press.

Yliruka, L. (2011). The Mirror method: A structure supporting expertise in social welfare services. *Social Work & Social Sciences Review, 15*(2), 9–37.

Index

Tables, figures, and boxes are indicated by *t*, *f*, and *b* following the page number.
For the benefit of digital users, indexed terms that span two pages (e.g., 52–53) may, on occasion, appear on only one of those pages.